The Moralist Tradition in France

THEODORE P. FRASER
College of the Holy Cross

RICHARD L. KOPP
Fairleigh Dickinson University
Madison

Library of Congress Number 81-69245
ISBN 0-86733-017-1

The authors wish to thank the following publishers for per-
mission to translate excerpts from their publications and
A. Knopf for the selected use of the Zeitlin translation of
Montaigne and the Philip Thody translation of Camus's
Notebooks (1935-1942):

Stock editions (Paris) for Jean Rostand, Pensées
d'un biologiste and Carnets d'un biologiste.

Editions Gallimard (Paris) for Alain, Propos
(Bibliothèque de la Pléiade); André Gide,
Romans, récits et soties (Bibliothèque de la
Pléiade) and Journal I, II (Bibliothèque de
la Pléiade); Paul Valery, Oeuvres II (Biblio-
thèque de la Pléiade).

Harcourt, Brace, Jovanovich (with Alfred A.
Knopf, Inc.) (New York) for Albert Camus,
Notebooks 1935-1942, transl. Philip Thody.

The authors wish to thank the following publishers for the use of excerpts from their publications:

Alfred A. Knopf, Inc. for Notebooks 1935-1942, Albert Camus, transl. Philip Thody; Fruits of the Earth, André Gide, transl. D. Bussy; Two Legends: Oedipus and Theseus, André Gide, transl. J. Russel; Journals of André Gide: Vols. I, II, transl. J. O'Brien; Essays, Montaigne, transl. Zeitlin.

Doubleday & Co. for A Biologist's Thoughts and A Biologist's Notebooks, J. Rostand, transl. Irma Brandeis.

Frederick Ungar Publishing Co. for Alain on Happiness (The Art of Being Happy, Bucephalus, The Misfortunes of Others), transl. Robert D. and Jane Cotrell.

This anthology is presented under the sponsorship of the
Maxwell Becton College of Arts and Sciences of Fairleigh
Dickinson University, Madison, Frederick H. Gaige, Dean.

The Moralist Tradition in France

Table of Selections

		Page
PREFACE		ix
INTRODUCTION		1
MONTAIGNE	Essays	30
ST. FRANCIS de SALES	Introduction to the Devout Life	52
PASCAL	Thoughts	66
LA ROCHEFOUCAULD	Maxims	79
LA BRUYERE	Characters	90
VAUVENARGUES	Reflections, Maxims and Portraits	113
VOLTAIRE	Philosophical Dictionary	130
ROUSSEAU	Emile	149
CHAMFORT	Maxims and Thoughts	162
JOUBERT	Thoughts, Maxims, Essays	175
STENDHAL	Thoughts and New Philosophy On Love	186
VALERY	Such As It Is	195
ALAIN	Discourses	209
GIDE	Fruits of the Earth New Fruits Diaries So be it... Theseus	226

		Page
J. ROSTAND	A Biologist's Notebook A Biologist's Thoughts	243
CAMUS	Notebooks (1935-1942)	255
REFERENCES		270

PREFACE

This anthology is designed to make the writings of the major
French moralists available in English translation in one
volume. Excepting such obvious luminaries on the world
literary scene as Montaigne, Pascal, Rousseau, Voltaire, and
Camus, many of the moralists have been generally neglected
and a few remain virtually unknown to American readers who
otherwise have a solid interest in literature, philosophy,
and intellectual history. The reason for this unfortunate
situation would seem to be largely explained by the absence
up to our own day of any general introductory work on the
tradition in English. To fill this lacuna, we have labored
on the present work which provides a critical essay on the
moralist tradition considered from literary and historical
perspectives, extensive individual author introductions,
and carefully selected texts of the most important and representative moralist authors from Montaigne to Camus.

With two exceptions the present authors are responsible for
the translation of all the prose selections in the work.
Both the Zeitlin and Thody translations of Montaigne and
Camus, respectively, were selected for their precise and
artful rendition. All of the other authors we have rendered
into English. Some (Vauvenargues, Joubert, Standhal, Alain,
and Rostand) have yet to be translated either in entirety
or in part; others have been translated in versions that
are either no longer available or that are dated and unsuit-
able for the modern reader. All of our final decisions
touching on the problems of translating this varied and

difficult texts were conditioned by one overriding concern: to mirror the meaning of the original passage as faithfully and as gracefully as possible.

Principally this anthology has been designed in connection with college courses in literature, philosophy, and the history of ideas. But of course, we also are eager to offer it to the much larger reading public interested in French writings and literature, and world literature.

We wish to acknowledge gratefully the interest expressed in this work by many of our friends and colleagues. We are particularly indebted to Reino Virtanen, Professor Emeritus of French, the University of Nebraska at Lincoln, for his thoughtful reading of our Introduction and helpful comments on the work and to Ervin Brody, Professor of Russian and Comparative Literature, Fairleigh Dickinson University (Madison), for his insightful commentary on several chapters. We also wish to thank William Green, Professor of History, Holy Cross College, Charles Mackey, Dean of Humanities, Simmons College, David O'Connell, Professor of French, the University of Illinois, Chicago Circle, and Dean Frederick Gaige, Fairleigh Dickinson University (Madison) for their comments and encouragement. Deep appreciation goes to Jane Ulrich for her unhesitating patience in putting the manuscript in this final form. This was a labor of love.

Finally, we wish to thank those students who inspired us, encouraged us, and by classroom interaction assured us that we had undertaken the right project.

INTRODUCTION

One of the most valid literary claims of the French is to possess a long succession of highly perceptive and gifted authors whom they designate as moralistes. Sainte-Beuve and subsequent French critics up to Sartre have fixed and evaluated this series, whose lineage, they claim, extends back to Montaigne and continues in a virtually unbroken line into the Twentieth Century. The title moraliste, conferred with honor on such seemingly disparate authors as Pascal, La Rochefoucauld, Vauvenargues, Rousseau, Stendhal, and Camus, to name only several, has a special meaning in French literature which its English equivalent, moralist, does not quite convey.

Though the English title seems to lack a precise definition, it does not denote for the French a professional philosopher concerned with "la morale" or moral philosophy taken as a discipline. The French moralist is rather a writer who has for his object an analysis of the human heart with special emphasis on the understanding of motive and conduct. Viewing man as he is--neither sinner nor saint but perhaps a composite of each, hence capable of both virtue and vice-- the moralist does not conduct his study of human nature along theoretical or abstract lines, but strives to give concrete application to his findings. In order to make us aware of our vices and foibles, the moralist therefore exposes human failings through observation and analysis and suggests norms or guidelines for conduct which may aid us to live "à propos", or honorably, to use one of Montaigne's favorite expressions.

1

The modern French philosopher and moralist Alain has described the matter and method of the moralists as consisting of "a total morality of human nature expressed in precepts, maxims, or general rules of conduct by means of which an impartial witness or observer gives counsel to his neighbor." Hence the observer not only paints but also judges the moral aspects involved in any given situation.

Alain goes on to say that the moralist cannot merely give advice since "the major difficulty seems always to reside in how to put such observations into practice for oneself; and this is the essential point in forming any moral judgment. A person cannot, after all, approve for himself acts which he would find reprehensible if performed by his neighbor."

In pursuing their project, the moralists share certain common attitudes and approaches. They are first of all supremely concrete and actual in their point of departure. Relying on sensory perceptions and personal observation gained through living, they consistently shun abstract speculation and prefer to deal with human beings in concrete situations. Always intensely interested in the psychological complexities of human nature, they strive to lay bare the deep springs of human motive and conduct. In their probings they reject any system which claims to have penetrated the ultimate mystery of the human personality and give the lie at every turn to any narrow determinism. Instead, they insist upon the multifaceted and essentially irrational cast of the human person. From this there often results an emphasis on the weakness of man's mind and will to direct him to wisdom and virtue. In La Rochefoucauld's words, "Folly pursues us at every stage of our lives;" and, "If anyone seems wise, it is only because his follies befit his age and station." Yet just as often these writers reveal an implicit and profound faith in the possibility of human nature that is incompatible with genuine skepticism or dark pessimism.

Whether or not they are believers, the moralists are strongly influenced by the Christian view of man and enter willy-nilly into the context of the Christian dialogue: Man is not as he feels he should be; he commits evil, though he would be good; he wants to be sincere but perceives his

2

propensity for deception and lies. Yet it is precisely this oscillation between good and evil that reveals the human creature to be a magnificent paradox, a startling and disconcerting contradiction. As Pascal perceives it: "The twofold nature of man is so evident that some have thought we have two souls. A single subject seemed to them incapable of such hidden variations from unmeasured presumption to a dreadful dejection of heart." And as he describes our vacillation from good to evil: "There is internal war in man between reason and the passions. If he had only passions without reason... But having both, he cannot be without strife, unable to be at peace with the one without being at war with the other. Thus is he always divided against and opposed to the self."

Taking this paradoxical dimension of human nature as axiomatic, the moralists regard personal integrity as a shifting balance of forces at war with one another. To foster a truer understanding of this conflict, they uncover the basic patterns of self deception and collective nonsense or prejudice which they see influencing human opinion and activity. They attack the time honored belief in the power of reason alone to lead man to wisdom and advocate instead the ideal of psychic wholeness which recognizes the positive effects of passion on human motivation and conduct. Vauvenargues says: "If our passions sometimes give us bolder advice than does thoughtful reflection, it is because they generally provide us with greater strength to bring matters to completion." Or more concisely: "Reason deceives us many more times than does the heart."

From Montaigne to Camus, then, the moralists place a strong emphasis on the ideal of living rather than on thinking. They further insist that an understanding of the total personality cannot be based on thought alone but must encompass sentiment as well; that life presents more examples of uncertainty and danger than any attempt to rationalize or systematize human behavior can explain; that the total growth and development of a human being does not depend alone on the process of acquiring intellectual knowledge; finally, that the human condition cannot be adequately appreciated or understood solely by speculative approaches--these are some of the dominant attitudes which the moralists bring to bear on their study of man.

The tools which they employ in their probings of human nature
consist of a keen, habitual use of psychological analysis, a
finely developed sense of what is "moral", and an aptitude
to recognizing the best and worst in human nature usually
without becoming hardened or cynical. Equal in importance
to these natural gifts is the marvelous vehicle of expression afforded them by their own language. Through practice
and evolution in the course of centuries, the French language has become an extraordinarily refined and accurate
means for expressing subtle analysis of moral nuances. And
this refinement of language has played a major role in allowing the moralists to write with admirable clarity and
conciseness.

Though they share in common the attitudes and procedures
just described, the moralists have consistently expressed
themselves in a diversified number of literary genres or,
more properly speaking, prose forms such as the essay, epi-
gram, maxim, aphorism, fable, moral portrait, reflection
dialogue, and discourse, to mention the most common. But
no matter which form the moralist employs, his work can be
identified as participating in the tradition by a tone of
high seriousness, thematic similarity, and a penetrating
analytical spirit which delicately describes and judges the
human phenomena it observes.

The unique function and preoccupation of these moralists
must be distinguished from that of the British moral philosophers of the 17th and 18th Centuries, also frequently referred to as moralists. Hobbes, Locke, Shaftesbury, Mande-
ville, and Adam Smith, among the most important, are moral
philosophers in a professional sense. They are intent on
founding a systematic approach to morality that posits general theories and they are far more concerned with the study
of man in the abstract than with the individual in concrete
situations. For the British moralist, his French counterpart seems more a satricial writer than a moralist since
he stops short of developing a comprehensive system but
merely points to the fact that human beings do not regulate
their lives by accepted principles of behavior and often
fall short of stating how man should act in a moral sense.
It is indeed true that the moralists aim at no prescriptive
or comprehensive systems but frame their observations and
judgments on human nature in fragmentary, non-sequential

comments derived directly from their study of human beings in the process of living.

The French moralists are not, however, merely very clever and gifted writers of satire though piquant portrayal of man in action often has an undeniably rich satirical vein. Yet the major goal of satire is to make us aware of our inconsistencies, foibles, and vices. And the satirist is therefore intent on illustrating the distance often existing in everyday life between the profession and practice of particular virtues; hence, he need not and rarely does go beyond providing us with such examples. For his part the moralist, while singling out human failings, offers, or at least suggests, means to avoid the moral pitfalls which his keen analysis has uncovered and presented for our examination. Using his method, he provides a message which falls somewhere between a Sunday school lecture of ready made do's and don'ts and a theoretical and involved code of ethical practice. Since for the practiced moralist the human creature is very often capricious and non-sequential in his actions, neither standard truisms on the one hand, nor abstract ethical theories on the other can effectively influence his conduct. Rather his follies must be pointed out to him through concrete example.

Finally, since they dare to reflect on the concrete evidence of evil and folly ever present in human existence, the moralists are sometimes disparagingly relegated to the rank of cynical commentators who are over impressed by the darker side of human nature. It is precisely because they so keenly and steadfastly insist on studying man as he is that the moralists refuse to adopt idealized or romanticized views of human nature which, though more pleasing, would be essentially false. Their experience convinces them that man remains substantially the same from age to age and must constantly be reminded of his foibles so as not to fall prey to complacency or moral blindness. Good is always mixed with evil, and wisdom with folly; egotism constantly stands in the way of our attempts to be sincere, and the good man the honnête homme, is the one daring to be true to his best instinct and striving valiantly to overcome his baser nature. In each century the moralists reiterate Socrates' enlightened counsel, "Know thyself", and they employ it incessantly as they study themselves and humanity. Introspection that is not divorced from the experience of

5

life thus becomes the basic formula both practiced and taught
by these commentators.

When Sainte-Beuve alluded to "cette série française" of moralists, he was referring to the authors whom he and other
French critics were to identify as such from the period
spanning the late Renaissance to the mid-Nineteenth Century.
He dedicated several of his articles in the Causeries de
lundi and Portraits littéraires to these writers whose deep
wisdom of human nature and motive, he believed, was one of
the crowning achievements of French literature. In these
references, he grouped them in what we could call historical
tiers or even emanations.

For Sainte-Beuve, the pioneer of the tradition and one of
its greatest geniuses was Montaigne, whose work continued
to feed and enrich subsequent writers "par cent retours"
(in hundreds of ways). In the first tier--the pinnacle--
he placed the classical authors born in the 1620's, Pascal
and La Rochefoucauld, who were distinguished by the depth
of their probings and the lucid conciseness of their literary style: "In the history of French language and literature La Rochefoucauld comes in date in the first rank after
Pascal, and even precedes him as a pure moralist. He has
the clearness and conciseness of phrase that Pascal alone
in that century had before him; which La Bruyère caught".
Both belonged to the "pure Louis XIV period" by their grand,
stern, and noble works. La Bruyère and Fénelon, writing in
the last decade of the century, represented the "radiant
end" of the classical period by the infinite grace of their
portrayal of man--more impressive by its refinement than
its originality

As continuers of the tradition in the Eighteenth Century,
Sainte-Beuve designated Vauvenargues, Chamfort, Voltaire,
and Rousseau. Of these he seemed to hold a preference for
Vauvenargues because of the latter's ardent attempt to rehabilitate the image of man which, according to Sainte-
Beuve, was somewhat vilified by the 17th Century moralists
(Pascal and La Rochefoucauld in particular) who assuredly
"did not flatter mankind". He presented Rousseau as having
pushed Vauvenargues' rehabilitation of man, "so far that
we might consider it exhausted. But there can be no stopping in so good a road". As for Voltaire, Sainte-Beuve
deemed him the worthy successor to La Rochefoucauld and

Pascal by the "purity and conciseness of expression" that characterized his works--a form of genius that would constitute the triumph of his century.

By his delicate and subtle presentation of themes summing up the moralist project and by his admirably lucid prose, Joubert, alone among the authors of the first half of the 19th Century, was judged by Sainte-Beuve as a worthy successor of the tradition. His Thoughts and Maxims, which were published posthumously in 1838, closed the circle and represented a fitting end of the moralist series for this critic.

Other French critics, contemporaries of Sainte-Beuve and those who would write later, designated the same authors as major moralists; they also came to regard the earlier authors--from Montaigne to La Bruyère--as representing a golden age of moralist literature by their more profound analysis of the human heart and the manifest perfection they brought to such literary forms as the essay, maxim, aphorism, thought, or portrait. Other authors were gradually added to the list: Fontenelle and Stendhal, Saint Francis de Sales as the Christian counterpart of Montaigne; and a partial listing of others certainly would include Charron, Nicole, Rivarol, Helvétius, Volney, Saint-Lambert, and De Maistre.

The moralists represented in this anthology comprise the principal authors designated and commented upon by the major French critics. Hence our choice is not arbitrary but respects the consensus of who are the most important from Montaigne to the mid-Nineteenth Century. In chronological order, they are Montaigne, Saint Francis de Sales, Pascal, La Rochefoucauld, La Bruyère, Vauvenargues, Voltaire, Rousseau, Chamfort, Joubert, and Stendhal. The common thread linking these authors is a marked penchant and talent in the study of the human heart, a keen interest in the sources of human motive and behavior, and the use of common or related literary modes of expression.

There also exists among the French today a commonly accepted extension of the term to encompass a number of modern authors whose preoccupation with moral observation and application distinguish them as continuers of this tradition. Even though many of them write fictional prose for the most part, these moderns reveal a fondness for moralist prose forms: maxims, thoughts, reflections, etc., and they record their most intimate thoughts using these forms. Frequently they echo or consciously refer to specific classical moralists, thereby revealing striking intellectual affinities and the desire to continue and to engage in the moral dialogue initiated by their predecessors.

From this category of modern moralists we have selected Paul Valéry, André Gide, Alain (Emile Chartier), Jean Rostand (the son of the author of Cyrano de Bergerac), and Albert Camus, since major aspects of the literary output of all these are strikingly allied with the matter, form, and intention of the earlier authors so designated. We perhaps could have included Jean-Paul Sartre--especially the Sartre who authored the critical essays in Situations or such moral treatises as Reflections on the Jewish Question. But in the decade before his death he had become much more the professional--and dogmatic--philosopher than a moralist, and his later philosophical works do not illustrate the spirit and methodology of the moralist exemplified in this collection.

Then, too, a number of modern novelists: Proust, Malraux, Mauriac, Saint-Exupéry,Bernanos, Julien Green, and other littérateurs can be considered moralists in the extended sense. While certainly not denying that a kindred spirit and intention often pervades the works of these writers, we feel that they do not demonstrate a sufficient degree of fidelity to the traditional prose forms and modus operandi of the earlier moralists to justify inclusion in a work specifically dedicated to such literature.

Moreover, such an extension of the term may be specious and confusing. If accepted, it renders meaningless all efforts to identify the specific elements of the moralist project as a distinctive current in French literature. To refute this process of mistaken identity, let us simply state the commonplace that fictional forms like the novel, when they artfully employ introspective analysis culminating in observations which we can apply to life, strive to subordinate their moral observations to the demands of a preconceived and an aesthetic whole. The structure of the novel cannot, therefore, approximate the non-sequential and fragmentary nature of moralist writings. Camus's judgment notwithstanding, that the greatest French moralists have not been the "composers of maxims" but the great psychological novelists, the fact remains that fiction is not the actual representation of reality, but, through its artful use of mimesis, arrangement, and willed distortion for aesthetic effect, is at least one step removed. It therefore lacks the rich and essential truth of concrete observation on human nature and conduct found in the works of the moralists.

The reason for this confusion in identity would seem to stem, at least in part, from the symbiotic existence of humanistic concerns and themes for which moralists and novelists have shared intense interest. In fact, it is precisely because all manner of French authors have constantly woven these humanistic and moral concerns into the fabric of their respective works that the French have claimed with such pride that theirs is a literature of moralistes par excellence. Despite such a convergence of aims and views, the modus operandi and the ultimate literary achievements of moralists and novelists must be distinguished on the point of fictional creation versus observed reality.

*

*   *

We present Montaigne first as the most important of the Renaissance moralists and indeed the most influential author of the entire series. In his Essays, he definitively laid the groundwork and fixed the method for all subsequent projects of self-study. In painting himself, Montaigne claimed that he was portraying humanity, "since every human being bears the entire form of the human condition."

Montaigne was also the first to challenge the aristocratic ideal of the Renaissance--stoical in nature--which limited moral perfection to an elite who were able to rise above mundane cares and human affliction by a supreme indifference

to the vicissitudes and trials of life, and the imperious
demands of the body. He admitted that such a moral ideal was
perhaps within reach of a few rare and "exalted" souls from
age to age, but he counseled for himself and mankind as a
whole the pursuit of a "lowly life" to be lived in conformity with what nature teaches us. The Essays therefore present a wise and practical philosophy of life which places
a high premium on tranquility of the soul and a spirit of
moderation in all things. This moral message is also color-
ed with a healthy skepticism regarding man's ability to
achieve an understanding of the great metaphysical questions.
Since such answers are beyond our ken, he urges that we turn
our attention to a cultivation of the self which should lead
to an appreciation of love of the life which we have been
given.

The supreme moralist, Montaigne refines his guidelines to
living an honorable life in the crucible of self-examination,
from which he draws wise observations which he gradually will
apply to man and his world. The Essays abound in literary
forms which become standard in moralist literature of all
succeeding generations. Montaigne, in fact, exhausts all
the forms in sustaining his dense "nervous" style. Aphorisms, maxims, reflections, portraits, dialogues, all are
woven into the rich fabric of his writings and no other moralist surpasses him in psychological depth or the artful
rendering of his prose.

Montaigne's work marks the successful attempt of French
humanists to break with both a rigid Christian stoicism and
the Florentine tradition of neo-Platonism which had become
extremely bookish and largely derivative from the new learning of the earlier Italian Renaissance. By his fresh and
personal approach to the study of human nature in its most
elementary forms, Montaigne therefore freed subsequent moralists from the stifling traditions of the past and laid
the groundwork for their on-going project.

Saint Francis de Sales, the leading figure of the Devout
School of Humanism of the late Renaissance, is the other
moralist included from this period. Though differing from
Montaigne in his overriding desire to inculcate piety and
commitment to a religious ideal in the readers of his Introduction to a Devout Life, he shared Montaigne's ideal of

10

a life lived wisely and in conformity with human nature, provided it be enlightened by God's grace. The quintessential Christian humanist, Francis de Sales in no way felt constrained to reject the world but rather to sanctify it. And like Montaigne, he found to be repugnant moral attitudes which would denigrate the worth and beauty of a human existence lived à propos. The cultivated Christian is an ideal which must be obtained, and none of the gifts which God gives to his creatures can be refused. Man, in his thought, has therefore the obligation to cultivate the mind, heart, and body.

In epistolary form Saint Francis offered extremely practical and mild mannered counsels--constantly supported by charming similes or parallels drawn from the world of nature: the birds, bees, all manner of animals, flowers, herbs, vegetation--all of which developed a "smiling" and attractive approach to virtue. In such a manner he succeeded in prescribing a concrete means to attain sanctity which was remarkably free from the heavy didacticism and moral rigidity which characterized Catholic spirituality after the Council of Trent. His gentle and persuasive message enhanced all that is human and was thus substantially in harmony with Montaigne's "smiling philosophy". It is for this reason that Saint Francis is considered to have had the same humanizing effect upon theology that Montaigne had on moral philosophy.

The Seventeenth Century developed what Taine would later term "a literature of the salon" which, as a cultural phenomenon, exerted a profound influence on moralist works of the period. The salons were social or literary centers where writers, artists, scientists, and fashionable people would gather to discuss with wit and refinement topics dealing with sentiment, literature, grammar, and vocabulary, to name the most important subjects. Presided over by such influential and intelligent women as the Marquise de Rambouillet, Mme. de Sablé, and Mlle. de Scudéry, the salons were largely instrumental in refining language and manners while encouraging subtle analysis of the passions and sentiments--particularly that of love.

The salons fostered the strong vogue in the 17th Century for aphoristic prose forms and character which were to become the favorite vehicles for writers to give permanent expression

11

to the piquant observations on human conduct and social mores discussed at these fashionable gatherings. Long a literary staple and dating back at least to Hippocrates (5th Century B.C.), the aphorism was revitalized and markedly refined in the salons of the 17th Century. It can in fact be said that the aphorism--traditionally a truism or commonplace expression--was elevated in the "workshops" of the salon to a new art form and was transformed into an instrument capable of recording the most subtle observations regarding sentiment, motive, and conduct.

This is particularly true of La Rochefoucauld's maxim, itself an aphorism in form but going one step beyond the function of this humble, traditional genre. As Professor Cruickshank has explained it: "Both the aphorism and maxim formulate what is claimed to be a general truth, but the maxim goes on to recommend or imply a role of conduct arising from this truth."[1]

To clarify this distinction, we offer the following examples: Pascal presents us with an aphorism in his famous statement: "It is the heart which experiences God and not reason". La Rochefoucauld's judgment: "What usually keeps us from opening our hearts to our friends is less our mistrust of them than of ourselves" is, however, a maxim because it performs a dual operation. It first expresses the truism that we do not willingly confide as a rule in others but it further posits a "mistrust" of self as the probable reason for our reluctance to engage in such confidences. Though there is this difference, strictly speaking, between an aphorism and a maxim, we shall for convenience's sake refer to them interchangeably and shall further include in the category of aphoristic prose forms the maxim, thought, apophthegm, reflection, and sentence (judgment).

We can appreciate the distance traversed by La Rochefoucauld and other 17th Century moralists in the development of aphoristic forms if we compare them with some of the earliest examples. Among the aphorisms of Publius Syrus (1st. Century

1 French Literature and its Background, vol. 2, The Seventeenth Century, ed. John Cruickshank (Oxford: Oxford Press, 1969), p. 138.

12

B.C.), one of the most gifted and well known of ancient
aphorists, we read:

> "The poor man lacks a little but the
> miser lacks everything."

> "Money is your slave if you know how
> to use it well, and your master if
> you do not."

> "A bad conscience often shelters us
> from danger but never from fear."

Let us now examine the new degree of refinement observed in
Pascal's aphorisms:

> "To make light of philosophy is truly
> to philosophize."

> "We never do evil so completely and so
> cheerfully as when we do it out of
> conscience."

From the pedestrian and practical commonplaces of Syrus to
Pascal's subtle shades of meaning one has the impression of
having crossed an abyss. For example, in Syrus' third aphorism above, "conscience" is intended to express a concept
with clearly defined meaning and with no troubling aspects.
In his use of the word in the second aphorism, Pascal casts
the positive meaning of the term into doubt as he stresses
questionable forces which "conscience" stealthily conceals
even from itself; and he even suggests that what we call
"conscience" is often not a guide to avoid evil.

The transformation of the aphorism reaches its apogee in La
Rochefoucauld's artful rendition of the maxim. We read, for
example: "We think we lead when we are being led, and while
making for one goal with our minds, we are unconsciously
drawn toward another by our hearts."

This maxim contains an extraordinary richness of insight and
expression. La Rochefoucauld is able, in fact, to describe
the conflict between head and heart--the disturbing and fundamental force for disintegration of psychic wholeness operative in all of us--in the very act of disruption. This

13

maxim thus becomes a disquieting statement that causes us to pause and reflect anew upon this troubling phenomenon which we know to be a common failing in all of us.

Another form to undergo remarkable refinement in 17th Century literary circles was the portrait or character sketch. Enjoying a long history dating back to Theophrastus (372-287 B.C.) the art of portraiture had long been a major component of French literature. Joinville, Commynes, and Froissart--Medieval memorialists and chroniclers--had relied heavily on this genre to portray historical figures of major importance in their chronicles of kings and nobles. The portrait's popularity continued to grow in the Renaissance, due in no small measure to the enormous influence exerted by Plutarch's Lives, once more made available by the new learning. Brantôme, Marguerite de Navarre and, indeed, Montaigne himself delighted in sketching the moral and physical traits of their contemporaries in deliciously frank and realistic terms revealing the period's unabashed lack of prudishness and its fondness for moral exempla upon which to establish rules for conduct.

A new approach to portraiture emerged in the 17th Century as moralists and other writers pursued the goal of examining and commenting upon human motive and conduct in a timeless quantum--a method they felt, which would make their works true and relevant for all times. The preference became that of drawing literary portraits depicting "types" of humanity reminiscent of Theophrastus' Characters. La Fontaine, Pascal, Molière, and La Bruyère, each in his own way, clothed moral attitudes in concrete and descriptive terms of reality aimed at creating a gallery of universal types. La Fontaine's wise and foolish animals who instruct humans in the Fables, Molière's prototypes of the miser, hypocrite, pedant, etc., and Pascal's finely etched vignettes of magistrates, kings, hunters, and gamblers whom he creates to dramatize our inability to recognize the true dimensions of the human condition--all are living persons whose moral dilemmas we experience in our own age.

The finest 17th Century portrait artist is La Bruyère. Composing his major work, Les Caractères, at the close of the century, he artfully linked together aphoristic expressions conveying his observations on human conduct and society with moral portraits describing fictional characters to illustrate his findings. In this vast fresco of most aspects of the human being in society, La Bruyère was not merely content to define moral attitudes or situations in abstract terms but he dramatized them in his sketches of fictional "characters".

He declared, for example, in the section "Of Gifts of Fortune", that "Nothing makes us better understand what trifling things Providence thinks he bestows on men in granting them wealth, money, dignities, and other advantages than the manner in which they are distributed and the kind of men who have the largest share".

This thoughtful reflection is followed almost immediately by a portrait graphically illustrating one such person to whom Providence had whimsically, indifferently, and unjustly bestowed such gifts and presents: a boy abbot. "This youth, so ruddy, so florid, and so redolent of health, is lord of an abbey and of ten other benefices; they bring in altogether one hundred and twenty thousand livres a year, which are paid him in golden coin. Elsewhere there are a hundred and twenty indigent families who have no fire to warm themselves during winter, no clothes to cover themselves, and who are often wanting bread; they are in a wretched and piteous state of poverty. What an inequality! And does this not clearly prove that there must be a future state?"

It can be seen, then, that La Bruyère achieved the moralist intention of expressing not only a particular moral or psychological truth, but also of grounding his observation in apt concrete description. He thus mitigated to a certain extent the very abstract nature of Pascal's and La Rochefoucauld's moral observations by providing in his portraits much of the color, moral climate, and ceremony in French society of his day. Yet for all that, his "caractères" have enduring truth for every age.

It would not be accurate to imply that the aphorism and portrait were the exclusive, or in some cases, even the predominant forms used by the 17th Century moralists. Though they perfected them, these writers employed all manner of short prose forms. Pascal preferred the "thought"--a more extended reflection than could usually be accommodated by the aphorism and resembling the form of the "meditation" developed by Marcus Aurelius, among others. Even La

Rochefaucauld did not write exclusively in maxims but framed
some of his extended reflections (the two most remarkable
being "On Self Love" and "The Falsity of a Scorn for Death")
in forms which more resembled short philosophical treatises
or discourses. La Bruyère, the most eclectic of the three,
consistently varied his use of maxims, reflections, and portraits to conform to his changing patterns of thought.

What is essentially characteristic of the rich outpouring of
moralist commentary is the non-sequential and non-systematic
approach it consistently followed in its study of mankind.
No one of these authors has a final statement to make about
human nature. So complex is the human psyche and so impon-
derable the ways of the human heart that any comprehensive
system or summing up on the matter would seem to them vain
and pretentious. This preference for fragmented literary
forms, then, emphasizes the moralist credo that no final
judgment of man should, or indeed, can be made.

Hence there emerges from these Seventeenth-Century authors
a strong sense of existential anguish and futility elicited
by the spectacle of man, who in Pascal's vision, is set ad-
rift, a prey to his own fears and inadequacies, a mere speck
in the frightening void of the immeasurable universe. Though
certainly Pascal and, to a lesser degree, the other moralists
postulate a search for God and an acceptance of the Christian
religion as the ultimate bulkwark against human insufficiency,
so much emphasis is placed on man's moral weakness, ruthless
self-interest, and spiritual blindness that the possibility
of conversion is itself shrouded in pessimism. In this respect, the Renaissance's preference for Christian stoicism--
first decisively challenged by Montaigne--has been dealt a
mortal blow.

Products of an extremely conservative age, the 17th Century
moralists excell in an ingenious study of human motive viewed
in the confines of the self. Rarely do they turn their vision
to judge the validity or justice of their own society. They
accept as a matter of course the principles of monarchy and
Catholicism. The flaws that they perceive in the moral conduct of the nobility and powerful churchmen are, therefore,
only living proof of the inability of humans to live up to
the standards that both institutions preach. La Bruyère comments with sadness on the egoistic cruelty and venality of
the courtier and poignantly describes the dire plight of the

peasant while Pascal decries the vanity and pomp of kings
and the arbitrary nature of justice administered by magistrates. Neither, however, proposes programs for social
change. Keen observers who elevate their findings on human
conduct to a level of detached analyses, they are primarily
concerned with the reform of the individual and do not press
for changes in the social and political spheres. The 17th
Century moralists, in sum, provide us with an essentially
static and timeless view of the moral interior of man and
the social geography of the period. This fundamentally descriptive approach will be sharply altered by moralist writers of the following century.

The changing moral attitudes of the 18th Century were the
result of a slow and gradual process of change. Initially
the moralists and philosophers of the period were far from
radical; Diderot even maintained that many of the philosophes could find intellectual contemporaries in Louis XIV's
reign. The elegant salons still existed as a means of refining ideas and mundane figures like Fontenelle, Rivarol,
and, of course, Voltaire upheld the tradition of the subtle
conversationalist. Yet an entirely new spirit came to ani-
mate these aristocratic gatherings. No longer was it deemed sufficient to observe the ways of human beings from a
leisurely vantage point but rather the motivation now was
to prepare the way for social action. Armchair analysis
for the gratification of an elite gave way to the more
serious aims of enlightening society as a whole. The rumb-
lings of social discontent dramatically served to transform
the salons into foyers for the expansion of philosophical
ideas.

The most marked change in the moralist approach during the
18th Century was the shift in emphasis from the study of
the individual as a self-contained moral entity to that of
a man as a social being with consequent obligations to the
social order. Hence, the moralist would no longer take for
his goal the perfection of the individual or the aristocratic ideal of the wholly interior approach to values. Rather
would he come to view personal intentions as ultimately
linked to social ends. If, for example, Vauvenargues agrees
with La Rochefoucauld that the individual is generally motivated by the demands of "intérêt" (self-seeking), he does
nevertheless insist that a distinction must always be made
between the ruthless egotism of a Hobbes and legitimate

self-interest that serves society through compassionate and generous actions. The first, he would claim, is unworthy and reprehensible; and the second is human, totally legitimate, and the foundation upon which the good of society reposes. As he sums it up: "To blend particular interests with the general constitutes the basis for all moral systems".

Such a different perspective could not help but open to scrutiny the established religious and social systems of the age. Bayle and Voltaire labored to separate moral laws from religious dogma which, they felt, was often even contrary to authentic moral truth. Helvetius went as far as to say that laws should not be founded upon any religious system regardless of the truth it may contain, and even Rousseau, though exalting feeling at the expense of rationalism, also aimed to reform the human heart and ultimately society itself by his vivid comparison of corrupt contemporary man with what he might have been in nature. Even that seemingly confirmed cynic, Chamfort, who continually lashed out against the enormously corrupt society of the late ancien régime in his mordant maxims and thoughts on the "Perfected Civilization", believed that human beings could aspire to virtue if supported and educated by a humane and well intentioned social order. With Rousseau and the other moralists he shared the view that mankind was capable of at least limited happiness, and he agreed with Rousseau that the key to this was to find a simpler existence: "Happiness is like watches. The least complicated give the least trouble..." Hence a utilitarian, rational philosophy with reform for its purpose was supported at least in theory by the moralists.

Preoccupied as these writers were with rehabilitating the moral reputation of man and applying their observations to the social order, they perhaps seem a bit lacking in the finesse d'observation of their classical predecessors. Because they were more intent on describing man as a social being interacting with his fellows, they may be said to have less profoundly descended into the hidden recesses of the human heart; and the portrait of man which they paint seems less complex. Rousseau excepted, they tended to view the human being as a social entity for whom the only authentic virtues are social. Voltaire, in particular, restates these as embodying the qualities of justice, beneficence, and compassion for others.

18

If they are less acute in their probings of human nature, they succeed in restoring balance to the too somber and pessimistic emphasis on human weaknesses and failings developed by their 17th Century predecessors. Yet for all that, they were just as reluctant to formulate systems which might explicate once and for all the perennial complexities of the heart and mind. In fact, their impassioned and continuing attack on all metaphysical attempts to definitively explain the nature of man and the universe gives ample testimony to their belief that such matters went beyond the mind's capacity for understanding. Candide's deceptively simple formula to "cultivate one's garden" is perhaps the best summation of the limits that the moralists set for what can be most profitably pursued by man in this life--positive efforts to improve the human condition in the political and social arena through concerted action.

If these writers are more socially oriented, they remain faithful nonetheless to the moralist tenet of refusing to state more than can be observed. Their reflections are still based upon analysis and perception grounded in the realm of lived experience; and though there is a shift away from composing aphoristic forms in favor of more extended reflections, these observations are as non-systematic and fragmentary as those of their predecessors. In the end we see that the 18th Century moralists continue the method and spirit of the tradition while transferring the emphasis from a purely descriptive study of human nature to its application in the social sphere.

In the wake of the Revolution, that cataclysm which, in Hegel's words, "stood humanity on its head", French writers of the first part of the 19th Century turned their attention within to develop what the philosopher Maine de Biran termed "la moralité de réflexion" (the morality of reflection). Writing in 1816, he declared that the French, after living through such an extraordinary series of events, were frankly exhausted from intense political involvement. They were more disposed now "to turn inward" in order to experience the repose and consolation that could only be found in the intimate confines of the individual conscience. The aging Rousseau had prefigured such a literary retreat in his Rê-veries, in which he gave himself over to the bliss of conversing with his soul; and at the turn of the century, a

19

similar flight from the world soon became a cherished ideal. The moralist Joubert wrote of his desire to "retire into his tower", and in his Fragments of a Diary, Henri Amiel cere- moniously prostrated himself before "the sanctuary of the inner conscience". The young Stendhal, torn by the attrac- tion of society and his passionate efforts to retain in tact the strength and purity of his inner being, admonished him- self in his earliest journal: "You return to what is base through your love of society and its pleasures. Yet you must encounter these as often as possible so as to continue to be disgusted by them".

Such a climate created a new vogue for religious sensibi- lity which the Enlightenment had, in the main, strongly dis- credited. It became acceptable once again to believe in some form of deity which responded to the deepest aspira- tions of the soul; and even if one did not believe, it was no longer fashionable to excoriate those who did or to label them as bigots or fanatics. Needless to say, the forms of faith which developed through inner reflection were both highly personal and individualistic. Eschewing traditional dogma, the generations following the Revolution were clear- ly indebted to Rousseau's "religion of the heart", and there were many who warmed to the moral sentiments so eloquently revealed to the young Emile by the Savoyard vicar.

A natural result of the return to religion was the ten- dency to reject the primacy of the rational faculty in weighing the goodness or justice of human actions. The 18th Century moralists had experienced this change in attitude by their refusal to go as far as many of the philosophers in venerating reason as the summum bonum which, after di- vesting man of ignorance and superstition, would usher in a more perfect social order. By their emphasis on human wholeness, those moralists preferred to regard both reason and feeling as essential components in the quest for good- ness and justice. When faced with the necessity of judging the relative merits of each, however, they were inclined to stress the limitations of reason as compared with the pro- founder insights provided by the heart. In a telling max- im, Vauvenargues had declared that "Reason deceives us more often than nature"; and Rivarol had gone so far as to state that "The heart of man is that part of him which is infin- ite; intelligence has its own limits and one does not love God with all one's mind, but with all one's heart."

20

Rousseau was more extreme in postulating the virtually infinite superiority of sentiment over reason, as he declared
that "The depraved man is he who thinks".

In the 19th Century, writers, in general, further downgraded
the wisdom of reason and went beyond the delicate balance--
more poetic than real--which their predecessors had attempted to achieve. The passionate nature of man was now elevated to the position traditionally enjoyed by the rational
faculty and came itself to be the touchstone for authentic
and correct moral judgment. The honnête homme was now the
one who dared to feel. Joubert declared that "To think
about what we do not feel is tantamount to lying"; and
Stendhal, combining passionate feeling and a determined program for action in the development of his genius, concluded
that "Man cannot perform anything well unless it be supported by the passions".

That the above are not isolated instances can be proved by
turning to other major 19th Century figures. The philos-
opher-historian Guizot advanced the thesis that human instincts and feelings, when universally experienced, were
the most reliable means of guiding the mind to what was
true and just, and he substantiated this process by basing
it upon "les droits du coeur", (the rights of the heart).
And Auguste Comte went so far as to state as a general principle that "le sentiment doit toujours dominer l'intelligence" (feeling must always dominate our intelligence).

It would, of course, be highly inappropriate to weigh in
the same balance the intimate and personal observations of
Joubert, Stendhal, or Amiel with the works of historians
and philosophers such as Guizot and Comte, who were intent
on influencing the political sector with humanitarian programs for the improvement of French society. Yet it is
essential to note that the new emphasis given to the individual conscience and the importance attached to "les
droits du coeur" were central to most 19th Century political and philosophical projects. While the moralists preferred to turn inward to record their personal reflections,
others would opt to affect humanity as a whole through
grand plans for humanitarian reform. Moralist observations
thus coexisted throughout the century with social tracts
and treatises by political philosophers and historians,

with both domains sharing similar concern for the rights and essential dignity of the individual.

While faithful to the 18th Century's demand that moral analysis no longer serve the sole purpose of self-enrichment, the new century also brought renewed importance to introspective examination as the starting point. Hence the 19th Century's predilection to turn within was based upon the firm belief that only through such an intimate self-appraisal could one gain proper insight into what is truly desirable for man. Joubert, who early had espoused a life of quiet retirement, nevertheless declared from the innermost chamber of his "tower": "A private conscience, an individual moral code, and a personal religion? Certainly not: Such concerns by their very nature cannot be private."

In this respect the 19th Century writers and moralists struck a healthy balance between the profound psychological analysis given to the human in the classical period and the more prescriptive aim taken by the Enlightenment authors. Though agreeing with the latter that knowledge accrued through personal analysis should indeed be applied to societal needs, these 19th Century authors reaffirmed their debt to the classical moralists in their belief that self-awareness enhanced by inner reflection had first to be achieved before any collective effort could be made to understand or improve the social order.

The influence of positivism and subsequent deterministic theories advanced by the natural scientists, particularly in the second half of the century, did not provide a fertile climate for traditional moralist literary forms. Yet the seeds of decline had already been sown in the early part of the century by the romantic preference for personal journals examining in minute detail the "vital movement of the soul". With such an emphasis on the personal I, the unique cast of the individual was exalted to the detriment of more universal judgments and observations on human beings. In such a climate, the time honored function of the maxim and thought--to elevate personal observation to the level of the general with resulting application to human motive and conduct--seemed, if not intrinsically faulty, then at least rash and audacious.

22

Moreover, the burgeoning of sociological and political systems such as those forwarded by Comte, Saint-Simon, Fourier, and Marx which emphasized the collective nature of human experience seemed, at least at this time, to render obsolete introspective and non-systematic reflections on man which were not based on ideological tenets, or which did not press for partisan support for them. It is, therefore, not surprising that the "série française" of traditional moralists identified by Sainte-Beuve ended about mid-century, with Joubert and Stendhal closing the cycle.

Joubert is the last French writer of any consequence who chose to express himself almost exclusively in maxims and thoughts (he also cultivated short forms of the essay). He never faltered, moreover, in the belief that even in his own day the maxim remained an especially effective vehicle to advance all forms of knowledge. As he expressed it: "A maxim is the exact and noble expression of an important and uncontestable truth. Good maxims contain in germ all potential good. Once strongly engrained in the memory, they nourish the will." During his entire life, Joubert expended his energies on a grand design to reconcile the legacy of enlightenment rationalism with the vogue for religious mysticism of his own period, to which he was strongly drawn. And the title he gave to his collected musings, Thoughts, Maxims, and Essays, is a clear indication of his conscious determination to continue, in form and spirit, the moralist tradition and to engage in a dialogue with his predecessors.

Though primarily renowned as one of France's greatest novelists, Stendhal (Henri Beyle) was also an important moralist. Utilizing a wide variety of aphoristic forms, he recorded in his personal journals and in his very perceptive treatise on love, De l'amour, his intimate reflections on human nature, the passions, the role of the artist, and the nature of society, to mention the most important. His main goal in composing such works was to derive and set to paper ethical standards upon which to fix his personal life. The title of the earliest Stendhalian journal, Pensées et nova filosofia, (Thoughts and New Philosophy), is revealing as a summation of his intention: to formulate a "new philosophy of life" based upon an energetic program of self-realization devised through reflection and the systematic use of the will.

In the course of Stendhal's writings there occurs a major shift in emphasis from a preference for the briefer aphorism-maxim to the extended thought-reflection which was to become his principal mode of expression in these works. "Since, he remarked, every general maxim is in some way false, to write only in maxims is to demonstrate a bad method of writing."

Stendhal provides a fascinating case in point to prove that the moralist tradition could fully adapt itself to record the individual's search for meaning and fulfillment despite the complexities of the modern age. In his use of analysis and observation, he faithfully adhered to the moralist method yet he interiorized and personalized his findings to a degree unknown to his predecessors and developed a dynamic, clear-sighted program for personal growth which he referred to as the "culte du moi" (the cult of the self). By his emphasis on the self-fulfilling power of the will in the pursuit of truth and happiness, Stendhal strongly influenced the moral teachings of Nietzsche and a host of modern philosophers for whom this is a central doctrine.

If the tradition ends in a formal sense with Stendhal, it is far from a dead letter in modern France. Indeed there exists a posterity of authors who continue the literary prose forms and the moralist analysis of the human. This renewed attention accorded to moralist literature in our own century can be attributed to at least two factors: There is first the powerful influence of the German philosophers Schopenhauer, Nietzsche, and Lictenberg--themselves much indebted to moralist thought--who show a decided predilection for aphoristic forms.[2] The second reason was the profound

---

2   Consider Nietzsche's appraisal of the importance of the moralists: "Reading Montaigne, La Rochefoucauld, La Bruyère, Fontenelle, Vauvenargues, Chamfort, one is nearer the ancients than with any group of six authors of other countries...They contain more real thoughts than all the books of German philosophers together. To glow with a thought, to be burnt up by it--that is French". Or, "...The much more uncomfortable grand fait is that all the great French moralists had a will and character of their own, from Montaigne, Charron, La Rochefoucauld, up to Chamfort and Stendhal. As an artist one has no

crisis in faith and the collapse of tradtional values which
occurred in the wake of the Great War. There developed as
a result a growing distrust of moral and political systems on
a grand scale. Renewed emphasis was consequently applied to
ethical concerns strictly relevant to the individual's search
for meaning and understanding of the self and the universe.
In such a post-war climate, aphoristic forms were once again
deemed natural and appropriate vehicles for expressing the
intuitive and non-sequential patterns of thought which were
part of the intensely subjective literature of the period.

The modern moralists presented in this anthology are most
eclectic in their use of traditional prose forms. Though
they share Stendhal's preference for the extended thought or
reflection, they often employ shorter forms which serve as
effective means to express a brief remark, spontaneous insight, or spark of intuition. In fact, it can be said that
these authors exhaust the entire range of aphoristic forms
and utilize them to support and give form to the free flow
of their thought patterns.

Paul Valéry reveals the most striking fidelity to this literary continuity. In his prodigious and unflagging effort
to divest the human mind of myths and dubious beliefs acquired by tradition, this philosopher-poet composed finely
etched observations and reflections representative of the
best of the earlier moralists. From the age of twenty,
Valéry would rise each day before dawn and spend several
hours refining and recording his current thoughts. These
remarks, which he labeled variously, "Odds and Ends,"
"Rhumbs," "Analecta," and "Bad Thoughts and Not So Bad,"
are remarkably diverse, provocative, and challenging by

---

2 (cont'd.) home in Europe except Paris". Concerning his
    preference for aphorisms: "A good aphorism is too hard
    for the ravages of time, and is not eaten away in thou-
    sands of years, although it serves every age nourishment:
    in this it is the most paradoxical thing in literature,
    the eternal expressed in the transitory, the food which is
    always valued, like salt, and never becomes stale as
    even salt does". Human All-Too Human in The Complete
    Works of Frederich Nietzsche , ed. Oscar Levy, Vol. 7,
    (New York: Macmillan, 1924), p. 302 and p. 83.

their high seriousness. They run the gamut of human investigation from philosophy to ethics, to history, science, literature, and art.

André Gide's role as a moralist is best seen through the poetic prose of his early work, Fruits of the Earth, and the mature prose of the Journal. In the first, he recorded his personal liberation from ethical and moral constraints which he felt had stifled the free development of his "authentic" self. This youthful paen to fervor and sincerity recorded the initial abandonment of the cerebral life for self-fulfillment. In the volumes of the Journal, Gide set down his painstaking efforts to develop an understanding of the self as well as what is generally termed the experience of reality, with which we all must come to grips. Ultimately concluding that neither the self nor the framework of reality are permanently fixed states, he preferred to record the oscillations of his innermost being which was constantly nourished by a carefully cultivated mind and an aesthetic pursuit of wisdom. The journals thus became a fascinating record of a voyage of self-discovery and, as such, are reminiscent of Montaigne's earlier experiment in the Essays.

Then there is Alain (Emile Chartier), whose concise definition of the moralist project is given above. A philosopher in the non-systematic sense dear to the French, he exerted tremendous influence on many young intellectuals in the period between the two world wars both as teacher and writer.

During his career, he evolved an extremely personal moral philosophy based primarily on sense perception and matters of interest drawn from his vast humanistic background. Alain strongly believed that philosophy is a discipline that cannot be separated from other forms of human thought --religion, art, literature, politics, science--or from life itself. In putting his thoughts into writing, he virtually created a new genre which he called the Propos (Discourses), philosophical sketches so artfully rendered that they resemble short prose poems.

In his Discourses, Alain demonstrated keen interest in almost every manner of thing of interest to humans. He dealt with the passions, political happenings, leading personalities, war, God, popular manners of speech, habits, customs, animals, plants, and framed his musings in the context of everyday experience, in the absence of which, he felt, the mind can only operate in a void. With this method he developed a practical, warm, and down-to-earth approach to life. He stressed the concept that the will should accommodate itself with the world as it is and with human nature as one experiences it through study of the self and others. Accordingly, such a program should lead to a full measure of happiness in the course of any human life. In both aim and spirit, then, Alain's works are totally reminiscent of the moralist tradition and his finely chiseled experiments in prose achieve a similar clarity and conciseness of expression.

That the moralist forms could be assimilated in the world of science has been amply demonstrated by Jean Rostand. This famous biologist-writer gathered together his reflections on the nature of man in two volumes: A Biologist's Thoughts, and A Biologist's Notebooks. An avid reader of the moralists and particularly attracted by Pascal's views, he consistently relates the results of his biological research to passages from various authors and moralists. His reflections frequently recast celebrated Pascalian "thoughts" making them parallel or contrasting with conclusions drawn from biology and genetics. He thereby gives to Pascal's view of man and the universe new and striking dimensions by this application of scientific theory. He effects a similar transformation of passages taken from other moralists by tempering classical and traditional psychological insights with his own biological meditations on "the substance of man."

The most recent and best known of the modern moralists is certainly Albert Camus. Designated somewhat disparagingly by Sartre--in the heat of their monumental quarrel in the early 50's--as the last great decendant of the French moralist tradition, he has often been designated by modern critics as the most important secular moralist of our age.

Although all of Camus' works--fictional or non-fictional--reveal the moralist's deep concern and understanding of modern man's desperate struggle to live fully and ethically in the world, his affinity to the methods and aims of the tradition is most apparent in the Carnets (Notebooks). Published in two volumes encompassing the period from 1935-1951, the Notebooks constitute a logbook in which Camus

recorded the state and progress of his inner life. He jotted
down anecdotes, snippets of conversations heard by chance,
reflections or comments elicited by his readings on all manner of authors and contemporary figures, fragments from works
in progress, comments on the world situation, and many aphorisms and reflections--all of which reveal the evolving patterns of his moral and artistic development.

Though extremely fragmentary and not originally intended for
publication, the Notebooks thus provide an admirable index
to his moralist preoccupation. In his varied observations
and reflections based on self study and life experience, he
agonizes over his own growth as an artist who strives to remain true to his personal vision and values. At the same
time he formulates his commitment to the struggle of modern
man, whose freedom and dignity, he feels, are menaced from
all sides by forms of political collectivism intent on de-
humanizing him and imposing brutal tyrannies in the name of
futurist goals.

*

*   *

In his celebrated essay on "Paris and the Senses," Matthew
Arnold defined what he felt was the unique contribution made
by the French for the moral edification of the rest of the
world; one century later his statement remains extremely perceptive and convincing in explaining what constitutes the
great appeal and influence that French authors in general--
and certainly the moralists in particular--have enjoyed
among multitudes of non-French readers.

Arnold's theory revolves about his judgment that in her literature, France alone has kept intact the Greek tradition of
fidelity to nature, which explains "her attractiveness for
everybody, and her success and her repeated disasters."[3]

---

3 "The True Greatness of the Old Testament" in Dissent and
   Dogma, Complete Works of Matthew Arnold, ed. R.H. Sapor,
   Vol. 6. (Ann Arbor: University of Michigan Press, 1960-
   77), pp. 388-392.

In Arnold's viewpoint this tradition has led to the ideal of "l'homme moyen sensuel" (the average sensual man), whose world capital is Paris and whose aspiration we all share. In his words, "We all have in us this homme sensuel,the man of the 'wishes of the flesh and of the current thoughts': but we develop him under checks and doubts, and unsystematically and often grossly. France, on the other hand, develops him confidently and harmoniously. She makes the most of him because she knows what she is about and keeps in a mean, as her climate is in mean, and her situation."

Arnold then goes on to analyze the "tact and measure, good sense, and logic" with which the French have evolved this concept, as well as their intention to "develop the senses, the apparent self, all round in good faith, without misgivings, without violence." As a result, France "has much reasonableness and clearness in all her notions and arrangements, a sort of balance even in conduct."

Though Arnold chose to deal with the ethos of "l'homme moyen sensuel" as a product of French literature as a whole, the moralists have played the dominant role in the evolution of "a balanced and measured approach to the development of the apparent self" which lies at the root of the concept. For it is uncontestable that without the long and uninterrupted study of human nature carried forth by Montaigne, Pascal, La Rochefoucauld, and the others, there would have existed no sure foundation upon which to base such an ethical ideal.

By its very definition, then, the concept of the "average sensual man" is a result of the long-range study conducted by the moralists on human character and motive. And in the final analysis this morality does not postulate a fixed absolute--such as saintliness or cynicism--but a frequently shifting mean between the best and worst of human responses.

"Ni bête ni ange" (neither saint nor sinner), capable of virtue, love, and justice, yet forever needing the sagacity to say no to those forces--interior or exterior--which flatter and encourage our baser instincts; such is the doctrine of moral realism refined by the moralists and comprising the core of Arnold's concept of the "average sensual man." And such is the wise and measured view of human nature which France, primarily through its moralists, has bequeathed to the rest of the world.

Chapter 1

MICHEL EYQUEM de MONTAIGNE
(1533-1592)

Since their initial publication nearly four-hundred years
ago, Montaigne's Essays remain the most remarkable-and suc-
cessful-experiment in the investigation of the self. For
Montaigne such an enterprise was his ultimate concern and
the one which he pursued relentlessly in all his writings:
"I study myself," he declared in an early essay, "more than
any other subject. It is my metaphysics, it is my physics
...I who have no other profession, find within me such infinite depth and variety that I have reaped no other fruits
from my learning than to become aware how much there remains
for me to learn."

Michel Eyquem de Montaigne was born the 28th of February,
1533, in the chateau of Montaigne some sixty kilometers
from Bordeaux. The son of a rich merchant from that city,
he was the first of his line to assume the name of his property, since his family had been titled only fifty years before his birth.

His father, Pierre Eyquem, a veteran of the Italian wars
and an enthusiastic student of the new Renaissance learning,
provided him with a remarkable education. The young boy
was awakened to the sound of music each morning so as not
to disturb his natural cheerfulness and equilibrium. He
was instructed by a tutor who taught him Latin as a living

language before he learned his native tongue. Latin remained his second language and this fact greatly accounts for
the seemingly effortless ability with which he incorporated
copious quotations from the ancients into the body of the
essays, usually without pedantry or ostentation.

When only six years of age Montaigne was sent to the Collège
de Guyenne in Bordeaux, one of the most illustrious of French
Renaissance schools. Here he apparently suffered a great
deal because of the rigid discipline, primitive hygienic conditions, and the rigid and narrow attitudes of some of his
teachers. Moreover, he was far advanced beyond students of
his own age. His father intervened and arranged for the boy
to receive private instruction from tutors outside the
Collège. One of these, "a man of greatest understanding,"
allowed the boy to follow his natural literary tastes, and
Montaigne devoured the works of Ovid, Virgil, Cicero,
Terence, and Plautus, in particular. When thirteen he had
completed his secondary studies and began the study of law,
most probably at the University of Toulouse.

In 1554, at the age of twenty-one, he succeeded his father
as counselor of the cour des aides of Perigueux and, in a
short period, became a representative to the Parliament of
Bordeaux (1557). Though he referred very seldom to his official duties, he must have gained many insights during his
thirteen years as legal counsel which prompted him to de-
nounce, in many subsequent passages of the Essays, the in-
adequacy of human systems of justice and the cruelty that
they sometimes mask or even condone.

Upon his entry into Parliament he met the friend and ruling
passion of his life. Etienne de la Boétie, also a member
of this body and a well-known humanist scholar and poet,
profoundly influenced Montaigne's ethical views during this
period. In fact, the stoical rigor of the earlier essays,
with their emphasis on the contemplation of death as the
supreme end of life, stems largely from this association.
When La Boétie died only four years later, Montaigne never
forgot the brave and serene countenance assumed by his
friend during the closing moments of his life. Montaigne
later wrote the moving essay "Of Friendship" to describe
his love for La Boétie and to discourse with deep feeling
on the nature of friendship itself.

31

The year that he entered Parliament, Montaigne also married Françoise de la Chassaigne in what does not seem to have been a warm or particularly sharing union. Though he devotes several passages of the Essays to comments on marriage as a state of life, he tells us very little of his own, and of his wife, only that she took excellent care of many of the material problems inherent in running his extensive estate. From the marriage were born six daughters; and only one survived to adulthood.

In 1568, Montaigne suffered the loss of his beloved father but not before the latter, a few months before his death, had asked him to translate a somewhat obscure work by Raymond Sebond, a fifteenth-century Catalan theologian. Sebond's treatise, the Book of Creatures or Natural Theology, constituted his attempt to demonstrate the existence and nature of God by the use of analogies drawn from the various levels of creation. The work ultimately claimed that such a proof could be derived by the use of unaided reason alone, and presumably for this reason, it was placed on the Index of of Prohibited Books in 1558. Montaigne's father wished to vindicate Sebond's thesis and provide a version in the vernacular apparently to stem the tide of anti-Christian and "rational" attacks against religious belief which had been making headway in France during the turbulent years of religious strife.

One year later, Montaigne published his translation of the huge tome. The immediate acclaim which it won him along with his unconsoled and persistent grief at the loss of his father and dearest friend confirmed his decision to retire from active life in 1571. In his well stocked library, Montaigne now hoped to devote himself exclusively to reading, contemplation, and jotting down his sundry musings. This regime gradually resulted in the composition of "essais" --brief written attempts or trials in prose. The first volume, comprising Books I and II of the "essais," was subsequently published in 1581.

Plagued by kidney stones, Montaigne took an extended leave from his chateau in 1581 to take the cure for the malady at various thermal stations in France, Switzerland, Germany, and Italy. This voyage also afforded him the opportunity to travel through the principal cities of these countries and greatly increased his plentiful stock of observations on human mores and social conventions. Many of these fresh insights he would later incorporate in the more lengthy and universal essays he wrote after 1581.

The tourist Montaigne was forced to return to Bordeaux as the city's elected mayor in 1582 and he held this post for the next four years. His first impulse had been to reject the honor straightaway, but Henry III had virtually commanded him to accept. So effectively did he discharge his duties that he was enthusiastically elected for another term in 1584. He, in fact, proved to be a talented mediator between the rival factions of the Protestants and the Catholic League which were tearing the city apart.

Ultimately he sided with the Catholic cause less through religious conviction than innate political conservatism and a strong loyalty to the monarchy; and he viewed the Protestants as dangerous purveyors of civil war and sedition.

When the plague ravaged Bordeaux in 1585, he refused to return to supervise the election of his successor and has ever since been seriously taken to task by critics for this prudent but hardly inspiring retreat to the relative safety of his own property. Such a decision was, however, totally in accord with his absolute insistence that the mayor of Bordeaux and Michel de Montaigne were two entirely different entities and that he would only lend and never give his person totally to this political office.

He spent the years from 1585 to his death in 1592 in the "tower" of his chateau enjoying the repose that he had so fervently sought since his abortive retirement. During these years he revised and often considerably altered the "essais" of the first two books and finished the thirteen chapters of Book Three. The revised and new writings were combined in the complete edition of the "works" of 1588.

After his death, the final additions and revisions he had made after 1588 were incorporated into the "essais" by Mlle. Marie de Gournay, a highly intelligent and passionately devoted woman whom he met in Picardy during one of his final trips to Paris, where he had been summoned to advise Henry IV. To this woman, his "covenant daughter", as he called her, he entrusted the editing of what would become the posthumous and definitive editions of 1595 and 1611.

When he retired from public life, Montaigne occupied himself initially with the Renaissance practice of jotting down and collecting pithy sayings--aphorisms, apothegms, proverbs, anecdotes, etc.--from his rich background and current readings of the literature of the ancients. His frame of reference was always that of the moralist--an intense interest in human character, conduct, and motive. Following the influence of his beloved authors (especially Seneca and Plutarch), he reveled in analyzing deeds and the moral qualities that governed them in all areas of human endeavor seen through exemplary characters.

Not content after a time with merely collecting kernels of wisdom or analyzing conduct provided by classical authorities, he subjected his data to a searching self-analysis which caused him to depart markedly from the literature of the ancients. Rather than regarding his intimate feelings as secondary, as they had, he compared his deepest opinions and feelings on the self with comments that he read. Nor did he seek to conceal this process but made it the primary object of his writings. That is to say, these topics were reflected from and refracted through his particular temperament. Gradually he became convinced that his views did not reflect himself alone but were truly representative of all humanity. Thus he subsequently amplified the earlier assertion, "I am the groundwork of my book," by the claim: "Each man bears the entire form of the human condition." It is by this process of self-analysis through his musings and writings and their subsequent application to all mankind that Montaigne cast the mold for all future moralist literature.

It would be a vain exercise to try to draw from the Essays any systematic or sustained doctrine. In fact, Montaigne took great pains to refute systems which purported to explain human nature in any definitive fashion. Rather, his message reposes on a conviction that at first glance appears somewhat unsettling: that is, the amazing complexity

34

of man. What each of us possesses that is least bad is our own particular make-up--the "forme maîtresse"--which individualizes each one of us from the other. We cannot, he says, transform this radically, but each of us alone can realize its potential and be the sole judge of its relative excellence. "You alone, he says, are the one who knows if you are cowardly or cruel, loyal or deceitful: others do not see you and only appraise you through uncertain conjectures."

Montaigne ultimately proposes a moral code which rests upon the notion of the conscience. Often betrayed by our imagination and buffeted by conflicting passions in a world of constant flux, we are called upon to develop and refine a moral sense by which we can control our passions and give order and balance to life. Only then can we live worthwhile and virtuous lives.

Imbued as they are with such wise and human counsel, it is not surprising that very early in the Seventeenth Century the Essays were already being described as "the breviary of decent people"; or that in our own century, Montaigne remains certainly the most influential and perhaps the most widely read of all French moralists.

ON REPENTANCE

Others form man; I describe him, and portray a particular
one, ill fashioned enough, and whom, if I had to mold him
anew, I should certainly make very different from what he is.
But that's past recalling. Now, the features of my portrait
are not random, though they change and vary. The world is
but a perennial merry-go-round. All things therein are incessantly in motion, the earth, the rocks of the Caucasus,
the pyramids of Egypt, both with the general movement and
their own. Constancy itself is nothing but a more languid
motion. I cannot fix any object; it keeps tottering and
reeling by a natural intoxication. I take it as it is at
the instant that I am occupied with it. I do not paint its
being. I paint its passage: not a passage from one age to
another, or, as people say, from seven years to seven years,
but from day to day, from minute to minute. I must accommodate my history to the times. I may presently change, not
only by fortune, but also by intention. It is a record of
various and changeable occurrences, and of unsettled and, as
sometimes happens, contradictory ideas, whether it be that I
am then another self or that I take hold of subjects by
other circumstances and considerations. So it is that I may
perhaps contradict myself, but the truth, as Demades said,
I do not contradict. Could my soul once take footing, I
would not essay, I would resolve; but it is always in a
state of apprenticeship and trial.

I set forth a life that is humble and without distinction:
it all comes to the same thing. All of moral philosophy can
be applied as well to a common and private life as to one of
richer stuff. Every man carries in himself the entire form
of the human condition.

Authors communicate themselves to people by some special and external mark; I, the first of any by my universal being, as Michel de Montaigne, not as a grammarian, a poet, or a lawyer. If the world find fault that I speak too much of myself, I find fault that they do not so much as think of themselves.

But is it reasonable that, being so private in my way of living, I should aspire to present myself to public knowledge? And is it reasonable, too, that I should offer to the world, where style and art have so much credit and authority, the crude and simple products of Nature, and of a rather weak nature besides? Is it not like building a wall without stone or some such material, to construct books without learning and without art? The fancies of music are guided by art, mine by chance.

This, at least, I have in keeping with the rules, that no man ever treated of a subject which he understood and knew better than I do the one that I have undertaken, and that in this I am the most learned man alive; secondly, that no man ever penetrated further into his matter, nor more thoroughly analyzed its elements and connections, nor more exactly and fully arrived at the end he had proposed for his labors. To accomplish it, I need bring nothing but fidelity to the work; and it is there, the most pure and sincere that is to be found anywhere. I speak truth, not as completely as I should like, but as much as I dare; and I dare a little more as I grow older, for it seems that custom allows to age more liberty of prattling and more indiscretion in talking of oneself. It cannot happen here, as I often see elsewhere, that the craftsman and his product contradict one another: "Can a man who is so sensible in conversation have written so foolish a book?" or" "Do such learned writings proceed from a man so feeble in conversation?"

If the talk of a man is ordinary and his writing distinguished, it means that his ability lies in the place from which he borrowed it, and not in himself. A learned man is not learned in all things; but a man of talent is always a man of talent, even in ignorance.

Here my book and I go hand in hand together, and keep the same pace. Elsewhere, men may commend or censure the work

apart from the workman; here they cannot. Who touches the
one, touches the other. He who shall judge the one without
knowing the other will wrong himself more than me; he who
has come to know the work gives me all the satisfaction I
desire. Happy beyond my desert if I enjoy only this much of
public approbation, to make men of understanding feel that I
was capable of profiting by learning, had I had it, and that
I deserved to be better assisted by my memory.

Let me excuse myself here for what I often repeat, that I
rarely repent, and that my conscience is satisfied with itself, not as the conscience of an angel or of a horse, but
as the conscience of a man; always adding this refrain, not
by way of formality, but in sincere and real submission,
that I speak as one who questions and does not know, purely
and simply referring myself for the decision to the common
and legitimate beliefs. I do not teach, I relate.

There is no vice truly a vice which is not harmful, and
which a sound judgment does not condemn; for there is in it
so manifest an ugliness and disadvantage that they are perhaps in the right who say that it is caused chiefly by stupidity and ignorance. So hard is it to imagine that a man
may know it without hating it. Malice sucks up the greater
part of its own venom and poisons itself with it. Vice
leaves repentance in the soul like an ulcer in the flesh,
which is always scratching itself and drawing blood. For
reason effaces all other griefs and sorrows, but it causes
that of repentance, which is so much more grievous since it
springs from within; as the cold and heat of fevers are more
sharply felt than that which comes from without. I hold for
vices (but each according to its measure) not only those
which reason and nature condemn, but also those which the
opinion of men has created, even though it be a false and
erroneous opinion, provided it has the authority of law and
custom.

There is likewise no good action which does not gladden a
well-born nature. There is assuredly a kind of gratification in well-doing that causes inward rejoicing, and there
is a generous pride that accompanies a good conscience. A
soul daringly wicked may perhaps arm itself with security,
but with this complacency and satisfaction it cannot supply

38

itself. It is no little pleasure to feel oneself preserved
from the contagion of so depraved an age, and to say to oneself: "If anyone should look into my very soul, he would
yet not find me guilty either of the affliction or ruin of
anyone, or of revenge or envy, or of offending the public
laws, or of innovation and disturbance, or of failing in my
word; and though the licence of the time permits and teaches
everyone to do so, yet have I not laid my hand on any Frenchman's goods or thrust my fingers into his purse, and have
lived only on what is my own, in war as well as in peace;
neither have I set any man to work without paying him his
hire." These testimonies of a good conscience are pleasant,
and this natural rejoicing is very beneficial to us, and the
only reward that we can never lack.

To ground the recompense of virtuous actions upon the approbation of others is to adopt too uncertain and shaky a foundation. Especially in so corrupt and ignorant an age as
this, the good opinion of the people is injurious. On whom
can you rely to see what is commendable? God defend me from
being an honest man according to the descriptions of honor
I see every man give of himself daily. "Those things which
once were vices are now moral."

Some of my friends have at times taken it upon them to school
and lecture me with great plainness, either of their own
accord or at my request, as if acquitting themselves of an
office which for a well-composed soul surpasses, not only
in utility but in kindness, all other duties of friendship.
I have always received it with the most open arms of cour-
tesy and gratitude. But to speak of it now in all sincerity,
I have found so much falseness both in their blame and
praise that if I had sinned instead of doing well, I should
hardly have committed a sin according to their value. Those
of us in particular who live private lives, not exposed to
any other view than our actions, and, according to that pattern, sometimes hug and sometimes flog ourselves. I have my
own laws and my court-room to judge me, and I refer to these
more than to any other authority. I do indeed restrain my
actions according to others, but I extend them only according to myself. No one but yourself knows if you are cowardly and cruel, or loyal and devout. Others do not see you,
they guess about you by uncertain conjectures. They do not

so much see your nature as your art. Therefore do not hold
by their opinions; hold by your own. "You must use your own
judgment. In the matter of virtues and vices, a man's own
conscience carries great weight: take that away, and everything lies in ruins."

But the saying that repentance follows close upon the sin
does not seem to have in view sin in its high estate, which
is lodged in us as in its proper domicile. We may disown
and retract the vices which take us by surprise and into
which we are hurried by passion; but those which by long habit are rooted and anchored in a strong and vigorous will are
not capable of being disputed. Repentance is nothing more
than a recanting of the will and an opposition to our fancies, which leads us about in all directions. It makes this
person disown his former virtue and continence:

> Why to my youth was not the wisdom given
>   Which now I share?
> Or with my old desires why come not back
>   Youth's cheeks as fair?

It is a rare life that preserves its orderly procedure even
in private. Everyone can play his part in the farce and
represent an honest character on the stage; but within, and
in his own bosom, where all is permitted, where all is concealed, to be disciplined there-that is the point! The
state nearest to it is to be so in our own house, in our
ordinary actions, for which we are accountable to no man;
where there is no study, or artifice. And therefore Bias,
describing an ideal domestic establishment, says it is one
of which the master is the same within, of his own free will,
as he is without, from fear of the law and of what people
might say. And it was a worthy saying of Julius Drusus to
the workmen who offered, for three thousand crowns, to put
his house into such a condition that his neighbours would
no longer be able to look into it as they had done. "I will
give you," he said, "six thousand, if you will make it possible for everybody to see into it from all sides." It is
observed to the honor of Agesilas that in his travels he
was accustomed to take up his lodgings in churches, so that
the people and the gods themselves might see into his private actions. Some men have seemed miraculous to the world,

40

in whom their wives and valets have never observed anything that was even noteworthy. Few men have been admired by their own household.

No one has been a prophet, not only in his own house, but in his own country, says the experience of history. It is the same in things of no consequence. And in this following humble example a reflection of greater ones may be seen. In my region of Gascony they think it a droll thing to see me in print; the farther off from my own lair the knowledge of me spreads, the more high am I valued. I buy the printers in Guyenne; elsewhere they buy me. On this circumstance do those people base their expectations, who keep concealed while living and present, to gain a reputation when they are dead and absent. I prefer to have less of it, and only throw myself upon the world for that part of it that I actually draw on. Beyond that, I hold it quit.

See this fellow whom the people, after a public function, escort to his door with loud acclaim. Along with his gown he puts off the part he has been playing; his descent is as deep as his climb was high. Within, in himself, all is in confusion and base. And even though order should exist there, it requires a lively and well-sifted judgment to perceive it in those humble and private actions. Besides, order is a dull and sombre virtue. To enter a breach, conduct an embassy, govern a people, are brilliant actions. To scold, laugh, sell, pay, love, hate, to hold pleasant and reasonable communion with oneself and one's family, not to let go of oneself nor to be false to oneself, that is a rarer and more difficult matter, and not observed so much. Retired lives, whatever people may say, are thereby subject to duties as severe and strenuous as those of other lives, if not more so. And private persons, says Aristotle, render a higher and more difficult service to virtue than do those who are in authority. We prepare ourselves for eminent occasions more out of glory than conscience. The shortest way to arrive at glory would be to do for the sake of conscience what we do for the sake of glory. And the virtue of Alexander in his great theater seems to me to display much less vigor than that of Socrates in his humble and obscure activity. I can easily imagine Socrates in the place of Alexander, but Alexander in that of Socrates, I cannot. If you will ask the former what he can do, he will answer: "Subdue the world"; if you put the same question to the latter, he will say: "Carry on human life conformably with its natural condition": a skill of much more general importance, more difficult, and more legitimate.

The worth of the soul does not consist in mounting aloft, but in walking at an orderly pace. Its greatness is not exercised in greatness, but in a middle state. As those who judge and test our inner being make no great account of the luster of our public actions, and see that these are only drops and thin tricklings of water oozing from a thick and slimy bottom; so likewise they who judge us by this brave outward appearance, infer a similar quality in our internal constitution, and are unable to couple common faculties, just like their own, with these other faculties that astonish them and are so far beyond their scope. So we endow demons with monstrous shapes. And who does not picture Tamerlane with raised eyebrows, open nostrils, a dreadful visage, and a prodigious stature, which is the figure that the imagination has constructed from the report of his name? Once upon a time, if I had been brought into the presence of Erasmus, it would have been hard for me not to take for adages and apothegms anything he might have said to his serving-man and his hostess. We find it more in keeping to imagine an artisan on his commode or on his wife than a great president, venerable by his bearing and his talent. From their high thrones, it seems to us, they will hardly abase themselves so low as to live.

As vicious souls are often incited by some extraneous impulse to do good, so are virtuous souls to do evil. We must therefore judge them by their settled state, when they are at home, if they ever are; or at least when they are closest to repose and to their natural state. Natural inclinations are assisted and reinforced by education, but they are scarcely altered and overcome. A thousand natures in my time have escaped toward virtue or toward vice contrary to a training that led in the opposite direction:

> As when wild beasts, long time in cages shut,
> Grow tame and lay aside their threatening looks,
> Learning to suffer the control of man;
> But if a little warm blood touch their mouths,

Their savage fury and their rage return,
At the forgotten taste their jaws distend,
They burn with thirst, and hardly can be kept
From springing at their trembling master's throat.

These original qualities are not to be rooted out; they may
be covered, they may be concealed. The Latin tongue is, as
it were, natural to me; I understand it better than French,
but it is forty years since I have made any use of it for
speaking or writing. Yet in extreme and sudden states of
excitement, such as I have fallen into two or three times
in my life (once, when I saw my father, though in perfect
health, fall upon me in a swoon), the first words that rush-
ed from the depths of my breast were always in Latin, Nature
surging up and forcibly expressing herself in spite of long
disuse. The same experience is related of many others.

They who in my time have attempted to revise the morals of
the world by new ideas, reform external vices; the essential
vices they leave as they were, if they do not increase them.
And the increase is what is to be feared. We are apt to
rest from all other well-doing on the strength of these
external, arbitrary reforms which are less costly and bring
greater recognition, and by this means we atone at a cheap
rate for the other natural, consubstantial, and internal
vices. Consider a little how our own experience in the matter stands. There is no man who, if he listens to himself,
does not discover within himself an individual principle, a
ruling principle, which struggles against education and a-
gainst the tempest of passions that are hostile to it. For
my part, I am not much agitated by sudden gusts; I am nearly
always in my place, like heavy and cumbersome bodies. If I
am not at home, I am always very close by. My excesses do
not carry me very far away. There is in them nothing
strange or extreme; and yet I have healthy and vigorous
changes of feeling.

The true condemnation, the one which affects the common run
of men, is that even their retirement is full of corruption
and filth; their idea of reform is blurred, their penitence
is sick and faulty, almost as much as is their sin. Some,
either because they are by nature cemented to vice, or because of long habit are no longer aware of its ugliness.

43

Others (of the group to which I belong) feel the weight of vice, but they offset it with pleasure, or some other circumstance; they suffer it and submit to it, for a certain price, but viciously and basely, nevertheless. Yet it might be possible to imagine a disproportion so great between the pleasure and the sin that the pleasure might with justice excuse the sin, as we say that utility excuses it; not only if it were incidental, something apart from the sin itself, as in theft, but in the very exercise of the sin, as in the enjoyment of women, where the provocation is violent and, it is said, sometimes irresistible.

The other day at Armagnac, on the estate of a kinsman of mine, I saw a country fellow whom everybody called by his nickname, Thief. He gave the story of his life as follows: Born a beggar and realizing that by toiling with his hands for a living he would never succeed in protecting himself against want, he decided to become a thief, and by the aid of his physical strength he had practiced his trade throughout his youth in safety. For he gathered his harvest and his vintage from other men's lands, but at such a great distance and in such great heaps that it is hard to imagine how one man could have carried off so much in a single night on his own shoulders. And besides, he was careful to equalize and distribute the damage that he did so that the loss to each individual was of little consequence. Now, in his old age, he is rich for a man in his position, thanks to this business which he openly confesses. And to make his peace with God for his ill-gotten gains, he says he is daily engaged in compensating with favors the successors of those whom he robbed; and if he does not finish his task (for to do it all at once is out of his power), he will charge his heirs with it, in proportion to the wrong which he alone knows he has done to each. By this description, be it true or false, it appears that this man regards theft as a dishonest action and hates it, but not so much as he hates poverty; he repents of it quite simply, but in so far as his wrong action was counterbalanced and rewarded by certain benefits, he does not repent of it. That is not what I mean by that habit which incorporates us with vice and brings even our understanding into conformity with it, nor by that furious whirlwind which in gusts confuses and blinds our soul and hurls us for the time, judgment and all,

44

into the power of vice.

Customarily, whatever I do, I do it as a whole, and I move in one piece. I have hardly a motion that hides from my reason, and that is not guided by the consent of nearly all parts of me, without division, without internal sedition. My judgment has all the blame or all the praise of it. And the blame it once has, it always has, for almost since its birth it has been one: the same inclination, the same road, the same strength. And in the matter of general opinions, I established myself in youth in the position where I had to stay.

There are sins that are impetuous, instantaneous, and sudden: let us set them aside. But with respect to those other sins, so many times repeated, meditated, and considered, or constitutional sins, even sins flowing from our profession and vocation, I cannot conceive that they should have remained lodged for so long a time in the very same heart unless the reason and the conscience of the man who harbors them constantly wills and means that it should be so. And the repentance which, according to his boast, overcomes him at a certain prescribed moment is for me a little hard to imagine and conceive.

I do not follow the opinion of the Pythagorean sect, that men take up a new soul when they return to the images of the gods to receive their oracles. Unless he meant to say that it must needs be extrinsic, new, and borrowed for the time being: their own showing so little sign of the purification and cleanness that is becoming to such a function.

They act quite contrary to the Stoical precepts, which do indeed command us to correct the imperfections and vices which we acknowledge to be in us, but forbid us to be troubled and chagrined on account of them. Those men make us believe that they feel great regret and remorse within; but of amendment and correction, or cessation, there is no symptom. Yet there can be no cure if the disease is not thrown off. If repentance were heavy in the scale of the balance, it would weigh down the sin. I know of no quality so easy to counterfeit as piety, if the conduct of life is not brought into conformity with it. Its essence is abstruse and occult; its forms are easy and ceremonial.

45

For my own part, I may desire in general to be other than I
am; I may dislike and condemn my whole nature and implore
God for my entire reformation and for pardon of my natural
infirmity. But this I ought not to call repentance, I think,
any more than my dissatisfaction at not being an angel or
Cato. My actions are ordered in conformity with what I am
and with my condition. I can do no better. And repentance
does not properly affect things that are not in our power;
regret, indeed, does. I can imagine innumerable natures
loftier and more orderly than mine; I do not for all that
improve my faculties, just as neither my arm nor my mind
grows more vigorous by conceiving those of another to be so.
If to imagine and desire a nobler way of acting than our produced repentance of our own, we should have to repent of our
most innocent actions, inasmuch as we may well suppose that
in a more excellent nature they would have been performed
with greater dignity and perfection; and we should wish to
do likewise.

When I reflect on the behavior of my youth in comparison
with that of my old age, I find that in general I have conducted myself with order in both, according to my notion;
that is all that my resistance can do. I am not flattering
myself: in similar circumstances I should always be the same
man. It is not a spot, but rather a dye with which I am
stained all over. I know of no superficial, half-way, and
merely formal repentance. It must affect me in every part
before I can call it so; it must pierce my bowels and afflict
them as deeply and as entirely as God sees into them.

As to business, many good opportunities have escaped me for
want of successful management. And yet my plans were well
enough laid, in relation to the circumstances they were
faced with; it is their way always to choose the easiest
and safest course. I find that in my former deliberations
I have, according to my rule, proceeded wisely, considering
the state of the business that was put before me, and I
should do the same a thousand years from now in similar situations. I do not consider what it is at this moment, but
what it was when I deliberated.

The strength of every decision is related to time; circumstances and things ceaselessly revolve and shift about. In

my life, I have committed some serious and grievous errors, not for lack of good judgment, but for lack of good fortune. In the objects which we handle there are secret elements, not to be guessed at, particularly in the natures of men; mute conditions, that make no show, unknown sometimes by the possessor himself, that are brought out and awakened by occasions as they arise. If my prudence was unable to penetrate into and foresee them, I am not in the least aggrieved at it. Its function is confined within its own limits. It is the event that gets the better of me, and if it favors the side that I have rejected, there is no remedy. I do not blame myself; I accuse my fortune, not my effort. This cannot be called repentance.

Phocion had given the Athenians some advice which was not followed. When the affair nevertheless, contrary to his opinion, passed off prosperously, someone said to him: "Well, Phocion, are you glad that things go so well?" "I am indeed glad, he replied, that it has turned out thus, but I do not repent of having counselled otherwise." When my friends apply to me for advice, I give it freely and clearly, without hesitating, as nearly everybody does, at the thought that, the matter being subject to chance, it may turn out contrary to my idea and they may reproach me for my advice: about that I am quite indifferent. For they will be wrong to blame me, and I had no right to refuse them that office.

I have hardly anyone   but myself to blame for my errors or mishaps, because in fact, I rarely make use of the advice of others, unless by way of respectful formality, except when I have need of scientific information or knowledge of fact. But in things where I stand in need of nothing but judgment, other men's reasons may serve to support me, but have little effect in deterring me. I lend a favorable and courteous ear to all of them but, as far as I can remember, I have hitherto trusted to none but my own. In my view they are but flies and atoms that lead my will hither and yon. I set small value on my opinions, but I set just as little on those of other men. Fortune pays me properly. If I do not accept advice, I give still less. I am consulted very little, but I am heeded even less; and I know of no public or private undertaking that has been reformed and set right by my advice. Even those whom Fortune had in some manner tied

to my direction, have been more disposed to let themselves be
guided by any other minds. And as a man who is as jealous of
the rights of my repose as of the rights of my authority, I
would rather have it so. By letting me alone, people humor
me in what I profess, which is to be settled and contained
wholly within myself. It is my pleasure not to be interested
in the affairs of others and not to be involved in any responsibility for them.

With respect to any affair when once it is over, I have little regret, however it may have turned out. For this idea
relieves me of worry: that the thing had to happen that way.
It is seen to be part of the great stream of the universe and
of the chain of Stoical causes. Your imagination cannot by
wish or thought disturb one iota without overturning the
whole order of things both past and future.

As to the rest, I hate that repentance which the arrival of
old age brings with it. The ancient who said that he was
obliged to the years for having rid him of sensual pleasure
was of a different opinion from mine. I can never be behol-
den to impotence for any good it may do me. "Nor will providence ever appear so unfriendly to her own work that de-
bility should be ranked among the best things." Our desires
are few in old age; a profound satiety overcomes us after
the act. In this I see no manifestation of conscience. Melancholy and weakness imprint in us a sluggish and rheumatic
virtue. We must not let ourselves be so wholly carried a-
way by natural changes that our judgment is corrupted by them.
Youth and pleasure did not formerly disable me from recognizing the face of vice in sensual pleasure; nor does the
distaste which the years bring me disable me from recognizing that of sensual pleasure in vice. Now that I am no longer in it, I judge of it as though I were. I, who agitate
it briskly and attentively, find that my reason is the very
same that it was in my licentious years, unless, perhaps,
in so far as it is weakened and impaired by growing old.
And I find that though it refuses to embroil me with this
pleasure out of consideration for the good of my bodily
health, it would not refuse it, any more than formerly, for
the sake of my spiritual health. I do not regard it as more
valiant for being out of the battle. My temptations are so
broken and mortified that they are not worth its resistance.

By merely stretching out my hands, I exorcize them. Should it be confronted with the old concupiscence, I fear it would have less strength to resist it than it formerly had. I do not see that of itself it judges things otherwise than it did then, nor that it is endowed with any new light. So, if there is any improvement in it, it is a maimed sort of improvement. It is a miserable kind of remedy to owe one's health to the disease!

It does not belong to our misfortune to perform this function; it belongs to the good fortune of our judgment to do so. I cannot be made to do anything by evils and afflictions, except to curse them. That is for people who can only be aroused by the lashes of a whip. My reason runs a freer course in prosperity. It is much more distraught and taken up with absorbing pains than pleasures. I see much more clearly in fair weather. The admonitions of health, as they are more cheerful, so too are they more useful than those of sickness. I advanced as far as was in my power toward a reformed and well-regulated life when I had health to enjoy. I should be ashamed and resentful that the wretchedness and misfortune of my decrepitude should be given the preference over my good, healthful, sprightly, vigorous years, and that I should be estimated not by what I have been, but by what I have ceased to be. In my opinion it is happy living, not (as Antisthenes said) happy dying that constitutes human felicity. I have not strained myself to tack on in monstrous fashion the tail of a philosopher to the head and body of a libertine, nor to have this wretched remainder of existence disown and belie the fairest, richest, and longest part of my life. I wish to present myself and to be seen uniformly throughout. If I had to live my life over again, I should live it just as I have lived it. I neither complain of the past nor fear the future. And if I do not deceive myself, my inner movements have been approximately like my outward ones. It is one of the principal obligations that I have to my fortune, that the course of my bodily states has been run according to the season suited to each one. I have seen the grass, the flower, and the fruit; and now I see the withering up. Happily, since it is natural I endure much more mildly the infirmities that I have, because they come in their own time, and also because they make me remember more kindly the long felicity of my past

49

life. So also it may well be that my wisdom is of the same
proportions in this age as in the other, but it used to be
much more enterprising and of better grace when it was fresh,
gay, and natural, than now that it is bowed down, peevish,
and painful. I repudiate, therefore, those casual and sorrowful changes.

God must touch our hearts. Our conscience must improve itself by the reinforcement of our reason, not by the weaken-
ing of our appetites. In itself sensual pleasure is neither
pale nor discolored, though it appear so to dim and bleary
eyes. Temperance should be loved for its own sake and out
of reverence to God, who has commanded it, and chastity too;
what a catarrh imposes on us and what I owe to the favor of
my colic, is neither chastity nor temperance. A man cannot
boast that he despises and resists sensual pleasure if he
does not see it, if he is not acquainted with it, with its
charms, its powers, and most alluring beauty. I know them
both, I am in a position to speak. But it seems to me that
in old age our souls are subject to more troublesome ail-
ments and imperfections than in youth. I used to say this
when I was young; then they pointed out to me my beardless
chin. I still say it, now that my grey hairs give me the
authority to do it. We give the name of wisdom to the harshness of our humors and the distaste of present things. But
in truth, we do not so much give up our vices as we change
them, and, in my opinion, for the worse. Aside from a silly
and tottering pride, a tedious garrulity, bristling and un-
sociable humors, supersitition, and an absurd eagerness for
riches after the use of them has been lost, I find there
more envy, injustice, and malice. Old age imprints more
wrinkles in our minds than in our faces; and never, or very
rarely, do we find a soul that in growing old does not acquire a sour and musty smell. Man moves altogether both
toward his growth and toward his decay.

As I observe the wisdom of Socrates and many circumstances
of his condemnation, I dare to believe that he in some way
purposely lent himself to it by prevarication, seeing that,
at the age of seventy years, he would soon have to suffer
the stupefaction of the rich activity of his mind and the
dimming of its accustomed brilliance.

What metamorphoses do I see old age bring about daily in many of my acquaintances! It is a powerful malady, and it steals upon us naturally and imperceptibly. It takes a great provision of study and great precaution to avoid the imperfections with which it loads us, or at least to slow up our progress. I feel that, despite all my defenses, it gains inch by inch upon me. I resist as long as I can. But I myself do not know where it will bring me in the end. But come what may, I am content the world should know from what height I have fallen.

Chapter 2

SAINT FRANCIS DE SALES
(1567-1622)

A contemporary of Montaigne, Francis de Sales shared many of
the same beliefs and aspirations of this secular humanist.
It can be said, in fact, that this Catholic saint prescribed
a similar path to moral development in the realm of Christian
spirituality. Like Montaigne, he was profoundly aware of the
weaknesses and vicissitudes of human nature, knew its limits,
and placed no more demands on it than could reasonably be expected; and like Montaigne, he was a brilliant and erudite
humanist who had at his fingertips an imposing knowledge of
the literature of the ancients. Yet as a learned and saintly priest, his strongest and most cherished intellectual influences were derived from Holy Scripture and the writings of
the Church Fathers which, he believed, had brought to perfection the moral teachings of the ancients through the light
or revelation. Armed with this formidable background, he was
able to effect a delicate synthesis of the moral acumen of
antiquity with Christian teachings, thus realizing the most
accomplished form of Christian humanism to appear in the
Renaissance.

Francis de Sales was born in 1567 of an aristocratic family
in the château de Sales near Thorens in Savoy. His father
intended him for high government service and Francis received
the best education available at the time. He gained a solid
humanistic background at the Collège de Clermont in Paris and

also studied theology at the Sorbonne. Soon after this he
was sent to prepare for a course in law at the University of
Padua. Irresistibly drawn to the priesthood despite strenuous parental opposition, he was ordained at the age of
twenty-five.

He was first assigned as a parish priest in the province of
Chablais in Savoy where the Reformation had recently made
enormous inroads. His immediate task was thus one of evan-
gelization in what was regarded as a missionary diocese.
Francis was initially ignored by the fiercely independent inhabitants of this mountain province and he had to resort to
disseminating brief written articles on the Catholic faith
which he had slipped under the doors of the recalcitrant con-
verts to Calvinism. Gradually many were enticed to hear
Francis' sermons and soon overflow crowds packed his church
to hear him.

Unlike other preachers of the day, Francis strictly avoided
obscure quotations from Greek and Latin or subtle theological
disquisitions. He instead interspersed his sermons with
topics grounded in everyday life which reflected a keen
psychological insight into the spiritual needs and dominant
interests of his contemporaries. Endowed with a marvelous
speaking voice and a suavity of manner that immediately broke
down all forms of resistance, he was able to make each listen-
er believe that the sermon was delivered for him alone. The
moral message was always and ever how to achieve a better
measure of self-knowledge in order to live a more authentically Christian life. In the pulpit Francis always appeared
to be meditating and never declaiming; not the slightest
note of harshness or accusation ever marred his irresistibly
appealing and pertinent moral lessons. It is a historical
fact that after a few years of his ministry the inhabitants
of his region returned almost en masse to the old faith.

Because of his immense popularity and brilliant success, he
was made Bishop of Geneva at the age of thirty-five. His
fame spread to Paris and, shortly after his consecration, he
delivered a series of sermons in the Royal Chapel at the invitation of Henry IV. So impressedwas Henry that he begged
Francis to remain in Paris. But Francis resisted all pressures and refused to forsake "his poor bride," as he called

his mountain diocese of Geneva, for the "rich wife" or impos
ing see of Paris. Francis also later refused to be elevated
to the rank of Cardinal when offered this promotion by Pope
Leo XI. To the very end of his life he remained in what he
considered his authentic calling: a director of souls.

And indeed he was brilliant in this capacity. The first of
his two great treatises, the Introduction to the Devout Life,
took form as the collection of written conversations and letters originally addressed to several of his spiritual daugh-
ters--Madame de Chantal and Madame de Charmoisey in partic-
ular--from the most aristocratic families of Geneva whom he
was leading to religious perfection. These letters of spiritual direction were masterpieces of persuasion and read as
easily as Francis spoke in his sermons. Urged to bring them
together in a volume, he arranged them topically and addressed them to the fictitious "Philothée" or lover of God. They
immediately enjoyed astounding success: over forty editions
had already been published in France by the time of his death
in 1622 and they had been translated into fifteen languages.
In 1616 he published his second great work, the Treatise on
the Love of God, which was a more systematic and theological-
ly grounded study incorporating Neo-Platonic philosophy with
Christian morality. He was canonized by Pope Alexander VII
in 1665 and was declared the patron saint of Catholic jour-
nalists by Pope Pius XI in 1923.

What is the major aim of Saint Francis de Sales in the Introduction to the Devout Life? Simply to lead the soul to God.
And the first condition for this spiritual journey is interior peace of mind and the knowledge and possession of the
self. One must, he says, "hold his soul in his hands," and
learn how to dispose of and decisively control the ego. Man
in the state of nature is never at rest but is constantly
buffeted by natural appetites that prevent his achieving
order and balance. Grace alone restores peace and tranquility to the soul. Contrary to Montaigne's doctrine that man
can achieve harmony in himself by conforming to nature's
teachings and that perfection implies a purely human or natural process, Francis taught that such a harmony can only be
found in God. Man can therefore realize himself fully only
through seeking the love of God.

_To introduce man to the salutary operation of grace, Francis proposed a program of discipline remarkably free of the harsh measures that had traditionally been prescribed for the attainment of sanctity. He did not declare war on human nature nor did he counsel harsh or rigorous forms of mortification. The essential elements of his program are rather the cultivation of humility and gentleness, since all practices that do violence to the soul frighten and unhinge it.

The devotion that he counseled, then, has nothing harsh or unsettling about it; it accomodates itself perfectly to the legitimate demands of all states of life, and it is by no means necessary to embrace the life of the cloister in order to attain perfection. True devotion permeates every aspect of life and rather than turning the Christian away from human involvement, it enriches his human existence. The ultimate test of whether or not a soul finds itself on the path of true devotion is the extent to which charity dominates all its thoughts and actions. In Francis' words, "Devotion is nothing more than spiritual agility and vitality by means of which charity accomplishes its operations in us and we in it both happily and whole-heartedly."

The Christian aspiring to perfection exemplifies in his actions and attitudes a cheerful optimism and a total acceptance of whatever life may bring. He must forever banish from his inner thoughts anguish, impatience, and sadness. The latter state is especially reprehensible for "a sad saint is indeed a wretched one." To be truly Christian one must also refuse none of the natural gifts that God has given; the soul and the body must be developed together, for the cultivation of the one as opposed to the other results in an unbalanced and thoroughly unattractive human being. Modesty, gentleness, and compassion provide an exterior shield to fend off the strident demands of the ego.

Yet nothing can be gained if there is not present a constant vigilance against all forms of self-love and base desires which wean the soul away from the love of God. A discipline of steel joined to mildness of character thus provides the basic mechanism of Salesian spirituality. The end result should be a humane and civil form of devotion which leads the soul to God with none of the ugly grimaces, contortions, and exaggerated exercises too often erroneously associated with sanctity.

Like Montaigne, this Christian humanist fervently believed it necessary to respect and cultivate the essential self. For Francis, every soul had its "particular difference," as he termed it. Aware through introspection of the moral choices open to it, it must strike its own balance in order to check the many impulses to degradation present in all of us. Through its unique spiritual experience, it must chart its own path to perfection by employing its particular form of wisdom. "Each soul, he declared, is like a great kingdom which, to preserve itself, possesses its own laws and directives unique to itself."

To this fervent humanistic belief in the essential freedom and responsibility of the individual to develop his own particular being, Francis grafted the neo-platonic concept that love and beauty are mystically united in their highest forms in the love of God. Through divine grace each soul possesses the real potential to create a unique form of human beauty. In existential terms, this truth places the responsibility for the achievement of a beautiful life squarely on the shoulders of each human being, and, "The more beautiful our souls become, the more authentically do we exist." The touchstone of all moral endeavor, then, is the cultivation of a morally beautiful Christian who attracts others to God through the noble and immensely attractive edifice which his own life gradually becomes.

The following passages from the Introduction to the Devout Life present some of the major themes and means to perfection advanced by this gentle moralist who successfully fused the secular aspirations of Renassiance humanism to the operations of Divine Grace.

That Devotion is Suitable to All Sorts of Vocations and Professions

At the time of creation, God commanded the plants to bring forth fruit, each according to its kind and so does He command Christians, the living plants of his Church, to bear the fruits of devotion, each according to his ability and vocation. Devotion should be differently exercised by the gentleman, the artist, valet, prince, widow, maiden, and married woman and we should further adapt the practice of devotion to the strength, occupation, and duties of the individual. I ask you, would it be right for a bishop to live the solitary life of a Carthusian? Or if husbands did not wish to earn any more money than Capuchins; if artisans spent all day in church, and those in religious life were constantly exposed to all manner of encounters and obligations to render service to those in the world, as a bishop must, would not such forms of devotion be considered silly and out of season? Such faults often occur, however, and the world, which is incapable or unwilling to discern the difference between devotion and the indiscretions of those who think they are devout, disparages true devotion which never embodies such disorder.

No, devotion when it is authentic harms nothing and perfects everything. Yet when it runs counter to a person's legitimate vocation, it is certainly false and without foundation. "The bee, says Aristotle, draws its honey from flowers without affecting them, and leaves them as whole and fresh as it found them." True devotion operates even more effectively since not only does it do no harm to any kind of vocation or occupation but even decorates and embellishes it. All sorts of gems thrown into honey seem to become more glittering each according to its particular color and every individual better fulfills his vocation when he joins it to the practice of devotion. The family becomes more peaceful, the love of husbands for their wives more sincere, the prince's obligation more assured, and all vocations are rendered more agreeable and satisfying.

It is an error, if not a heresy, to wish to banish the devout life from the company of soldiers, from the artisan's shop, from the court of princes or the households of married people. It is true that devotion which is purely contemplative and monastic cannot be exercised in these vocations. But there are many other forms which perfect those who live in the world. (I:3)

Of Patience

"You have need of patience so that in doing the will of God you may bear away the promise," says the Apostle Paul. And our Savior himself has said: "In your patience you shall possess your souls." Indeed Man's greatest happiness is to possess his soul, and the more perfect our patience, the more perfectly do we possess it. Never forget that our Lord has saved us through suffering, and we, too, should work out our salvation by enduring afflictions, pains, injuries, contradictions, and displeasures with all possible meekness.

Do not limit your patience to this or that kind of injury and affliction, but extend it generally to all the trials that God may be pleased to send you. There are some who refuse to suffer any tribulations save those that are honorable: for example, to be wounded or taken prisoner during war, to be persecuted for religious reasons, or to be impoverished by a lawsuit from which they emerge victorious. These people love not tribulation but the honor that it brings. The true, patient servant of God bears up equally under trials accompanied either by ignominy or honor. To be scorned, denounced, and accused by the wicked is pleasing to a man of good heart; but to be reproved, accused, and treated badly by good men, friends, or relatives is a real test of patience. As the sting of the bee smarts more than that of the fly, the evils and contradictions we endure from good men are far more difficult to bear than from the wicked. And it is surely not rare that two virtuous and well-intentioned men foment dissensions and even persecutions one against the other.

Be patient not only as regards the major burdens and afflictions that may befall you, but also be patient with accidental circumstances that may arise from them. Many would be content to endure evils provided that they were not really touched by them. I would not be vexed at being poor, says one, if it would not prevent me from serving my friends, giving my children a good education, or living as honorably as I would like. Poverty would not worry me, says another, were it not that the world would think that it happened through my own fault. Another would be quite indifferent to slander provided that no one would believe the slanderer.

58

Others are willing, so they think, to suffer some part of a given evil but not the whole. They insist that they do not complain on account of their illness but because they greatly inconvenience those about them. But I maintain that we must patiently accept not only sickness but the kind that God wishes, in the place He wishes it, among persons that He wishes, and with the inconveniences that He wishes. The same must be said of all other tribulations.

When evil comes to you, then, try to counter it with remedies that are within your power and in accord with God's will, for to do otherwise would be to tempt His divine Majesty. Having done this, wait with resignation for the results that God permits. If it please Him that your remedies overcome the evil, humbly give Him thanks. If it be His will that the opposite occurs, bless Him with patience.

Let me advise you to follow the advice of Saint Gregory: "Whenever you are justly accused of a fault, humble yourself and confess that you deserve the charge brought against you. If it be false, defend yourself by meekly denying your guilt for you owe this respect to truth and to the edification of your neighbor. But if after your true and lawful defense they should continue to accuse you, do not be the least concerned nor try to press your defense; because, having discharged your duty to truth, you must do the same to humility. In this way you neither offend against the care you must have of your reputation, nor the affection you owe to peace and humility of heart.

Complain as little as possible of the wrongs which have been done you; for, as a rule, he that complains, sins, because self-love magnifies the injuries we suffer and makes us believe them greater than they really are. Above all, never complain to persons who are ready to be indignant and think evil. If complaints be necessary, either to remedy the offense or restore quiet to your mind, let them be made to souls who are calm and who truly love God. Otherwise, instead of easing your heart, it will be provoked to greater pain. Instead of extracting the thorn, it will be sunk deeper."

Many, when they are sick, afflicted, and offended by others, refrain from complaining or showing a sensibility of what they suffer, lest they should appear to be showing weakness. But they still seek many artifices, that others should not only pity their sufferings and afflictions, but also admire their patience and courage. Now this is not a true patience, but rather a delicate ambition and vanity. "They have glory, says the Apostle, but not with God." The truly patient person neither complains himself nor desires to be pitied by others; he speaks of his sufferings simply, plainly, and sincerely, without complaining or exaggerating. He patiently receives condolence, unless he is pitied for an evil which he does not suffer, for then he modestly declares that he does not suffer on that account, and thus he remains in this way at peace between truth and patience, bearing the evil but not complaining of it.

Remember that the bees, while making their honey, live upon a very bitter food, and that we are never better able to do acts of great gentleness, nor to compose the honey of excellent virtues, than while we eat the bread of bitterness and live in the midst of pain. And as honey made from the flowers of thyme, a small bitter herb, is the best, so virtue exercised in the bitterness of the meanest and most abject tribulations is the most excellent of all.

Look often with your inner eyes on Christ Jesus crucified, naked, blasphemed, slandered, forsaken, and overwhelmed with all sorts of troubles, sorrows, and labors; and remember that all your sufferings, either in quality or quantity, are not comparable to His, and that you can never suffer anything for Him equal to that which he has suffered for you. (III:3)

Of Conversations and Solitude

To seek society or avoid it--these are two extremes equally blamable in the devotion of those who live in the world. To shun society smacks of disdain and contempt of our neighbors; to be too taken with it is a mark of sloth and idleness. We should love our neighbor as ourselves, and to prove that we love him we must not avoid being with him. And to testify that we love ourselves, we ought to dwell within ourselves when we are by ourselves, "Know first yourself, says Saint Bernard, and then others." If, then, nothing presses you to go out into company or to receive company at home, remain within yourself and get to know yourself in your own heart. But if company visits you, or any just cause prompts you to go out, go in God's name and see your neighbor with a good heart and a happy countenance.

Evil conversations are those which are conducted for some bad intention or which occur when the participants are vicious, indiscreet, and morally lax. We must flee from them as bees get out of the way of a swarm of gadflies and hornets. Just as the breath and saliva of those bitten by rabid dogs are extremely dangerous for children and others of delicate constitution, so these vicious and lewd people can only be approached to the peril of anyone whose devotion is still tender and weak.

There are some conversations which are useless for anything except recreation and consist merely in relaxation from serious occupations. As to these, though we must not be overly attracted to them, yet we may allow them to occupy the leisure destined for recreation.

Other conversations have politeness for their object, as in the case of friendly visits and certain gatherings to do honor to our neighbors. With respect to these, as we ought not be overscrupulous in the practice of them, so neither must we be harsh in condemning them, but modestly fulfill our duty in their regard, so that we may avoid both rudeness and levity.

Finally, there are useful conversations, such as those engaged in by devout and virtuous people and it would be of tremendous benefit for you to take part in them. A vine planted among olive trees bears succulent grapes which have a slight taste of olives, and a soul which is often in the company of virtuous people comes to resemble them. Drones cannot make honey by themselves but help the bees to produce it. It is, therefore, of greatest advantage to you to cultivate such company.

In all social contacts, sincerity, simplicity, meekness, and modesty are always preferred. There are some persons who make no gesture or motion without so much artificiality as to weary the company. And as he who could not speak without singing would be a burden to the rest of mankind, so they who affect an artificial carriage, and do nothing without affectation, are very disagreeable in company, for in such persons there is always some kind of presumption. Let a moderate cheerfulness as well as modesty always prevail in your conversation.

Besides that mental solitude which I earlier observed, whereby you may retreat even amid the greatest distractions, you ought also to love actual solitude. Not that you need to go into the desert as did Saint Mary the Egyptian, Saint Paul, Saint Anthony and the ancient solitaries; but that you should remain for some time alone by yourself where you may at leisure withdraw your spirit into your heart and refresh your soul with pious meditations, holy thoughts, or spiritual reading. Saint Nazianzen, speaking of himself, says, "I used to walk by myself at sunset, and pass the time on the seashore; for I was accustomed to make use of this recreation to refresh myself, and to shake off a little my usual weariness." And afterward he relates the good thoughts he had. And when the apostles one day had told our Lord how they had preached and how much they had done, he said to them, "Come ye apart into a desert place, and rest a little." (III:24)

Of Being Just and Reasonable

We are men only through our reason, and yet it is rare to find a truly reasonable man. This is all the more true because self-love usually leads us astray from reason and conducts us imperceptibly toward a multitude of minor but dangerous injustices and iniquities which, like the little foxes mentioned in the Song of Songs, destroy the vines. No one pays them any attention because they are so tiny, yet they are numerous enough to do great damage. And are not the things that I am going to mention as unjust and unreasonable? We condemn our neighbor for the slightest infraction but excuse ourselves in far more important matters. We want to sell dearly but buy cheaply; we want everything

62

we say taken in good part, but we are extremely touchy about what others say of us.

If we become attached to some exercise, we scorn all others and banish any that do not please our tastes. If a servant is clumsy or unattractive, we take a quick dislike to him, find fault with all that he does, and never let off grieving him. But if someone charms us by physical beauty, he can do no wrong. There are virtuous children whose parents refuse to deal with them because of some physical imperfection and there are others of vicious temperament who are favored because of certain bodily grace or attractiveness. On the whole, we prefer the rich to the poor though they often are not at all as virtuous. We even prefer those who dress best. We proudly exact our rights but desire others to be courteous and humble in demanding theirs. We assert our rank punctiliously but would have others humble and condescending. We are quick to complain about our neighbor but tolerate no complaint about ourselves. What we do for others always seems very considerable, but what others do for us is as nothing. In short, we have two hearts--one gentle, gracious, and courteous towards ourselves, and the other hard, severe, and rigorous toward our neighbor; and we have two scales-- one which weighs to our advantage and the other to the detriment of others.

Be just and even handed in all your dealings and actions. Put yourself in your neighbor's place and you will judge well. Make yourself the seller while you are buying and the buyer while you are selling, and you will thus sell and buy justly. Injustice in buying and selling is mean because it does not oblige us to make restitution inasmuch as we remain only within the limits of strictness in that which is favorable to ourselves. But it does not clear us of our obligations to make amends, for, in the final analysis, it is only treachery to do otherwise. Believe me, a man of a generous, just, and courteous disposition is never the loser. So examine your heart often and see whether it has such regard for your neighbor as you would want him to have for you, for this is the secret of true reason. Trajan, blamed by his confidents for making the imperial majesty, as they thought, too accessible, said, "Ought I not be such an emperor toward private citizens as I would want an emperor to be toward me were I myself a private man?" (III:36)

Of Humility to Outward Things

Elias said to a poor widow, "Borrow some pots and pour oil
into them." In order to receive God's grace in our hearts,
we must empty them of our own vanity. A falcon, screeching
and surveying birds of prey, terrifies them by its strength
and secret power. And this is why doves prefer it to all
other birds and live in confidence in its environs. In a
similar way humility repels Satan and keeps intact in us the
graces and gifts of the Holy Spirit. It is for this reason
that all the saints have honored this worthy virtue more
than any other moral precept.

We call that glory vain which we assume to ourselves, either
for what is not in us, or for what is in us and is ours, but
yet does not merit the glory we give it. Some people become proud and haughty by riding a fine steed, or by wear-
ing fine clothes and a plume in their hat; but who does not
see how silly this is? For if there be any glory in such
things, it belongs to the horse, the tailor, and the bird.
And how cowardly it is to borrow one's esteem from a horse,
an elegant suit of clothes, or a feather. Others value
themselves because of a dignified moustache, a well trimmed
beard, curly hair, delicate hands, or the ability to sing,
dance, and play. But are they not weaklings in their attempts to enhance their reputation by such frivolous and
foolish considerations? Others, with a bit of learning,
want to be honored by the whole world, as if everyone should
become their student and accept them as their teachers.
These are called pedants. Others strut vainly about because
of their good looks and think they are admired by everyone.
All this is extremely vain, foolish, and impertinent; and
the glory which is raised on such weak foundations is justly esteemed vain and frivolous.

Thus, to know if a man is really good, wise, learned, and
generous, we must see if his qualifications tend to humility, modesty, and submission; for then they shall be good
indeed. But if they are only for show, they shall be so
much the less genuine, in the same proportion as they are
more apparent. The virtues and good qualities of men that

64

are bred and nourished by pride, boasting, and vanity have only the superficial appearance of good.

Honors, rank, and titles are like saffron, which thrives best and grows more abundantly when trodden underfoot. It is no distinction to be handsome if we consider ourselves so. Beauty, to have good grace, should be neglected; and knowledge is a disgrace when it puffs us up and degenerates into pedantry.

If we are punctilious as to rank, place, and titles, besides exposing our qualities to be examined, tried, and contradicted, we render them vile and contemptible; for as honor is beautiful when freely given, so it becomes base when exacted or sought after. When the peacock spreads his tail in order to be admired, in raising up his beautiful feathers, he ruffles all the rest, and shows off his least attractive parts. So honors being a pleasant consolation to those that view them from afar, without stopping to amuse themselves with them or to be earnest about them. Those who affect them, or feed on them, are exceedingly blamable and worthy of reprehension.

The pursuit and love of virtue begins by making us virtuous; but the pursuit and love of honor makes us contemptible and worthy of blame. High-minded persons take no delight in the petty considerations of rank, honor, and salutation; they have other things to perform; such weakness only belongs to idle spirits.

He that may have pearls never loads himself with shells; and such as aspire to virtue do not trouble themselves about honors. (IV:3)

Chapter 3

BLAISE PASCAL (1623-1662)

Blaise Pascal was considered a prodigy as a child. He continues to be considered a true genius. His discoveries in
mathematics and physics are still impressive achievements
by today's standards. But these two areas of knowledge do
not delineate the extent of his mental power. He also invented a machine to do arithmetic calculations, conceived
the first public transportation, or busline, in France, and
composed what most scholars consider the most perfect, most
classical prose of the Seventeenth Century.

Contemporary with Pascal's life was the development of a
religious divergence within the Catholic Church, Jansenism.
This movement, with its stoical approach to life and death,
salvation and perdition, was condemned by the Jesuits when
its doctrine of predestination was first proclaimed (1640).
The Jesuits took particular offense at this anti-humanistic
stance, and for the next century and more, a struggle raged
between the more worldly, compromising Jesuits and the
strict polemical Janenists.[*]

_____

[*]The excellent work of Saint-Beuve, Port-Royal, gives the
 history of the abbey where Jansenism found its seat and
  thrived until 1710 when Louis XIV attempted to destroy the
  movement by destroying its buildings and disbursing its
  population.

In his twenty-third year, Pascal was introduced to this new faith and he and his family were converted to it in the years following. Abandoning the comforts which were his because of his family wealth, Pascal embraced poverty as a road to salvation and in order to impose humility on his existence, he wore a belt fitted with nails; when men came to consult him because they respected his well-known genius, he unobtrusively pressed the nails into his flesh lest he become absorbed in the vanity of adulation which the world offers.

In the beautiful prose which he wrote in the second half of his life we see him as a Christian and social moralist. Perhaps a bit too spiritually oriented, Pascal never enjoyed a great following for his Christian ideals. One of his principal ideas, "The I is hateful", pits him directly against the enlightened humanism of Montaigne whose idea of knowing oneself in order to know the rest of humanity has influenced western thinking up to the present. As a social moralist, however, he continues to please and convince by his sincerity and humor. His attraction to absolute values--so easily attributed to his "scientific mind", but just as dependent upon his Jansenist convictions--inspired the transparent style and logical thinking of Stendhal, among others.

Like Du Bellay before him, Mozart, Byron and other great talents after him, Pascal lived a brief life of intense activity. His achievements are rare even today. Born in 1623 into a well-to-do middle class family, he lost his mother when he was an infant. His father, Etienne Pascal, a person of exceptional intelligence, raised Blaise and his two older sisters, Gilberte and Jacqueline, alone. Seeing that Blaise was extraordinarily clever, even precocious, he decided to educate his son himself; Blaise Pascal never went to school. By the age of ten he had a mastery of Euclydian mathematical principles. At eleven he wrote a treatise on sound and at sixteen an essay on conics (The Geometry of Conics). At nineteen he invented a machine to do arithmetic calculations. And at twenty-four he discussed his theory of the vacuum with Descartes. (A year later he made experiments proving that Nature does not abhor a vacuum but that physical pressures cause vacuums to be filled.) Pascal's Law (pressure on liquids in a closed place causes equal distribution of pressure) and the first attempt at public transportation in Paris are still other examples of his intellectual potential.

Around 1647 his family was subtly introduced to the new Christian life as interpreted by the Jansenist movement and Pascal gradually abandoned his scientific pursuits in favor of the pursuit of his salvation. He was not truly able to combine the two pursuits, convinced as he was that science and worldly matters were the reverse side of spiritual matters, therefore impossible to bring together. One of his own Thoughts attempts to explain this dichotomy: "The heart has its reasons which Reason does not know."

His own life over the next five years (1649-1654) illustrates this separation between the worldly and spiritual. This is usually referred to as his mundane period. It is then that he met the society of the brilliant salons; those same places that boasted atheistic guests (Théophile, Cyrano de Bergerac) and agnostics (the cynical and pessimistic La Rochefoucauld), and featured the charming ladies of the salon, none of whom seems to have been very taken by Pascal's concern with grace and salvation. Why, then, was he there? The answer remains unclear, but his thoughts on society suggest that he was seeking to understand how people spend their time while waiting for their final judgment. After five years, as his precarious health gradually worsened, he withdrew to a more retired existence meditating on man's fate. At Port-Royal he wrote the now classic Provincial Letters to defend his fellow Jansenists who were continually under attack by the Church and the government. There he lived a life of sacrifice and poverty as much as his wealth and privilege could permit to him and planned an apology of Christianity which, left incomplete at his death (1662), was published in 1670 with the editorial help of his surviving sister, Gilberte. It is this incomplete work which we know today as the Thoughts (Les Pensées).

While Pascal found it impossible to combine religion with everyday life of society, the comments he makes very frequently are moral judgments on mundane situations; as mentioned before, these are the ideas of Pascal which appeal to us most today. Probably the most shattering discovery of the half-century during which Pascal lived was that man and his planet were not the center of the universe; the world had become much smaller than previously thought. For Pascal, and some contemporaries (Descartes, Leibniz) this was cause for anguish concerning the fate of man. Man was seen in a potentially absurd situation reduced to a mere speck on a small planet in a vast universe. Some three centuries later the existentialists (e.g., Malraux, Sartre, Camus) would attempt to give man dignity by placing values on his emotions and his actions but Pascal's remarks remain in direct opposition: Man's dignity is found in his ability to think. He can be crushed like a little reed, but he knows he is being crushed and therein lies his superiority over all other creatures: Man is a "thinking reed".

His solutions to this dilemma seem a bit absolutist in the contemporary world: everything must be sacrificed to God; the things of this world offer no hope of salvation; man must suffer to mortify his existence in preparation for salvation; the atheists are the misled sheep; agnostics are confused.

But his observations on man's situation offer a greater rationalization on the need to find God as he moves through life. For example, the essential problem in life is to find inner peace; for Pascal this can only be found with God and His Son, Jesus Christ, and is available to all: "The grace of God makes itself known in great spirits by little things and in simple spirits by great things." Living in society is killing time; it is covering up the individual's lack of inner peace and diverting his attention from the true purpose of his life: to serve God.

Pascal was greatly admired for his scientific knowledge during his own lifetime, but his religious principles caused great consternation with the government authorities and their religious supporters, the Jesuits. After all, Pascal was the most articulate spokesman that the Jansenists were ever to have and the Jesuits never produced anyone of his caliber. In fact, there are many who believe that France as a whole never produced another mind of this caliber. He has remained an influence in the centuries after his own but rarely for the one subject of which he was most convinced: religion. Later writers have looked to him for the

art of his prose, his sincerity, his recognition of mankind's absurd situation in the universe: neither all flesh
nor all spirit, the human being is faced with problems experienced by no other creature. Then, too, most everyone
appreciates his comments on society and its demands which
force the individual to play a role other than the one leading to salvation.

Pascal's moralism applies to everyday life just as Montaigne's, but, whereas Montaigne's led to a humanism because
it seeks to define a good life for this world, Pascal's
seeks to transcend the values of this world in preparation
for the next life. It is at this point that Pascal becomes
separated from almost all other moralists except the most
aescetic, since one of the principal aims of the moraliste
is to come to terms with this life.

The Thoughts presented here reveal Pascal's concern with the
present life and the one he looked forward to. They also
prove that, no matter what may be our personal philosophy
of life, we can admire the production of a brilliant mind
in meditation.*

*The numbers follow the order established by Brunschvicg.

70

23. Physical science will not console me for the ignorance of morality in time of affliction. But the science of ethics will always console me for the ignorance of the physical sciences.

30. We do not choose as captain of a ship the traveler who is from the best family.

37. The charm of glory is so great that we love every object to which it is attached, even death.

40. How vain is painting which attracts admiration by resemblance to things which we do not admire in the original.

43. Little consoles us because little affects us.

44. Love and hate change the face of justice, and how much more just does a lawyer find his case when he has been well paid in advance....

47. Let everyone examine his thoughts. He will find them all concerned with the past or the future. We almost never think about the present, and if we do think about it, it is only to grasp an understanding of how to prepare for the future. The present is never our end.
The past and the present are our means; only the future is our end. Thus we never live, but we hope to live, and, always preparing ourselves to be happy, it is inevitable that we should never be so.

51. Why are you killing me? I am unarmed.--What? Don't you live on the other side of the water? My friend, if you lived on this side, I would be an assassin, and it would be unjust to kill you this way. But since you live on the other side, I am a hero, and that is just.

59. When it is a question whether we ought to go to war and kill so many men, condemn so many Spaniards to

death, it is one man alone who judges, and even he is
biased; there ought to be a third, unbiased, party.

64. This dog is mine, these poor children were saying.
This is my place in the sun. That is the beginning
and the picture of the usurpation of the entire earth.

70. If our condition were truly happy, we would not need
diversion from thinking about it.

97. Lust and force are the sources of all our actions.
Lust causes the voluntary ones, force the involuntary.

98. How is it that a cripple does not offend us and a fool
does? Because a cripple recognizes that we walk
straight and a fool says that we are the fools. If
not for that we would feel pity for him, not anger....

104. Nobility is a great advantage which puts a man of
eighteen in the forefront, known and respected as
another would have merited at fifty. That's thirty
years gained easily.

111. I can easily conceive of a man without hands, feet,
head, because it is only experience which teaches us
that the head is more necessary than the feet. But
I cannot conceive of a man without thought. He would
be a stone or a brute.

113. It is not from space that I must seek my dignity but
from the control of my thought. I will not gain anything in possessing worlds. By space the universe
surrounds me and swallows me up like a speck: by
thought I understand this.

114. The greatness of man is great in that he knows that
he is miserable; a tree does not know it is miserable,
but it is (also) to be great to know oneself miserable.

120. We are so presumptuous that we would like to be known
by everyone and even by the people who will come when
we are no longer here. And we are so vain that the

esteem of five or six people who surround us amuses us and contents us.

133. Men, not having been able to cure death, misery, and ignorance, have decided,to make themselves happy, not to think about them.

134. Notwithstanding these miseries, he wants to be happy and only wants to be happy, and cannot not wish to be so.
But how will he go about it? To succeed he would have to make himself immortal, but not being about to, he has decided to prevent himself from thinking about it.

135. I sense that I might not have been, because the self exists in my thoughts; therefore I who think would not have been, if my mother had been killed before I had been given life. Therefore I am not a necessary being. Nor am I eternal or infinite, but I see clearly that there is in nature a necessary being who is eternal and infinite.

166. We rush head on into the abyss after having placed something in front of us to prevent us from seeing it.

200. Man is only a reed, the feeblest in nature, but he is a thinking reed. It is not necessary for the entire universe to rise up in order to crush him; a vapor, a drop of water suffices to kill him. But if the universe were to crush him, man would still be nobler than that which kills him because he knows that he is dying and that the universe has the advantage over him. The universe knows nothing about this. All our dignity consists, then, in thought. It is on this point that we must elevate ourselves, not on space and time which we could not possibly fill. Let us strive, then, to think well: that is the principle of morality.

210. All men hate each other by nature. They have used lust as best they could to make it serve the public good. But that is only pretense and a false image

of charity, because in the end it is only hate.

413. He who would like to know fully the vanity of man has only to consider the causes and effects of love. The cause is a je ne sais quoi (Corneille). And its effects are frightening. This je ne sais quoi, such a small thing that one cannot recognize it, shakes the whole land, princes, armies, the entire world.
If Cleopatra's nose had been shorter, the whole face of the world would have been changed.

418. ...One must wager. It is not voluntary, you are involved. Which will you choose then? Let us see; since you must choose let us see which interests you the least. You have two things to lose: the true and the good, and two things to stake: your reason and your will, your knowledge and your happiness, and your nature has two things to avoid: error and misery. Your reason is no more shocked in choosing the one over the other since you must of necessity choose. That is one point settled. But your happiness? Let us weigh the gain and the loss in wagering that God is. Let us consider these two cases: if you win, you win all; and if you lose, you lose nothing: wager, then, without hesitating that He is...

423. The heart has its reasons which Reason does not know; we sense this in a thousand things.
I say that the heart loves the Universal Being naturally and itself naturally, in the measure that it gives itself to them, and it resists one or the other by will. You have rejected the one and preserved the other; is it by reason that you love yourself?

424. It is the heart which feels God's presence and not the mind. That which faith is: God felt by the heart, not the mind.

434. Let us imagine a number of men in chains, all condemned to death, some of whom are massacred each day in the sight of the others, and those who remain see their own fate in that of their fellows, and await their turn, looking at each other in sorrow and despair. That is the image of man's fate.

510. The more clever one is, the more one finds clever men. Ordinary people do not find any difference between men.

578. Eloquence is a painting of thought, and thus those who, after having painted it, add more, make a picture instead of a portrait.

592. If the Jews had all been converted by Jesus Christ we would have no one but doubtful witnesses. And if they had been exterminated, we would not have any witnesses at all.

597. The I is hateful...In a word the I has two qualities. It is unjust in itself in that it makes itself the center of everything. It is disagreeable to others in that it wishes to enslave them, because each I is the enemy and would like to be the tyrant of all the others...

620. Man is obviously made to think. It is all his dignity and all his merit; and his whole duty is to think properly. Now, the order of thought is to begin with the self, and his Author and his end. But what does everyone think about? Never about that, but about dancing, playing the lute, singing, becoming king, without thinking of what it is to be a king, to be a man.

622. Nothing is so unacceptable to man as to be in complete repose, without passions, without business, without diversion, without purpose.
He then feels his nothingness, his forlornness, his insufficiency, his dependence, his weakness, his emptiness.
There will immediately arise from his soul, boredom, gloom, sadness, chagrin, spleen, despair.

649. What Montaigne has of good can only be acquired with difficulty. What he has of bad, I mean besides his mores, could have been corrected in a moment if someone had warned him that he told too many stories and spoke too much about himself.

650. Have you never seen people who in order to complain
      of the lack of attention you pay to them flaunt be-
      fore you the example of important people who esteem
      them? I will answer that: Show me the merit with
      which you have charmed them and I too will esteem
      you.

670. Speaker of clever words, bad character.

671. Do you want people to believe good of you, don't
      speak about it.

675. Style. When we see a natural style we are surprised
      and delighted because we expected to see an author
      and we find a man. While those who have good taste
      and who on seeing a book expect to find a man are
      totally surprised to find an author. Plus poetice
      quam humane locutus es.
      They honor nature well who teach that she can speak
      of everything, even theology.

678. Man is neither angel nor beast and it is unfortunate
      that he who wishes to play the angel plays the beast.

688. What is the Ego?
      A man who places himself at the window to see the
      passersby, if I pass there, can I say that he placed
      himself there to see me? No, because he is not
      thinking about me in particular; and the one who
      loves someone because of his beauty, does he really
      love him? No, because smallpox, which will kill the
      beauty without killing the person, will cause him to
      stop loving.
      And if someone loves me for my judgment, for memory,
      does he love me, me? No, because I can lose these
      qualities without losing myself. Where then is this
      Ego if it is not in the body or in the soul? And
      how can one love the body or the soul except for
      these qualities which are not me since they are
      perishable? Could one love the substance of the
      soul of a person abstractly and some qualities
      which were there? That is not possible and would
      be unjust. Therefore we never love a person, but

only some qualities.

689. It is not in Montaigne but in myself that I find all that I see in him.

696. Let no one say that I have not said anything new; the placement of the subject is new. When we play tennis, we both play with the same ball, but one places it better.
I would as soon one said to me that I used the same words before. As if the same thoughts did not form another discourse by a different arrangement, just as the same words form other thoughts in different arrangement.

708. Popes. Kings dispose of their power, but popes cannot dispose of theirs.

720. Ethics and language are special but universal sciences.

750. Cromwell was going to ravage all Christianity; the royal family was doomed and his own forever powerful, except for a little grain of sand which formed in his ureter. Even Rome was about to tremble under him. But this stone having formed there, he died, his family ruined, peacefully, and the king restored.

770. The example of Alexander's chastity has not made so many continent as that of his drunkenness has made intemperate.
It is not shameful not to be as virtuous as he, and it seems excusable not to be more vicious than he. We do not believe ourselves to be completely sharing the vices of the common men when we see that we are sharing in the vices of great men. And yet in such matters we do not notice that they are ordinary men. Because however exalted they may be, they are still attached to the least of men in some way. They are not suspended in air, totally removed from our society. No, no, if they are greater then we are, it is that they hold their heads higher, but they have their feet on the ground just as we do.

They are all on the same level and stand on the same earth, and at that extremity they are as abased as we, as the least significant, as the children, as the beasts.

813. We never do evil so completely and so cheerfully as when we do it out of conscience.

IX*. No pleasure has any savor for me without communication, says Montaigne: a mark of man's esteem for man.

---

*This Thought remained unpublished until 1923.

Chapter 4

LA ROCHEFOUCAULD (1613-1680)

With the publication of La Rochefoucauld's Maximes (1665)
the moraliste can no longer be looked upon as a writer of
purely religious and philosophical interests. While La
Rochefoucauld presents many maxims which are influenced by
the religious and philosophical attitudes of his friends
and associates, most of them are derived from their social
conduct. La Rochefoucauld has created a fine art from the
relationships between human beings, and art that previously
seemed best expressed by poetry or novel. His writings
offer one of the best examples of the "literature of the
salon," as Taine called it. La Rochefoucauld was influenced by all the facets of salon life, especially in its
cultural and literary ideals.* It was as a result of his
experience with salon life that in a few words he was able
to reveal the essence of a human encounter; conciseness was
his aim, and he succeeded perhaps better than anyone else
writing in the French language.

La Rochefoucauld's contemporaries include Corneille,
Moliere, La Fontaine, and, of course, Mazarin and Louis XIV.
He was one of the figures who brought French classicism to
its peak in the mid-reign of the Sun-King. And he is frequently considered the best exemplar of classicism: if
this literary period is defined by its fidelity to clarity,
precision, brevity, avoidance of ambiguity, respect for the
* See Introduction, pp. 11-12

mind over the emotions, then La Rochefoucald could well be considered that ideal practitioner of classical literature.

The maxim was a pastime in the salons of the period, but it is thanks to La Rochefoucauld that the maxim has become an important literary genre of artful expression and original ideas. Alexander Pope described classicism as: "What oft was said, but ne'er so well expressed." Frequently it seems that La Rochefoucauld's work goes beyond this definition in that no one even seems to have said it before he did.

François VI, Prince de Marcillac, later duc de La Roche-foucauld (1650) was born in Paris in 1613 of an old noble family. The education of such a man was traditionally a preparation for military leadership, and at the age of six-teen he was a <u>maître de camp</u> and fought in Italy. For the next twenty-five years he divided his time between political and military activity and social activity. These two areas were closely related, however, because as the scion of an old noble family La Rochefoucauld was the natural enemy of attempts of both Cardinals Richelieu and Mazarin to strength-en the power of the monarchy at the expense of the nobility. La Rochefoucauld was a leader of the Fronde*, the rebellion which threatened the early reign of Louis XIV, and the so-ciety which he frequented was indeed elegant but it was made up of enemies of the cardinals and of the principle of absolute monarchy.

In the civil war which was the Fronde, the struggle was bitter and the price was high. La Rochefoucauld's castle was razed in retribution for his participation in this treasonous rebellion. His friend, Cinq-Mars (whom De Vigny idolized in his novel) was executed and his castle was al-so razed, except for the two towers which still stand in the Loire Valley as symbols of the triumph of the monarchy over rebellious vassals--or are they, perhaps, symbols of the righteous indignation of grand nobility whose tradi-tional role in government has been usurped? La Rochefou-cauld's pervasive pessimism suggests that both are wrong

---

*Fronde: slingshot; the government pretended that this re-bellion was really of minor importance, a game of children.

since both result from the folly of human nature.

In 1652 La Rochefoucauld fought in his last battle; he was seriously wounded by a musket shot in the face. He retired from public life for a while and when he returned France had changed. The Fronde had ended in victory for the monarchy. Louis XIV, who frequently forgave his enemies but never forgot what they had done, gave a substantial pension to this former frondeur who from then on used his wit to grace the salons of several prestigious socialites, among whom the most important to his career were Mme. de Sablé and Mme. de Lafayette.

In his retreat after the wounding, La Rochefoucauld, like several of his contemporaries, began writing his memoirs. But it was with the composition of the maxims, originally intended for private circulation, that he revealed himself to be a writer of the first quality. The creation and presentation of these maxims, aphorisms, etc., formed part of the precious atmosphere affected by the habitués of the elegant salons. Like the people in the salons themselves, these pastimes were not expected to be profound; they were parlor games. The inspiration and the expression evoked a true artistic talent. He directed five editions of the Maxims during the remainder of his life, adding new ones from recent experience, removing some or rephrasing them to tone down the mordant depression that frequently characterized the early ones and which frequently shocked his refined, elegant social milieu.

In the light of La Rochefoucauld's disappointments in politics, in the military and in society, it is not surprising to note that he was attracted by the stoical element which he found in the Jansenism which many of his social acquaintances had adopted. He seems unimpressed by the spiritual interpretations offered by Jansenism but totally enmeshed by its contention of man's unending involvement in evil in some form or another. For La Rochefoucauld, this evil takes the form of self-interest and he sees it in all our actions, the good as well as the bad.

He does not draw pessimistic conclusions from his maxims. Rather he uses the maxim to illustrate his pessimistic view

of life. He is misanthropic, in general, but he seems to
take special delight in misogyny. In his case, anti-femin-
ism is the result of just one complaint among his many
grievances against life. He is, quite simply, against just
about everyone he has met because just about everyone has
been cause for disappointment.

Perhaps the element which has most affected La Rochefoucauld's philosophical attitude is "amour-propre", a sentiment combining not simply love of oneself but also a cal-
culating and corrupting approach in protecting one's interests: "We all have sufficient strength to bear the misfortunes of others." It was in his first work, Mémoires (1662),
that he brought out his conviction that, in essence, everyone is motivated by this selfish approach to social conduct.
If at times he seems to have mellowed with age in writing
the Maxims, it is really the influence of mistresses he had
in later life, especially the novelist, Mme. de La Fayette.

The honnête-homme and the honnête-femme, the all-around
correct individual, are the creations of La Rochefoucauld's
society and even he respected that ideal. His writings,
however, show that he found such a person rare indeed because it is only by considering his criticism of the self-
interested people that we get a glimpse of the ideal.

Readers are frequently tempted to see in the Maxims the
complaints of a grumpy old man who failed in life. There
is surely some truth in that idea but hardly enough to
account for the importance of La Rochefoucauld in French
literature and world literature. The reversals which he
experienced, while they were personally his, were also
experienced by many people of a background similar to his.
They all experienced socio-political defeat at the hands
of "absolute monarchy". But the significance of La Rochefoucauld's Maxims is far greater than simply serving as an
apology for five percent of the French population of the
Seventeenth Century since they continue to offer an interpretation of human motivation whose truths are hard to deny,
if indeed they can be denied. The appearance of psycho-
analysis in the Twentieth Century has not weakened the
message of these words. And the author's style with its
precision and clarity has not been surpassed over the
centuries.

If we object to La Rochefoucauld's sayings, it is rarely that we find them untrue, rather we object to their severity. Even like the friends of La Rochefoucauld, we feel, as social beings, the need to compromise in dealing with others. While we may want him to be more understanding of the need for hypocrisy in everyday social life, we must also understand the absolute values by which La Rochefoucauld lived.

Critics of La Rochefoucauld exist today just as they have since 1665, and his answer to critics is as valid now as when he wrote it. Of course, it is in the form of a maxim: "What causes so much argument against maxims which reveal the heart of man is that people fear being revealed."

MAXIMS

1. Our virtues are most often merely our vices in disguise. What we consider as virtues are often only
   a grouping together of various acts and personal interests which good luck or our own ingenuity can
   cleverly arrange. It is not always through chastity
   that men are valiant and women chaste.

6. Passion often transforms the cleverest men into fools
   and makes even the most foolish clever.

10. In the human heart there is a never ending procreation
    of passions; hence the destruction of one almost al-
    ways establishes the rule of another.

11. Passions often engender their opposites. Avarice some-
    times begets extravagance and extravagance avarice.
    One is often resolute through weakness and daring
    through timidity.

17. The moderate nature of the fortunate stems from the
    tranquility that good fortune lends to their
    temperament.

19. We all have sufficient strength to bear the mis-
    fortunes of others.

22. Philosophy easily triumphs over past and future mis-
    fortunes but it is of no avail before present ills.

26. Neither death nor the sun can be observed directly.

29. The evil that we do does not bring us so much per-
    secution and hate as our good qualities.

31. If we did not have so many faults, we would not take
    so much pleasure in noting them in others.

44. The strength and weakness of the spirit are badly
    named; they are, in fact, only the good or bad
    disposition of the body's organs.

49. We are never as happy or as miserable as we imagine.

54. The philosophers' scorn for wealth was a hidden desire to avenge their merit for the injustice of fortune, by the scorn of the same goods of which it deprived them; it was a secret to protect them from the vilification of poverty; it was a detour to achieve the recognition which they could not have by wealth.

55. Hatred of favorites is nothing more than love of favor. The resentment of not possessing it is consoled and softened by the scorn that one holds for those who possess it; and we refuse our recognition, not being able to refuse them the hommage they receive from everyone else.

56. To get established in society, we do everything we can to appear established there.

57. Even though men boast of their great actions, they are often not the effects of great plans, but the effects of chance.

67. Grace is to the body what common sense is to the mind.

70. No disguise can long conceal love where it exists or simulate it where it is lacking.

73. You can find women who have never had an affair, but it is rare to find any who have had just one.

76. True love is like seeing ghosts: everyone talks about them, but few have ever seen one.

78. For most men the love of justice is only the fear of encountering injustice.

89. Everyone complains of their memory, but no one complains of their judgment.

90. In life we please more often by our faults than by our good qualities.

93. Old men love to give good advice in order to console themselves for no longer being able to set bad examples.

94. Great names abase instead of exalting those who do not know how to bear them.

110. We give nothing so liberally as our advice.

112. The faults of the mind increase with age as do those of the face.

122. If we resist our passions, it is more because of their weakness than our strength.

127. The real way to be fooled is to believe oneself more clever than others.

134. A person is never as ridiculous for the qualities he has as for those he pretends to have.

138. We prefer to speak evil of ourselves rather than not to be spoken of at all.

140. A witty man would often be rather embarrassed without the company of fools.

147. Few people are wise enough to prefer useful blame to treacherous praise.

158. Flattery is false coin which gains its value from our vanity.

166. Society rewards the appearance of merit more often than merit itself.

168. Hope, deceitful as it is serves at least to bring us to the end of life in an agreeable manner.

171. Virtues are lost in interest, as rivers are lost in the sea.

182. Vices enter into the composition of virtues, as poisons enter into the composition of remedies: prudence combines them and tempers them and uses them profitably against the ills of life.

195. What often keeps us from abandoning ourselves to one vice is that we have several.

200. Virtue would not go so far if it were not accompanied by vanity.

203. The truly honorable man never boasts of himself.

209. Who lives without folly is not as wise as he thinks.

212. Most people only judge men by their popularity, or their wealth.

216. Perfect valor means doing without being seen what we would have done in the sight of the whole world.

218. Hypocrisy is hommage that vice pays to virtue.

229. The good that we have received from someone requires that we respect the evil that he does us.

231. It is great folly to want to be wise all alone.

250. True eloquence is saying all that is proper and only saying what is proper.

259. The pleasure of love is to love, and we are happier for the passion that we have than for that which we give.

264. Pity is often a feeling of our own misfortunes in the misfortunes of others; it is a clever foresight of the ills which may befall us; we give help to others in order to oblige them to help us in similar occasions, and these services which we do them are, properly speaking, good deeds which we do for ourselves in advance.

273. There are people, who are approved by society, who have for all their merit only vices which are necessary for the affairs of life.

286. It is impossible to love a second time that which we have truly stopped loving.

291. Man's merit has its season just like fruit.

294. We always like those who admire us, and we do not always like those whom we admire.

303. Whatever good someone says of us, they never teach us anything new.

308. We have made a virtue of moderation to limit the ambition of great men and to console the mediocre for their lack of good fortune and merit.

311. If there are men whose ridiculousness has never appeared, it is that no one has looked carefully.

316. Weak people cannot be sincere.

329. Sometimes we think we hate flattery, but we only hate the manner of flattering.

330. We pardon in proportion to our love.

340. The wit of most women serves more to strengthen their folly than their reason.

342. The accent of the region where we are born remains in our mind, and in our heart, just as in our language.

347. We hardly find people of common sense beyond those who agree with us.

368. Most honorable women are hidden treasures who are only safe because no one is looking for them.

405. We arrive as novices at the different stages of life, and we often lack experience at each one despite our number of years.

423. Few people know how to be old.

456. We are sometimes fools with wit, but never with judgment.

490. We often go from love to ambition, but he hardly ever go from ambition to love.

499. We do not ordinarily count a woman's first affair until she has had a second.

528. The good and the evil which come to us do not touch us by their greatness, but by our sensitivity.

Chapter 5

JEAN DE LA BRUYÈRE (1645-1696)

Unlike Pascal and La Rochefoucauld, La Bruyère in his
Characters or Mores of this Century, does not appear to
develop his study of men and women by using so many abstract
terms or as many moral generalities as they do. Rather his
intention as he expressed it in his "Préface" was to provide as accurate and as concrete a portrait of his contemporaries and their society as was possible. "I am giving
back to my public, he said, what it has lent me. From it
I have derived the matter for this work...It [the public]
can study at its leisure this portrait that I have drawn
of it following nature." And he did indeed provide a
highly factual tableau, not devoid of satire, of France in
the declining years of Louis XIV's reign.

It was certainly not a flattering portrayal: At the nation's summit--the court--he sketched a vain and arrogant
nobility basely adulating a monarch who jealously (and
blindly) defended his prerogatives. Below this impreg-
nable and self-centered elite, he presented a venal and
vulgar bourgeoisie scrambling for power and recognition;
and at the base of this social pyramid he described, sometimes in outraged terms, the lamentable condition of the
peasant, saddled with outrageous taxes, decimated by wars,
and slowly dying of hunger. The France that he depicted
thus bore little resemblance to that prosperous and

glorious realm of the early years of Louis' reign, but was now a wretched nation almost surely heading toward some violent cataclysm.

So unattractive and accurate a presentation gained for La Bruyère, shortly after his death, the reputation of having been primarily a social critic and perhaps a forerunner of the Enlightenment reformers as well as a philosophe before his time. Yet despite the social criticism implied in his observations, La Bruyère remained a man of his age. He viewed society as being essentially static: He believed that the present ills were timeless and more or less constant; that sharp distinctions between the poor and rich would endure, and that the conservation of the monarchy was always preferable to unforeseen evils caused by political upheavals. His portrait of the monarchy and the Church was, on the whole, respectful of the powers that each incarnated, and he never wavered from his strong conviction that both received their legitimacy directly from God. His ultimate purpose in writing the Characters was, in fact, to indicate that only through belief in God and the practice of religion could one find sufficient strength to understand and accept the world as it was; and any hope for the amelioration of the human condition could only be realized in the world to come.

Through his acceptance of timeless social and religious infrastructures La Bruyère was, therefore, writing in the same traditional vein as Pascal and La Rochefoucauld. How then does one explain the more concrete and graphic portrayal of men and women and their particular milieus which emerges from his work?

In the first place, La Bruyère was by nature not so much a philosopher-moralist concerned with plumbing the depths of motive and conduct as he was an artist, or literary painter, who faithfully recorded in his prose what he observed of others. Then, too, there is the important fact of class difference. The greater part of the Characters describes the mores and mechanism of court life. As a member of the bourgeoisie, La Bruyère was able to view this inner circle of power through the eyes of an outsider; as such he developed a more impartial view of this power structure and could record its most subtle machinations objectively and with neither the desire nor, for that matter, the slightest possibility of competing for power or glory within its framework. Finally, his position as an outsider in its midst would also explain the frequently bitter tone he used to lament the callous indifference of those in power to toward the appalling misery of the masses.

*

*   *

Very little is known of La Bruyère's family or his early years. He was born in Paris in 1645. His father, probably originally a lawyer, had become Contrôleur Général des Rentes (Property Tax Assessor) of the city. As a youth La Bruyère studied law, as did most bright and ambitious sons of bourgeois origin. He apparently never practiced it; but through money provided by an uncle, he purchased the post of Municipal Treasurer of the city of Caen--a position he was never to grace with his presence. He was therefore able to live in Paris and take advantage of the rich opportunities the capital provided for observing French society.

Through the good graces of his friend, Bishop Bossuet, he was appointed history tutor to the young son of Louis II de Bourbon, the "Great Condé" and was retained at court with the title "Gentleman of Monsieur le Duc." From this vantage point, he obtained, as Sainte-Beuve was to express it, "a corner seat in the first loge to view the grand spectacle of human life and high comedy of his age." And indeed La Bruyère used to greatest advantage this first-hand contact with the court at Versailles and Chantilly in the completion of the Characters which was published in 1687.

This first publication consisted of a translation of Theophrastus' irreverent and piquant sketches of his Athenian counterparts. To this translation that he had long been preparing, he appended maxims and reflections on social mores of his own time, as well as several portraits depicting social types by means of which he rendered concrete his general observations. The portraits immediately created a succès de scandale and were greatly responsible for the wide popularity of the work since it was generally believed that he had composed a roman à clef using these literary portraits to designate actual contemporaries.

Though there is undoubtedly some truth to the charge, it
does not go very far in explaining La Bruyère's primary aim.
He was far more intent on creating universal types than
flesh and blood facsimiles. His literary "characters" consist of finely etched and stinging portraits of all manner
of humanity--cruel courtiers, pretentious society women,
irreverent and avaricious churchmen; then quintessential
"types"--the glutton, the rich man, the poor man, the
pedant, the hypocrite, and others all drawn from his own
society. These portraits are both universal in this de-
piction of moral qualities yet concrete in the psychological
and physical traits that render life to the individual per-
sonas. They constitute not only authentic portraits of men
and women of his age but also represent human types holding attitudes and approaches to life that eternally endure.
And it is as the most brilliant portraitist of moral conduct and attitudes that La Bruyère takes his place among
the French moralists.

In our own age the Characters have also been judged as a
revolutionary turning point in French prose style by the
modern French critic, Julian Benda, himself a severe critic
of modern society and an authority on La Bruyère. According
to Benda, the work was the first in French literature not
to be organized about a central theme, hence not composed
in subordination to an aesthetic whole, but presenting artistic prose of changing mood and tone for its own sake.
Benda, therefore, regards La Bruyère to be not only a major
moralist but also a pioneer in the development of literary
form: through his stated aim, to "bien définir et bien
peindre," he virtually set the pattern for the impression-
ist prose style and fluid composition ultimately carried
forward and refined by Flaubert, Stendhal, and the Goncourt
brothers--all masters of literary impressionism in the
19th Century.

CHARACTERS or MORES OF THIS CENTURY

I. On works of the mind:

1. Everything has been said and, after more than seven thousand years during which there have been men who have thought, we come too late; the finest and the best ideas on manners and morals have been gathered up and presented; we can only glean after the ancients and the most gifted among the moderns.

3. To make a book is as much a handicraft as to make a clock; something more than intelligence is demanded to become an author. A certain magistrate was going to be raised on the strength of his reputation to the highest legal office; he was a man of subtle mind, much worldly experience, but felt compelled to print a treatise on morality, which is uncommon on account of its absurdity.

10. In art there is a degree of perfection, as in Nature there is one of goodness and completion. Anyone who feels this and esteems it is endowed with a perfect taste; but he who does not feel it and loves what falls below or above it, is lacking in taste. Hence there does exist a good and a bad taste, and we are right to distinguish the difference between them.

17. Among the various expressions which can convey our thoughts, there is but one which is apt. We do not always hit upon it in writing or speaking, but, nevertheless, such a one certainly exists, and all the others are weak and do not satisfy a cultured man who wishes to make himself understood.

18. A good author, and one who writes carefully, often finds that the expression that he has been seeking for sometime, and of which he was unaware, proves when found at last, to be the most simple, the most natural, and the one that most likely first occurred to him spontaneously.

31. When a work you have read has given rise to lofty thoughts and has inspired you with noble and gallant feelings, look for no other rule to judge it by; it is excellent and written in a masterly form.

62. If I may say so, there are certain inferior or second-rate minds who seem capable only of becoming the receptacle, the register, or the warehouse of all the productions of other men of talent; they are plagiarists, translators, compilers; they never think but relate to what other authors have thought; and as any collection of thoughts requires some inventiveness, theirs is badly conceived and incorrect, which compels them to make it more lengthy than excellent. They have nothing original about them; they only know what they have learned, and only learn what the rest of the world does not want to know; a useless and dry science, devoid of usefulness and charm, worthless for conversation and unsuited to human intercourse, like an unusable coin. We are amazed when we read them, as well as exhausted by their conversation or their works. The nobility and the common people mistake them for learned men, but wise men dismiss them as pedants.

63. Criticism is often not a science but a trade which requires more health than intelligence, more work than talent, and more practice than genius. If it is undertaken by a person of less discernment than experience in literature, and treats of certain subjects, it corrupts both the judgment of the reader and the author whom it criticizes.

67. He who is only concerned with writing to please the taste of his age, values himself more than his writings. We should always aim for perfection, and then posterity will do us that justice which is sometimes refused to us by our contemporaries.

II. Of Personal Merit

1. What man is not convinced of his uselessness, though he be endowed with the rarest talents and the most extraordinary merit, when he considers that at his death he leaves a world that will not feel his loss, and where so many people can be found to replace him?

4. What a horrible ordeal it is for a man without patrons or cabal, who belongs to no party, but who is alone and has only great merit to commend him to break out of his obscurity and rise to the level of a fool who has found favor!

5. Hardly anyone ever notices the merit of others on his own initiative. Men are too engrossed in themselves to have the leisure for penetrating or discerning the worth of others, so that a person of great merit and even greater modesty may remain a long time in obscurity.

9. There is no business in this world so distressing as that of winning fame: life is over before we have barely launched our enterprise.

15. A gentleman repays himself for his zeal in performing his duty by the pleasure he experiences through such actions, and he does not miss the praise, esteem, and gratitude which he sometimes does not receive.

21. If it be happiness to be of noble parentage, it is no less so to have so much merit that nobody has to inquire whether we are noble or common.

38. I met Mopus through a visit he paid me before knowing me previously; he asks people he does not know to present him to others who also have not met him before; he writes to ladies whom he only knows by sight. He also worms his way into a company of highly respectable people, who have no idea who he is, and without waiting till they address him, or realizing that he is interrupting them, he often speaks in a ridiculous manner. On another occasion he enters a public

96

meeting, sits down where he pleases, without paying
attention to others or to himself; and if he has to
give up his place to a minister, he sits down in the
seat of a duke and peer of the realm; he becomes the
laughing stock of the entire gathering, yet is the only
one who maintains a serious countenance. He is like a
dog, who when driven out of the king's chair, jumps
into the pulpit. He looks upon what the world thinks
of him with indifference, without any embarrassment
and without the least bit of shame; he has no more
sense of modesty than the common fool.

44. The good man is one who benefits others; if he suffers
for the good which he does, he is still better; and if
he suffers at the hand of those to whom he has done
good, he exemplifies such a degree of perfection that
nothing can be added to it but an increase of his sufferings; if he dies because of them, his virtue cannot
rise higher; it is heroic, it is faultless.

III.   Of Women

1. Men and women seldom are in agreement about the merits
    of a woman, because their interests vary too much.
    Women do not like in one another those same charms
    which make them attractive to men; many manners and
    traits which kindle in the latter the strongest pas-
    sions, sow among them aversion and antipathy.

2. Some women possess an artificial grandeur which goes
    no farther than the way they move their eyes or toss
    their heads, their manner of walking, a dazzling wit
    which is impressive, and which is only admired because
    it is superficial. In a few others we find a simple
    and natural greatness, not dependent on gestures and
    bearing, which flows naturally from the heart, and is,
    apparently, the result of their noble birth; their
    merit, as unostenatatious as it is real, is accomp-
    anied by countless virtues, which, despite their modest
    nature, escape and become evident to all who can
    recognize them.

10. A handsome face is the most beautiful of all sights,
    and the sweetest music is the sound of the voice of a
    woman we love.

11. Charm is subjective; beauty is something more tangible
    and independent of opinion.

13. A beautiful woman, who also is endowed with the qual-
    ities of a cultivated man, is the most delightful com-
    panion one can have, for she combines the merits of
    both sexes.

16. Women become attached to men by the favors they grant
    them, but men are cured of their love through these
    same favors.

17. When a woman ceases to love a man, she even forgets the
    favors she has granted him.

24. A fickle woman is one who is no longer in love; a loose
    woman is one who is already in love with another person;

a flighty woman is one who neither knows if she loves nor whom; and an indifferent woman is one who loves nobody.

53. Women go to extremes; they are either better or worse than men.

55. Women surpass most men in love; but men are their betters in friendship. Men are the reason that women do not esteem one another.

67. It sometimes happens that a woman hides from a man all the passion she feels for him, while he feigns a passion for her which he does not feel.

78. Few wives are so perfect as not to prevent their husbands from repenting at least once a day for even having married, or at least from envying those who have never married.

IV. Of the Affections

1. Pure friendship is a taste which men of an inferior nature can never cultivate.

2. Friendship can continue to exist between persons of different sexes without ever becoming coarse or sensual; yet a woman always regards a man as a man, and so does a man regard a woman as a woman. Such a relationship is neither love nor pure friendship, but something quite unusual.

3. Love is born suddenly, without warning, through natural disposition or weakness; a glint of beauty perceived transforms us, determines us. Friendship, on the other hand, is formed gradually, in time, through intercourse and long familiarity. How much wit, kindness, and affection; how many services and amenities are needed among friends to accomplish in several years what, in a minute, a beautiful face or a fine hand can do.

4. Time, which strengthens friendships, weakens love.

7. Love and friendship are mutually exclusive.

13. Love which grows bit by bit is too much like friendship ever to become a violent passion.

27. In friendship we only see those faults which may be harmful to our friends; in those we love, we notice only those which make us suffer.

31. We have no more the power to be continually in love than we have not to love at all.

36. When a plain-looking woman is loved, it can only be with a great passion; for either she is loved because of some weakness on the part of her lover, or she has some secret charms more irresistible than those of beauty.

63. We must laugh before we are happy lest we die without having laughed at all.

72. All the passions are deceitful; they conceal themselves as well as they can from others and even from themselves. No vice exists which does not feign some resemblance with a certain virtue, and which does not take advantage of this supposed resemblance.

76. Men begin with love and end with ambition; they seldom find a more tranquil state till death.

79. There are certain sublime sentiments, certain noble and lofty deeds which we owe more to the goodness of our nature than to the strength of our mind.

V. Of Society and Conversation

1. A man must be very insipid to have no character at all.

7. What are you saying? What? I don't understand you. Would you be so kind as to say it again? I understand you still less. Finally, I guess your meaning; you are trying to tell me, Acis, that it is cold! Why don't you say it? You want me to know that it is raining or snowing; simply say that it rains or snows. You think that I am looking well and want to congratulate me; say that you think that I am looking well. But you may reply that it is so plain and clear that anybody might have spoken like this. But what does that matter, Acis? Is it such a bad thing to be understood when one speaks and to speak as everyone else does? There is one thing, Acis, which you and those like you who speak in riddles, completely lack; you are not in the least aware of it, and I know that I am going to surprise you very much. The thing that you lack is wit. But that is not all. There is too much of something else in you, which is the opinion that you have more intelligence than other people; this is the source of all your pompous gibberish, of your confusing phraseology, and of all your grand words without any meaning. When next I find you talking to anybody, or entering a room, I am going to pull your coat and whisper in your ear: "Do not pretend to be witty; be natural, it becomes you better; use, if you can, plain language, such as they use who you think are without wit;" then perhaps we shall think that you have some yourself.

16. The true spirit of conversation consists more in bringing out the cleverness of others than in showing a great deal of it yourself; he who goes away pleased with himself and his own wit after conversing with you is also very pleased with you. Most men would rather please than admire you; they are less interested in being instructed, and even amused, than to be appreciated and praised; the most delicate pleasure is that of pleasing another person.

18. It is a very sad state of affairs when people have neither enough intelligence to speak well nor enough discretion to say nothing; this is the root of all impertinence.

37. Not to be able to bear with the ill-tempered with whom the world abounds, indicates that a person is not good-tempered himself: small change is as necessary in the world as golden coin.

41. In society, good sense always gives way first. The most sensible people are often swayed by a most foolish and eccentric person; they study his weakness, his temperament, his whims, and come to terms with them; they avoid offending him, and everybody lets him have his way; when he has a cheerful expression, he is praised; they are grateful to him for not always being unbearable: He is feared, respected, obeyed, and sometimes even loved.

79. Hardly any other men but those born gentlemen or of great culture are capable of keeping a secret.

83. A wise man sometimes avoids the world, that he may not become too wearied of it.

VI.   Of the Gifts of Fortune

4.   As favor and wealth forsake a man, they permit us to
     discover in him the foolishness they concealed, and
     which no one perceived before.

7.   If a financier makes a bad move, the courtiers say of
     him, "He is only a bourgeois, a man who comes from
     nothing, a lout;" but if he is lucky, they ask to
     marry his daughter.

13. Let us not envy a certain class of men because of their
     enormous wealth; they have paid a very heavy price for
     it, and one that would not sit well with us; they have
     sacrificed their peace of mind, their health, their
     honor, and their good conscience; this is too much to
     pay, and there is no profit to be made from such a
     bargain.

18. Champagne, getting up from a prolonged dinner, his
     stomach bursting and his head swimming with the agree-
     able fumes of Avernay or Sillery, signs an order pre-
     sented to him which would deprive a whole province
     of its bread if the act is not contravened. He can
     be excused; how can any man whose digestive juices are
     just starting to flow be aware that somewhere there
     could be people dying of starvation?

40. A man is thirty years old before he thinks about making
     his fortune; but it is not completed at fifty; he begins
     to build in his old age, and when he dies, his house is
     finally ready to be painted and glazed.

47. There exist miseries in the world which make the heart
     ache; some people do not even have food; they fear the
     winter and are afraid to live. Others eat cultured
     fruit; the earth and the seasons are compelled to pro-
     vide them with delicacies; mere bourgeois, simply be-
     cause they have grown wealthy, have had the audacity
     to swallow in one morsel enough food to feed a hundred
     families. Protest as one will against such extremes,
     let me be neither happy or unhappy if I can help it;
     I find refuge in the middle course.

104

52.   There are but two ways of getting ahead in the world,
      either by your own ingenuity or by the folly of
      others.

58.   There are some sordid minds, full of slime and filth,
      as taken with interest and gain as superior souls are
      with glory and virtue; their only pleasure is to ac-
      quire money and never to lose it; they are ever on the
      alert and are always seeking their ten per cent; they
      are only occupied with their creditors; always anxious
      at the devaluation or calling in of currencies; totally
      absorbed and immersed in contracts, titles, and parch-
      ments. Such people are neither relatives, friends,
      citizens, Christians, and perhaps not even men: they
      have money.

83.   Giton has a fresh complexion, full face, drooping
      cheeks, a steady and confident look, broad shoulders,
      a large chest, and a firm and deliberate step. He
      speaks with confidence, makes a person repeat every
      word spoken to him, and is only mildly pleased with
      what he is told. He takes a large handkerchief out
      of his pocket, and blows his nose with a loud noise;
      he expectorates with force, and sneezes very loud. He
      sleeps by day and by night, and soundly; he snores in
      company. He occupies more space when eating or walking
      than anyone, and takes up the middle of the street when
      he walks with his equals; when he stops, they stop;
      when he goes forward, they go forward; all are control-
      led by what he does. He interrupts and corrects those
      who are speaking; no one interupts him, and people lis-
      ten to him as long as he is pleased to speak; for they
      agree with him and assume that the news he tells is
      true. If he sits down, he sinks into an easy chair,
      crosses his legs, frowns, pulls his hat down over his
      eyes so as to see no one, or suddenly draws it back
      to reveal a proud and insolent countenance. He is
      cheerful, ever laughing, impatient, impudent, iras-
      cible, a free thinker, and a politician full of secrets
      about intrigues of the day; he thinks he has talents
      and intelligence; he is rich.

<u>Phaedo</u> has sunken eyes, a ruddy complexion, a lean
body and gaunt features; he sleeps very little and is
easily awakened; he is absent-minded, pensive and,
even though somewhat intelligent, he appears stupid;
he forgets to say what he knows, or to talk about
events with which he is acquainted; when he occasionally says something, he does it badly; he thinks that
he bores the people to whom he is talking and therefore
tells his story briefly but drily; hence he is not
listened to since he makes no one laugh. He applauds
and laughs at other peoples' tales, always agrees with
them, runs and flies to do them sundry minor services.
He is overly obliging, flatters and serves them; he is
close-mouthed about his own affairs, and sometimes is
not truthful about them; he is superstitious, scrup-
ulous, and diffident. He moves lightly and quietly and
seems afraid to tread the ground; he walks with downcast eyes and dares not raise them to regard passers-
by; he never takes part in any conversation but places
himself behind whoever is speaking; furtively he absorbs all that has been said and withdraws if anyone
looks at him. He takes up no room nor does he fill
any space; he goes about with his arms hugging his
body, his hat over his eyes so he won't be seen, and
wraps himself snugly in his coat. No street or gallery
is so crowded and filled with people, but he finds a
way to get through easily and to slip through without
being noticed. If he is asked to sit down, he seats
himself on the very edge of a chair, speaks softly and
not very audibly; he however gives his opinion freely
on public affairs, is critical of the age, and but
poorly informed about the doings of the cabinet and
the ministers. He only opens his mouth to reply; he
coughs and blows his nose in his hat, he almost expec-
torates on himself and waits till he is alone to
sneeze, or if he has to, no one hears it, and no one
thus has to say: "God bless you." He is poor.

VIII.   Of the Court

1.   The most honorable reproach we can make against man
     is to tell him that he does not understand the court;
     there is scarcely a virtue which we do not credit him
     with when saying this.

6.   To people who live in the provinces, the court appears
     admirable; but if they visit it, its charms diminish,
     like those of a beautiful vista that we view too
     closely.

8.   The court does not make a man happy, but it prevents
     him from being so anywhere else.

30. How many people almost smother you with their demon-
     strations of affection, and pretend to love and esteem
     you in private, who are embarrassed if they meet you
     in public, and at the king's levee, or at mass, avoid
     your gaze, and try not to greet you. There are very
     few courtiers who have sufficient nobility of character
     or self-confidence to dare to honor in public a man
     of merit who does not hold great office.

40. You are an honest man and you are not concerned with
     pleasing or displeasing the court favorites. You are
     solely attached to your master and to your duty; you
     are a lost man.

IX. Of the Great

27. Ease of living, affluence, and the tranquility of a
     successful and prosperous career are the reasons why
     princes can take some pleasure in laughing at a dwarf,
     a monkey, a fool, or a wretched story; less fortunate
     men laugh only when they ought to.

56. As a general rule we should not talk about the great
     and the powerful; when we speak well of them, flattery
     is almost always involved; it is dangerous to speak
     ill of them while they are alive, and cowardly when
     they are dead.

X. Of the Sovereign and the State

1. After we have surveyed all forms of government without
   predilection for our own, we find it hard to choose any
   one; there is a mixture of good and evil in all of
   them; it is therefore most reasonable to love our
   native land above all the others, and to submit to it.

4. Under a despotic regime a feeling for one's native land
   cannot exist. Self-interest, fame, and service to
   one's prince take its place.

13. The French temperament requires that its sovereign con-
    duct himself with gravity.

30. How very fortunate is that station which every instant
    provides a man with the means of doing good to thou-
    sands of men! How dangerous is that post which every
    moment allows its holder to injure millions!

XI. On Mankind

1. Let us not become angry with men when we observe them to be cruel, ungrateful, proud, egotistical, and forgetful of others; such is their makeup; it is their nature to be so; we might just as well object when a stone falls or the flames of a fire mount.

2. In one sense men are not fickle, or are only so in trifles; they change their dress, language, exterior appearance, their rules for what is proper, and sometimes even their taste; but they always retain their bad morals, and cling steadfastly to what is evil, or to their indifference to virtue.

13. If poverty is the mother of all crimes, a lack of intelligence is their father.

17. There exist some very strange fathers who, during their entire lifetime, seem only intent on giving their children reasons to be consoled at their death.

33. If life is wretched, it is difficult to endure; if it is happy, it is horrible to lose it. Both amount to the same thing.

34. There is nothing that men are so intent on preserving, and yet are so careless about, as life.

41. We hope to grow old and yet we fear old-age; in other words, we cling to life and shun death.

42. A man is better advised to yield to nature and fear death, than to do battle constantly, provide himself with arguments and reflections, and be always struggling with himself in order not to fear it.

45. Humanly speaking, one good thing about death is that it puts an end to old age. A death which prevents decrepitude is more in season than one which ends it.

46. Men may feel regret that their life has been ill-spent, yet they are not always led by this reason to make a better use of the time they have still to live.

48. There are only three events of major importance for man: birth, life, and death. He is unconscious of his birth, he suffers when he dies, and he neglects to live.

102. Most men employ the first part of their life in making the last miserable.

111. There is nothing more unnatural in the world than to find an old man who is in love.

118. A venerable, old courtier who has good sense and a reliable memory, is a priceless treasure; he is full of anecdotes and maxims; he knows many curious facts and circumstances about the history of the age, which do not appear in books; and we may learn from him rules for our own conduct and manners, which are always reliable, because they are based on experience.

119. Young men can better endure solitude than old men because their passions keep their minds occupied.

128. One sees certain ferocious animals, male and female, scattered throughout the countryside, black, livid, and burned by the sun, tied, in a sense, to the land which they are always digging and turning over with an unconquerable stubbornness; they have a somewhat articulate voice, and when they straighten up, they exhibit a human face: indeed, they are men. At night they retire to their lairs where they live on black bread, water, and roots; they spare other men the trouble of sowing, ploughing, and of reaping for their sustenance, and, therefore, do not deserve to lack that bread that they themselves have sown.

140. There is as much difference between the neutral character which a man assumes and his real character as there is between a mask and an authentic human face.

152. If some men are not so good as they could be, the fault lies in their early upbringing.

XVI.   Of Free-Thinkers

15.   I feel that there is a God and I do not imagine that
there is none; this is enough for me, and all wordy
arguments seem worthless; I therefore conclude that
God exists, and this conclusion is inherent to my
nature.   I received these principles effortlessly in
my childhood, and I have preserved them since, too
naturally in my more advance years, ever to suspect
them to be false.   But there are some men who rid
themselves of these principles.   I question whether
there really are such people, but if there be such,
that only proves that monsters do exist.

24.   To what extremes will a man not be carried through his
zeal for a religion in whose truths he hardly believes,
and which he practices badly.

31.   There are two worlds: one which we inhabit for a brief
period of time and which we must leave never to return
to; another, to which we must shortly go, there to
live forever.   Interest, authority, friends, a great
reputation and great riches are useful in the first;
a disregard for all these things is useful for the
second.   It is up to us to choose.

Chapter 6

VAUVENARGUES (1715-1747)

Almost everything about the life of Vauvenargues seems tragic except his indomitable will which permitted him to rise
above personal misfortunes. Born with a weak constitution,
the victim of a virtually uninterrupted series of hideous
diseases, and frustrated in all attempts to achieve fame
and success, he nevertheless left to posterity a cogent
study of human passions that vigorously called into question the pessimistic views on human nature offered by La
Rochefoucauld and Pascal less than a century before.

Luc de Clapiers, Marquis de Vauvenargues was born in Aix-
en-Provence in 1715 of an illustrious but impoverished
noble family. Since his early years were rendered miserable by ill health, he could never attend school with other
children. Instead he virtually educated himself in the
family library of the chateau of Vauvenargues. Here he
read voraciously the classical authors and especially the
works of the stoics, Plutarch, Marcus Aurelius, and Seneca
in particular, from whom he derived no small consolation
to bear with his suffering.

Driven with the desire to make a brilliant career in the
military--an ambition gained from his readings of Plutarch--
he enlisted in the king's regiment and rose to the grade
of captain. He participated in the Italian campaign of

1734 and then was forced to endure the monotonous and des-
ultory life of an officer assigned to remote garrisons in
Besançon, Verdun, and Metz. During the campaign in Bohemia
(1741-1742), both his legs were severely frozen and in 1744
he was forced to resign his commission because of physical
complications.

He then tried to embark on a career in diplomacy--tradi-
tionally a respectable profession for sons of ruined nobil-
ity--but found all avenues of advancement blocked to him
for lack of political preferment. During the last few
years of his life he resided in a modest Parisian hotel
and dedicated himself totally to his writings. His health
gradually deteriorated even more: he was monstrously dis-
figured and blinded by small pox and contracted tuberculosis. He died in 1747 at the age of thirty-two, only one
year after the publication of some of his major writings:
the essay, Introduction to an Understanding of the Human
Mind and his principal moralist text, Reflections and
Maxims. During the last three years of his life he was
befriended by Voltaire who immensely respected his erudition
and who championed his works.

Vauvenargues left for posterity several essays, a collection
of maxims and reflections replete with a gallery of literary portraits (some of which rival the best produced by
La Bruyère), various dialogues, letters, and fragments, all
of which comprise two slender volumes in the modern edition.
In all of his writings he had a sole aim: to study the self
and to apply his findings to an understanding of all men.
This he called, "the unique goal of all thought and action,
and the object of my entire life."

With not the slightest interest in physical sciences, mathematics, or social sciences, he gave himself totally to a
study of ethics: the problem of how to attain justice and
happiness, how to teach himself and others to live in mut-
ual peace, and what virtues were especially essential to
develop all the rich potential of the human soul--such were
the topics of his moral probings and writings.

Agreeing with Pascal that man's primary state in nature is
that of solitude--the prison of the self--and that he can
gain knowledge of himself in this state, Vauvenargues was

led to postulate that the full and proper development of
the human soul could not be achieved through self-knowledge
alone, but through cooperation with others. Unlike Pascal,
he did not feel that society was necessarily a prison but
rather that it offered the foundation for spiritual union
with others. The key to such union was meaningful action;
action was necessary to develop one's individual, moral
perfection as well as to provide virtuous conduct that would
enrich not only the self but others in their efforts to act
with virtue.

Again disagreeing with Pascal, Vauvenargues did not view
human nature as irrevocably sunk in misery and imperfection
but as a malleable entity whose baser instincts could be
elevated by remedies and insights contained in human nature
itself. Hence, he fervently wished to teach men and women
to know how to draw upon their better qualities, and by
pointing out their own weaknesses to them, to be tolerant of
the failings they encountered in others.

For La Rochefoucauld's stern and depressing view that self-
interest constituted the spring of all human motive, Vauvenargues had, as he put it, only repugnance. He readily
admitted the acumen of much that the latter had observed
but, in the main, considered him an evil influence because
of his exaggerated points of view: "Whatever may have been
his intentions, their effect seems pernicious; his book,
filled with delicate invectives against hypocrisy, continues
in our own day to turn men away from virtue by persuading
them that there is truly no such thing..." In marshaling
his attack on this illustrious moralist, Vauvenargues passionately insisted that man was capable of acting both from
base self-interest and the most surprising altruism--that
to deny the one in favor of the other was to be woefully
and negligently ignorant of the total dimension of man's
moral potential.

In his conscious attempt to "rehabilitate" man's image of
himself which he felt had been darkened by the overly pessimistic analyses of his moralist predecessors, Vauvenargues also developed a penetrating analysis of the human
passions themselves. Far from being degrading, passions
in their most primitive state represent, be believed, a

115

dynamic vitalism that permits the individual to break out
of the prison of the self. Provided they be guided by lucid intelligence gained through self-study, they give us
the means to achieve virtue and permit us to go beyond the
boundaries of mere cold reason through generous impluse.
A number of maxims which he composed clearly present this
view of the beneficial potential of the passions and the
ultimate superiority of head over heart: "Reason deceives
us more often than does nature;" "Reason is unaware of the
concerns of the heart;" "If our passions sometimes give us
more advice than does thoughtful reflection, it is because
they provide us with greater strength to bring matters to
completion," to quote only a few.

Closely tied to this vital role which the passions play
in the development of the authentic self is Vauvenargues's
cosmic view of man as an integral part of nature ever in
movement. As a tiny entity in this vast "alliance" that
is nature, man is governed by the law of action which necessitates communication with others. In fact, he enjoys his
full being only through action, and each human act is "a
new being" which we cause to exist. Hence the more we act,
the more we produce and live, since the destiny of all human affairs is maintained only through continual generation.
And as a living organism the soul is subject to universal
physical laws; if it refuses to act then it ceases to expand its horizons, shrivels up, and dies, while if it lives
in harmony with the universal law of communication through
generous action, it expands and delivers itself from the
bondage of solitude. To live and grow, then, each individual soul must lose its unique identity, be swept toward
action, and function as part of the cosmic soul--the source
of vital strength and generosity.

This program of moral energy and generosity is all the more
inspiring because it was personally lived in the face of
seemingly unbearable sufferings and disappointments. As
true to his ideals as was Pascal, Vauvenargues refused to
let exterior factors that he could not control darken or
wear down his moral heroism. His thoughts and reflections
which engendered a love and confidence in the goodness of
life and which renewed faith in the potential for virtue
inherent in natural man would have a major impact on those

18th Century philosophers and moralists, in particular
Rousseau, who were to forward his project of rehabilitating man's image of himself as a creature naturally disposed to virtuous action.

1. It is easier to speak about new matters than to reconcile those that have been discussed.

2. The human mind is more penetrating than consistent; it embraces more than it can connect.

3. When a thought is too weak to sustain a simple statement, it is an indication that it should be rejected.

5. Obscurity is the realm of error.

6. There are possibly no errors that do not perish by themselves when once they are clearly perceived.

9. When an idea is presented to us as if it were a profound discovery, and if we should take the trouble to follow it through, we often find it to be a verity which "is the talk of the town."

12. Always giving moderate praise is a sign of mediocrity.

13. Fortunes that have been made in a hurry, of no matter what sort, are the least permanent, because they are rarely the product of merit. The fruit of prudent toil is always slow to ripen.

16. As early as youth, burning ambition exiles all other pleasures and rules supreme.

19. Courage has more resources against disgrace than does reason.

22. Servitude debases men until they become enamoured of it.

24. It is not in reason's power to repair all of nature's defects.

25. Before attacking an abuse, we should try to weaken its foundations.

27. We do not have the right to make miserable those whom we cannot make virtuous.

28. We cannot be just if we are not merciful.

31. Our errors and dissensions in the realm of morality sometimes stem from a tendency to regard man as capable of being absolutely depraved or completely good.

36. Youth's storms are encircled by radiant days.

39. Even in love, habit is everything.

43. When we distinguish what we respect from what we love, we are almost certainly being narrow-minded. Lofty souls love naturally everything that is worthy of their esteem.

45. When we feel we do not have the qualities to be respected by someone, we are very close to hating such a person.

59. We have so little virtue that we deem ourselves ridiculous for esteeming glory.

60. The pursuit of wealth makes many demands; we have to be flexible, amusing, charming, scheming, offensive to no one, pleasing to women and men of rank; we have to be able to mix business with pleasure, hide our secrets, endure boredom night and day, and thrice play quadrill without moving from our chairs. And even after all of this, we are still sure of nothing. How much disgust and tedium would be spared if we dared to court glory on the basis of merit alone?

64. He who dresses before eight in the morning to attend a trial, to see an exposition of paintings at the Louvre, to be present at a rehearsal of a play that will soon be given, in short, who fancies himself well qualified to appraise the works of others in every category, often is a person lacking only taste and intelligence.

66. We often offend others when we extol them in terms which set limits to their merits. Few people are modest enough to endure our praise without being troubled by it.

67. It is difficult to esteem others as they would like to be.

68. Just as we console ourselves when we do not possess great talents, so should we be consoled for not holding positions of importance. We can be above both of these by the noble qualities of the heart.

70. Why should peace of mind be considered as the ultimate proof that a person is virtuous? Good health provides it.

73. The moderation one finds in the weak is true mediocrity.

77. It is not true that the poor are morally superior to the rich.

83. People who feel they no longer need others become impossible to deal with.

87. All men feel that they deserve a more important office than the one they hold. But Nature, which has not given them the ability, also makes them feel content in their present states.

94. People who are merely clever never hold the highest rank anywhere.

107. The maxims that men compose reveal their hearts.

111. Few maxims are true in all respects.

119. Few of us would be happy if it were the right of others to decide upon our occupations and our diversions.

123. Reason deceives us more often than does Nature.

124. Reason does not know the concerns of the heart.

125. If our passions sometimes give us more bold advice than does thoughtful reflection, it is because they provide greater strength to bring matters to completion.

127. Great or lofty thoughts have their source in the heart.

130. Magnanimity does not have to account for the prudence of its motives.

131. No one is more subject to error than people who act only upon reflecting.

133. Conscience is the most changeable rule of all. Healthy people have an arrogant conscience; the weak and miserable a fainthearted one; the irresolute have one that is troubled; and so on. Conscience is, therefore, an organ obeying the feelings that dominate us and the opinions that control us.

140. There is no falser standard by which to judge a life than by the way one dies.

141. It is most unjust to demand that a soul downcast and overcome by the blows of a terrible sickness maintain the same strength that it has displayed in former times. Are we surprised because a sick person can no longer walk, sit up, or support himself? Would it not be stranger if he were to remain the same man as he had been when in vigorous health? If we have a migraine or have slept badly, people excuse us for being incompetent the following day, and no one suspects us of being inattentive. Shall we refuse a dying man the same privilege that we grant to one with a headache, and shall we dare to assume that he has never been courageous while in good health, because he may seem to lack it on his deathbed?

142. If we are to accomplish great things, we must live as if we were never going to die.

143. The thought of death beguiles us because it makes us forgetful of living.

148. A lack of appetite is not an indication of health, nor is a good appetite one of sickness, but just the contrary! Yet we judge the soul by other standards. We suppose a strong soul to be unmoved by the passions; since youth is a more ardent and active period than old age, we regard it as a long period of fever; and we situate man's prime of life in his declining years.

149. The mind is the eye of the soul and is not its strength. Its strength is in the heart, that is, the passions. The most enlightened reason cannot make us act or will. Is it enough to have good vision to wish to walk, or must we not also have feet and the strength of will to set them in motion?

150. Reason and feeling reconcile and complement each other in turn. Whoever consults the one and avoids the other deprives himself imprudently of part of the help granted us to know how to act.

151. We perhaps owe the greatest successes of the mind to the passions.

154. The passions have taught men reason.

155. During the childhood of the human race and that of all individuals, feeling has always come before thought and has been its first teacher.

156. Young men suffer less from their own mistakes than from the prudence of the old.

159. The counsels of old age emit light without heat, like a winter sun.

160. The most common pretense of those who make others unhappy is that they want what is best for them.

164. Whatever does not offend society lies outside the jurisdiction of justice.

174. The most detestable, yet the most common and most ancient form of ingratitude, is that practiced by children toward their fathers.

175. We are hardly grateful to our friends for esteeming our good qualities if they so much as notice our faults.

184. To flee from force, we were obliged to submit to justice: Justice or force, we had to choose one or the other as our master, so slightly disposed were we to be free.

188. Among kings, nations, and individuals, the strongest abrogates to himself rights over the weakest, and the same rule is followed by animals, matter, the elements, etc., so that everything is fulfilled in the universe through violence. This rule, which we condemn with some appearance of justice, is the most general, the most absolute, the most immutable, and the most ancient of nature's laws.

191. It is good to be steadfast in character and flexible in the way we think.

198. Fire, air, spirit, light, all subsist through movement; on the one hand, there results the intercommunication and union of all being; and on the other, the concord and harmony of the universe. Yet this natural law, usually so fruitful, we find to be a defect in regard to man. Since he must obey it and yet cannot remain at rest, we must conclude that he is out of place.

199. Man offers himself repose only to be freed from toil and subjugation; yet he is only happy when in action and loves this alone.

203. A very intelligent person admires few things, and the same is true for one who is very limited. Admiration marks the boundaries of our knowledge and is less an indication of the perfection of things than the imperfection of our minds.

215.   A good mind can make connections between things; the
       ability to compare insignificant and very important
       facts broadens the mind; such accuracy would there-
       fore seem to be the first requirement and an abso-
       lutely essential condition for the truly universal
       mind.

217.   I do not agree at all with the maxim which holds that
       a cultivated man should know a little bit about every-
       thing. It is almost always useless, and sometimes
       even pernicious, to have a superficial and shallow
       knowledge of things. It is true that most men are
       hardly capable of knowing anything in depth, yet it
       is also true that the superficial knowledge which
       they seek only serves to flatter their vanity. Such
       knowledge is harmful to those who possess real intel-
       ligence, since it necessarily diverts such people from
       their principal objective, consumes their efforts in
       minute details and in matters alien to their needs
       and natural talents and, finally, it serves not at
       all, despite claims to the contrary, to indicate the
       broad scope of their minds. In all periods there
       have been people of mediocre intelligence who have
       known a great deal and, conversely, those with super-
       ior minds who have known very little. Ignorance is,
       therefore, neither a defect of the mind, nor is know-
       ledge a proof of genius.

227.   It is false to hold that equality is inherent in
       nature; for nature has nothing equal about it. Its
       sovereign law is that of subordination and dependence.

235.   We must have great resources of strength in mind and
       heart to appreciate sincerity when it wounds us or
       to practice it without offense; few people have
       enough depth to endure the truth and to tell it.

245.   When fortune wishes to humiliate the wise, it sur-
       prises them in those unimportant occasions when we
       act without our customary precaution or defense. The
       cleverest person in the world cannot prevent insigni-
       ficant blunders from sometimes bringing major mis-
       fortunes in their wake. Our reputations and fortunes

can be lost through a bit of heedlessness, just as
we may break a leg while walking about a room.

253. Neither the gifts nor blows of fortune can equal those
of nature, which surpasses it both in harshness and
in kindness.

256. People of rank do not discuss such insignificant matters as common people; yet common people are not engrossed in such frivolous things as people of rank.

270. Until we have hit upon the secret of how to perfect
men's minds, every step we take toward the truth
shall not prevent people from reasoning badly. And
the more we make them advance beyond common opinion,
the more shall we place them in danger of error.

281. It is most unfortunate that men cannot ordinarily possess a certain talent without somehow wanting to dis-
parage others. If they are refined, they discredit
strength; if they are geometers or physicists, they
write against poetry and eloquent discourse. People
of the fashionable world, who seem unaware that those
excelling in a particular field tend to criticize
others of talent, are greatly swayed by such judgments.
When metaphysics and algebra are fashionable, philosophers and mathematicians are the ones who determine
the reputation of poets and musicians, and vice-versa.
In such a way do the ruling minds subject others to
their courts of justice and, most frequently, to their
own errors.

283. Philosophers have too lightly adopted out of envy the
maxim which states, "People should not be praised until they die." I maintain, on the contrary, that
people should receive praise at whatever point during
their lives that they have deserved it; that when
jealousy and slander combine to attack their virtues
and talents in order to dishonor them, we must dare
to stand up for them. It is unjust criticism that we
should always fear to risk, and not true praise.

287. We are most mistaken to think that any given fault
      must totally exclude every virtue, or to consider
      the marriage of good and evil as monstrous or enig-
      matic. It is our lack of discernment that prevents
      us from reconciling many things.

291. If there be a love of self that is naturally compas-
      sionate and helpful, and another which is egotistical,
      cruel, unjust, boundless, and unreasoning, why must
      we confuse the two?

298. We are capable of friendship, virtue, humaneness,
      compassion, and reason. O my friends, what, then,
      is virtue?

299. If the illustrious author of the Maximes had resembled
      his portrayal of mankind, would he deserve our praise
      and the idolotrous veneration of his proselytes?

313. We have neither the strength nor the opportunity to
      do all the good and the evil that we contemplate.

316. The indifference which we feel for truth in the moral
      sense stems from our determination to follow our pas-
      sions, no matter what the cost; and this is what pre-
      vents us from hesitating when we must act, despite the
      incertitude of our opinions. As they say, it is of
      little importance to know wherein lies the truth, if
      we know where pleasure can be found.

321. Who is astonished at the errors of the Ancients when
      he considers that even today, in this the most philo-
      sophical of centuries, many intelligent people would
      not dare be seated at a table with thirteen settings.

324. The brief duration of our life can neither dissuade
      us of its pleasures nor console us for its afflication

386. My passions and thoughts die only to be reborn, as I
      myself die in my bed each night only to revive again
      with new-found energy and freshness. This experience
      that I have of death reassures me against the decline
      and disintegration of my body. When I perceive that

the vital principle of my soul calls back into life its extinguished thoughts, I understand that He Who created my body is able, with still more reason, to give it back its being. I say with an astonished heart: What have you done with these fickle matters that weighed so heavily in your thoughts. Retrace your steps, oh fleeting objects. As I speak, my soul awakens; these mortal images hear me, and forms of things past obediently reappear before me. O eternal world soul, thus shall your salutary voice lay claim to its works, and the earth, seized with fear, shall return what it had pilfered.

398. When imbued with some great truth which we feel passionately, we should never fear to declare it, even though it may have been expressed by others. Every thought is a new one when its author expresses it in a manner that is his own.

420. The works of great men, so often studied and imitated, conserve, despite the passages of time, their own original character. This is because most other men do not possess the power to conceive or to express as perfectly even those concepts with which they are most familiar. It is precisely this lively, perfect manner of thinking and writing which distinguishes genius in all categories and which assures that the most simple and common ideas, once touched upon by these great minds, can never age.

477. Understanding which comes from the heart is alone true and solid.

499. We would be less eager to seek the esteem of others if we were more certain that we deserved it.

505. It is my belief that there are scarcely any authors who have been content with their century.

538. During old age we no longer make friends. All those whom we lose can therefore never be replaced.

546. The soul's most perfect quality is to have a capacity for pleasure.

562. The worst evil that fortune can bring to a man is to
cause him to be born with modest talents and great
ambition.

579. Courageous souls cannot be disgraced by poverty, nor
can base souls be exalted by wealth. We can gain re-
nown in obscurity or suffer disgrace in an exalted
post. Fortune, which we commonly hold to be supreme,
can do almost nothing without the aid of [our] nature.

602. One cannot have a great mind and very little wit.

624. The cold and dreary days of autumn symbolize the
approach of old age. There is nothing in nature which
is not an image of human life, because human life itself is an image of everything; and the entire universe
is governed by the same laws.

664. It is sometimes a wasted effort to write on exalted
topics and universal truths. How many volumes have
been dedicated to the immortality of the soul, the
composition of bodies and spirits, movement, space,
etc.! These lofty topics attract our imagination and
gain universal respect for the author by dealing with
matters that go beyond the reach of the mind. But
very few of these treatises are really useful. It is
better to become interested in real, instructive, and
profitable topics than in these sublime speculations
from which nothing can be concluded that is reasonable
nor definite. Men need to know many less important
matters and should be instructed in them before all
else.

681. Women ordinarily have more vanity than character, and
more character than virtue.

682. We have to be very foolish to like society when we
are fond neither of women nor gambling.

695. We should put little men in minor occupations in which
they may labor with natural disposition and egotism.
Far from disdaining their lowly functions, they deem
them an honor. There are people who like to distribute
hay, imprison a soldier whose tie is not properly in

place, or use the cane at drill. They are haughty, arrogant, self-sufficient, and very happy with their subaltern roles. A man of superior talents would feel humiliated at what gives them happiness and would probably not discharge his duties.

749. Childhood's first gasp of breath is for liberty.

757. The first days of springtime have fewer charms than the burgeoning virtues of a young man.

799. Maxims are the sallies of philosophers.

758. The first light of dawn is not so sweet as the first vision of glory.

769. We usually set out to make our fortune using talents which we do not possess.

803. Nature bestows different talents on men. Some are born to invent and others to embellish. But the gilder attracts more attention than the architect.

824. The hatred of the weak is not so dangerous as their friendship.

934. Newton, Pascal, Bossuet, Racine, and Fénelon, in short, the most enlightened men of the world, in the most philosophical of the centuries, and at the height of their genius and the prime of life, believed in Jesus Christ. While dying le Grand Condé repeated these noble words: "Yes, we shall see God as He is,-- sicuti est, facie ad faciem."

Chapter 7

VOLTAIRE (1694-1778)

It is rare indeed for an author to have the distinction of
having his name associated with a historical period. We
find it quite acceptable to read about the Age of Augustus,
or the Age of Elizabeth I or of Louis XIV; all were exceptional political and social leaders. But the Age of Voltaire gets its name from a writer--not the best France has
produced--a writer whose name was not Voltaire to begin
with. The destiny of this pseudonym is not the only touch
of irony in Voltaire's existence. In fact, irony seems to
have pursued Voltaire all his life and he was quick to
realize how this attitude could be used to further his
career and to win the individual battles in his life-long
war on ignorance, intolerance, persecution, and injustice.

He was born so frail that it was thought he would not survive to be baptized in church. Yet he lived, with many
frailties, for eighty-four years. He was anti-aristocratic,
but many of his friends were from the aristocracy, and he
created an aristocratic air to his name--"Arouet de Voltaire"
--in order to take advantage of any influence which "de"
might have in society. He made his reputation early as a
playwright--he is often considered the Racine of the Eighteenth Century--but he is known principally for two other
works today: Candide and the Philosophical Dictionary. In
his own day his literary production rivaled his industrial

achievements, he was among the wealthiest entrepreneurs in Europe, one of Europe's wealthiest private individuals. He wrote ceaselessly of "goût" (good taste) and freedom but he was not a stranger to unbecoming behavior and his prejudices could well have interfered with the freedom of those he attacked. In most ways he was a revolutionary spirit: his social ideas were not emotional and personal as were those of Rousseau; Voltaire is more superficial, more inclined to the tastes of everyday people, less intellectual. And these attitudes would probably not have led him to support the excesses of the Revolution and the rise of the rabble to positions of social and political importance--out of their destined class, which, he thought, should serve a supportive role in society.

Voltaire was born into the comfortable bourgeoisie and aimed at a successful rise into French and European society and at a great increase in his initial modest wealth. He succeeded in the latter attempt more brilliantly than in the former. His disappointment came as he realized that no matter how well received he was by anyone of noble--or royal--distinction, he would always be received as a guest, never as an equal. His revenge on this situation takes the form of the wittiest, most satirical literature that France has produced.

François-Marie Arouet was born in 1694 during the depressing later years of the repentent Louis XIV. His father, a comfortable Parisian notary, wanted him to be a lawyer in order that the young man would never be poor or wanting. But the young man's perenially poor health does not seem to have encouraged the regular life of a lawyer and the sharpness of his innate intelligence made him realize at an early age that there was glory for him in France's preferred literary genre, the theater. In 1720 he produced his first tragedy, Oedipus, which was a success. His career as the 18th century Racine was launched and it lasted until his death, in 1778, a month after the success of his last tragedy, Irène. It was around the time of this first success that he began signing his name Arouet de Voltaire, after a village (Airvault) near his family property. The adopted name remained even as Arouet gradually faded.

His social involvement also began as the newly acclaimed
playwright was introduced to aristocrats whose recognition
he sought at the same time that he loathed what they represented. He also attended their salons. A critical piece
written against the Regency earned him a brief (11 months)
stay in the Bastille (1726) and exile in England for three
years. This adventure, along with a public beating by ruf-
fians hired by the Chevalier de Rohan to teach the upstart
not to criticize the aristocracy, must be counted among the
important lessons of Voltaire's social education.

In England, he met Locke and Bolingbroke among others. He
discovered the various religious sects flourishing there,
the rules of society and government and, of course, the
works of Shakespeare, hitherto unknown to the supposedly
cosmopolitan Frenchmen of his time. He wrote about all of
these subjects, on his return to France (1729), in the
English Letters.

Never abandoning the theater, he also wrote novels and poems.
At the same time he embarked on his industrial enterprises
which included the manufacture of silks, laces, watches,
along with beekeeping; his interests were indeed varied.
When a twelve year alliance with Mme. du Châtelet ended
with her death (1749), he accepted a long refused invitation
to live at the court of Prussia with Frederick II. This
promising relationship faded when the two titans of enlightenment found it unbearable to live under the same roof.
Voltaire returned to France disillusioned with the great of
this world to begin the long last phase of his life.

This phase includes, in addition to the continuing volumin-
ous correspondence and the theater: his most famous novela,
Candide (1759); endless attacks on the Church as the Infamous One which has caused so much death and destruction in
the world; his contributions to Diderot's Encyclopedia; his
own Philosophical Dictionary (1764); his famous Affairs in
defense of poor creatures caught up in society's merciless,
vengeful attacks on those suspected of offending the established religion (like the Calas family and the Chevalier de la
Barre); the purchase of two properties, one on each side
of the border of Switzerland, so that he could move com-
fortably and safely from one to the other as the political
climate changed in response to his many critical writings.

(The <u>Dictionary</u> was burned to signify official displeasure with <u>its</u> contents.)

When Voltaire returned to Paris (1778) for the performance of <u>Irène</u> at the Comédie Française it was after a half century of voluntary--but wise--exile. He was then a venerable old man whose ideas had won over many and silenced many others. He was vindicated in his struggle when his bust was crowned during a ceremony in his honor at the <u>Comédie</u>. Death was the only thing left for him. After eighty-four years of fragile health, he succumbed to living, in Paris, of course, where he still epitomizes the gallic good taste and sense of irony which are the hallmarks of French literature.

Although he contributed a few important articles to the <u>Encyclopedia</u> which Diderot directed for some twenty-one years, Voltaire was not satisfied with the restricted reading public to which these large, expensive, scholarly volumes would appeal. He decided to write a small, easily read and understood, dictionary which could be carried around and consulted by many more than the readers of the <u>Encyclopedia</u>. The "dictionnaire portatif", called the <u>Dictionnaire philosophique</u>, contains the essence of Voltaire's thoughts. It reveals the same caustic attitude to all the grievances which the author held in his lifetime though it lacks some of the brilliant satire found in his other masterpiece, <u>Candide</u>. But this is a serious piece; it is not an entertainment. The sickly old man seems to fear that time is running out on him and that he must simply, but directly, present his public with a list of the most important facts to be known, good and bad, before he dies.

It is, however, impossible to imagine Voltaire without a slight grin on his face, even when he attacks the most atrocious acts committed by one human being on another. He knew that the large public which he sought would be attracted by humor more than by dry sermons. And so, with an air of amusement before human stupidity he set off to attack, or justify, alphabetically from <u>abbé</u> to <u>virtue</u>, intolerance, greed, hate, tolerance, peace, etc., etc.

Organized religion is one of his special aversions. He was anti-Christian, anti-Jew, anti-Bible, anti-Church, anti-Clergy. While some articles remain exemplary for their sense of fairness and justice, others surely contributed to the revolutionary rejection of the Church and to the anti-semitism of the following centuries. In searching for individual freedom from governmental and religious interference in our lives, he seems to have needed a "whipping boy" at whom to point his accusing finger: Jews, Christian, peasants, even Jean-Jacques Rousseau.

While reading Voltaire, we must seek out not only the object of his prejudice (that is usually a most easy task) but also the purpose of his criticism and decide whether his conclusions justify his purpose. Otherwise we may be unnecessarily involved in his prejudices. We must always verify whether the reason for the attack still exists.

With his interest in civilized good taste, Voltaire's biggest contribution to civilization could well be his teaching of discernment. (We can profit by his example when we consider his own ideas.) Because still today, his work continues to warn against those institutions and attitudes which threaten to undo personal freedom in the name of the general good.

FRIENDSHIP (AMITIÉ)

This is the marriage of souls; it is a tacit contract between two impressionable and virtuous persons. I say impressionable, for a monk or a hermit may not be wicked at all and yet live without knowing friendship. I say virtuous, for the wicked have only accomplices, the voluptuous have companions in debauchery, the interested have associates, politicians assemble factions, the mass of idle men have connections, princes have courtiers; only virtuous men have friends. Cethegus was the accomplice of Catiline, and Maecenas the courtier of Octavius; but Cicero was the friend of Atticus.

What does this contract between two tender and honest minds produce? Its obligations are stronger or weaker according to their degree of sensitivity and the number of services rendered, etc.

The enthusiasm of friendship was stronger among the Greeks and Arabs than among us. The tales about friendship these nations have invented are admirable; we have none like them we are a little cold in everything.

Friendship was a matter of religion and legislation among the Greeks. The Thebans had a regiment of lovers: a fine regiment! Some have considered it a regiment of Sodomites; they are wrong; that is to mistake the accidental for the essence. Among the Greeks, friendship was prescribed by law and religion. Unfortunately, pederasty was tolerated by the mores; we should not attribute shameful abuses to the law.

GOOD, SUPREME GOOD (BIEN, SOUVERAIN BIEN)

Antiquity debated a good deal about the supreme good. It would have been just as well to ask, What is the supreme blue, or the supreme stew, the supreme walk, the supreme reading, etc. ?.

Everyone finds his good where he can, and has as much of it as he can, in his own fashion.

> *Quid dem? quid non dem? renuis tu, quod*
> *iubet alter*
>
> *(What should I give, what not give? You*
> *refuse what another commands.*
>
> Horace, *Epistles, II,ii,63)*
>
> *Castor gaudet equis; ovo prognatus eodem*
> *Pugnis*
>
> *(Castor delights in horses; he, born from*
> *the same egg,*
> *Likes fighting*
>
> Horace, *Satires, II,i,25-26)*

The greatest good is something that pleases you so much that you are completely unable to feel anything else, just as the greatest evil is something that deprives us of all feeling. These are the two extremes of human nature; and these two moments are short.

Neither extreme delight nor extreme torture can last a lifetime: the supreme good and the supreme evil are chimeras.

We have the beautiful fable of Crantor: Wealth, Pleasure, Health, Virtue, compete at the Olympic games; each claims the apple. Wealth says: "I am the supreme good, for with me all goods are purchased." Pleasure says: "The apple is mine for men desire wealth only to have me." Health asserts that without it there can be no pleasure, and wealth is useless. Finally, Virtue announces that it is superior to all three because with gold, pleasures, and health, a man may

136

make himself quite miserable if he behaves badly. Virtue
wins the apple.

The fable is quite clever, but it doesn't resolve the absurd question of supreme good. Virtue is not a good, it
is a duty; it is of a different nature, of a superior order.
It has nothing to do with painful or pleasant sensations.
The virtuous man with the stone and the gout, without help,
without friends, destitute of necessities, persecuted,
chained by a voluptuous tyrant who enjoys good health, is
miserable; and his insolent persecutor, caressing a new
mistress on his bed of purple, is happy. Say that the
persecuted sage is preferable to his insolent persecutor;
say that you like the one and detest the other; but confess
that the sage in chains is beside himself with rage. If the
sage will not admit this, he deceives you, he is a
charlatan.

DAVID

When a young peasant finds a kingdom while he is looking for asses, that is not a common occurrence; when another peasant cures his king of an attack of madness by playing the harp, that case is still quite rare; but when that little harp player becomes a king himself because he meets a village priest in some out of the way place who empties a bottle of olive oil on his head, the thing is even more marvelous.

When were these marvelous deeds written down and by whom? I have no idea; but I'm quite sure that it was neither by a Polybius nor a Tacitus. I greatly admire the worthy Jew, whoever he was, who wrote the true history of the mighty kingdom of the Hebrews for instruction of the universe, under the dictation and inspiration of the God of all the worlds; but I am displeased to see my friend David start by assembling a band of four hundred thieves, and come to an understanding, at the head of this troop of honest men, with Abimelech, the high priest, who arms him with the sword of Goliath and gives him consecrated loaves (1 Kings, chapter 21, verse 13).

I am a bit shocked that David, the anointed of the Lord, the man after God's own heart, should rebel against Saul, another anointed of the Lord, should depart with four hundred thieves to lay the country under contribution, rob good old Nabal, and immediately after Nabal is dead, marry his widow without delay (chapter 25, verses 10,11).

I have some reservations about his behavior toward the great king Achish, ruler of five or six villages in the canton of Gath, if I'm not mistaken. David, then at the head of six hundred brigands, made the rounds of the allies of Achish, his benefactor; he pillaged everywhere, he killed everybody, old men, women, babies at the breast. And why did he cut the throats of babies at the breast? "For fear," writes the divine Jewish author, "that these children might carry the news to king Achish" (chapter 27, verses 8,9,11).

The brigands got angry with him and wanted to stone him. What does this Jewish Mandarin do? He consults the Lord, who replies that he must attack the Amalekites, where these

138

brigands shall collect good booty and enrich themselves
(chapter 30).

Meanwhile, Saul, the anointed of the Lord, loses a battle
against the Philistines and is killed. A Jew brings the
news to David. David, who apparently had nothing on him
to give the courier for the *buona nuncia*, has him killed
by way of reward (II Kings, chapter 1, verse 10).

Ishbosheth succeeds his father Saul; David is strong enough
to make war on him: finally Ishbosheth is assassinated.

David seizes the whole kingdom; he surprises the little
town of Rabbah, and he puts all the inhabitants to death,
by means of quite extraordinary tortures; they are sawed in
two, they are torn to pieces with iron harrows, they are
burned in brick kilns; quite a noble and generous manner
of making war (II Kings, chapter 12).

After these fine expeditions, there was a famine of three
years in the land. I can well believe it, for given the
way in which good David made war, the soil must have been
poorly cultivated indeed.

The Lord is consulted and asked why there should be a famine. The reason was self-evident: surely when you have
peasants cooked in brick kilns or sawed in two, in a country
which barely produces any wheat, very few men remain to cultivate the earth; but the Lord replied that it was because
Saul had formerly killed Gibeonites.

What does good David do then? He calls together Gibeonites;
he tells them that Saul had done great evil in making war
on them; that unlike him, Saul was not after God's own
heart, that it was right to punish his race; and he gave
them seven of Saul's grandsons to hang-and they were hanged,
because there had been a famine (II Kings, chapter 21).

It is a pleasure to see how that imbecile, dom Calmet jus-
tifies and condones all these actions which would make us
shudder with horror if they were not incredible.

I won't mention here the abominable assassination of Uriah,

and the adultery of Bathsheba: it is familiar enough, and
the ways of God are so different from the ways of men that
he permitted Jesus Christ to be descended from this infamous Bathsheba, the whole race being purified by this holy
mystery.

I won't ask how Jurieu[*] had the insolence to persecute
the virtuous Bayle[**] for not approving all the actions of
good King David: but I do ask how they tolerated a man
like Jurieu molesting a man like Bayle.

---

[*]Pierre Jurieu (1637-1713), Traditionalist Protestant
theologian often involved in polemics with other
theologians.
[**]Pierre Bayle (1647-1706), Protestant theologian, author
of Dictionnaire historique et critique.

CIVIL AND ECCLESIASTICAL LAWS
(LOIS CIVILES ET ECCLÉSIASTIQUES)

Among the papers of a lawyer these notes were found; perhaps they deserve some scrutiny.

Let no ecclesiastical law ever have authority unless it has
the express sanction of the government. This is how Athens
and Rome always avoided religious disputes. These disputes
are the lot of nations which are, or have become, barbaric.

Let the magistrate alone have authority to permit or pro-
hibit work on feast days, because it does not become priests
to forbid men to cultivate their fields.

Let everything concerning marriages depend solely on the
magistrate, and let priests restrict themselves to the
august function of blessing them.

Let lending at interest be purely the business of the civil
law, because it alone presides over commerce.

Let all ecclesiastics be subjected to the government in all
cases, because they are subjects of the state.

Let us never suffer the ridiculous shame of paying a foreign
priest the first year's revenue from land which citizens
have given to a priest who is their fellow-citizen.

Let no priest ever have the authority of depriving a citizen
of the slightest right, on the pretext that the citizen is
a sinner, because the sinner priest should pray for other
sinners, and not judge them.

Let the magistrates, the farmers, and the priests pay the
expenses of the state equally, because all equally belong
to the state.

Let there be only one weight, one measure, one common law.

Let the sufferings of criminals be useful. A hanged man is
good for nothing, while a man condemned to public works
still serves his country and is a living lesson.

Let all the law be clear, uniform, and precise: to interpret it is almost always to corrupt it.

Let nothing be ignominious except vice.

Let taxes never be anything but proportional.

MORALITY (MORALE)

I have just read these words in a declamation of fourteen volumes, entitled *Histore du Bas-Empire:*

> "The Christians had morality; but the pagans had none."

Ah! monsieur Le Beau, author of these fourteen volumes, where did you get this nonsense? Eh! What about the morality of Socrates, of Zaleucus, of Charondas, of Cicero, of Epictetus, of Marcus Aurelius?

There is only one morality, monsieur Le Beau, as there is only one geometry. But, you will tell me, most men don't know geometry. Yes; but when they apply themselves to it a little, everybody is in agreement. Farmers, laborers, artisans, have not taken a course in morality; they have read neither the *Finibus* of Cicero nor the *Ethics* of Aristotle; but as soon as they reflect, they are the disciples of Cicero without knowing it: the Indian dyer, the Tartar shepherd, and the English sailor know right from wrong. Confucius did not invent a system of morality as men build systems in physics. He found it in the hearts of men.

This morality was in the heart of the praetor Festus when the Jews urged him to put Paul to death for bringing foreigners to their temple. "Know," he told them, "that the Romans never condemn anyone without hearing him." While the Jews lacked morality, or disregarded it, the Romans knew morality and glorified it.

There is no morality in superstition, it is not in ceremonies, it has nothing in common with dogmas. We cannot repeat too often that all dogmas are different, and that morality is the same among all men who make use of their reason. Hence, morality comes from God, like light. Our superstitions are nothing but darkness. Reader, reflect: work out this truth; draw your conclusions.

PRIDE (ORGUEIL)

In one of his letters, Cicero says to this friend with complete frankness: "If you have someone to whom you want me to turn over Gaul, send him to me." In another letter, he complains that he is tired of letters from some princes or other, who thank him for elevating their provinces into kingdoms, and he adds that he doesn't even know where these kingdoms are located.

It may be that Cicero who moreover often saw the sovereign Roman people applaud and obey him, and who was thanked by kings he didn't know, had some feelings of pride and vanity.

Although this feeling is not at all appropriate to an animal as pitiful as man, we might nevertheless forgive it in Cicero, a Caesar, a Scipio; but that in the heart of one of our semi-barbarian provinces a man who has bought a small office, and has mediocre verses printed, takes it into his head to be proud-that could keep us laughing for a long time.

PHILOSOPHER (PHILOSOPHE)

Philosopher, *lover of wisdom;* that is, *of truth.* All philosophers have had this double character; there is not a philosopher in antiquity who failed to set an example of virtue and to give lessons in moral truth to mankind. They could be wrong about natural science; but that is of so little importance to the conduct of life that philosophers did not need it. It required centuries to learn a part of the laws of nature. A day suffices for a sage to learn the duties of man.

The philosopher is not an enthusiast, he does not set himself up as a prophet, and he does not claim to be inspired by the gods; therefore I would not count among the philosophers the ancient Zoroaster, or Hermes, or the ancient Orpheus, or any of the legislators of whom the nations of Chaldea, Persia, Syria, Egypt, and Greece boasted. Those who called themselves the children of the gods were the fathers of imposture; and if they employed lies to teach truths, they were unworthy of teaching them. They were not philosophers: at best they were very prudent liars.

DEIST (THÉISTE)

The deist is a man firmly convinced of the existence of a
supreme Being, as good as it is powerful, which has created
all the extended, vegetating, feeling, and reflecting
beings; which perpetuates their species, which punishes
crimes without cruelty, and rewards virtuous actions with
kindness.

The deist does not know how God punishes, how he protects,
how he forgives; for he is not rash enough to flatter himself that he knows how God acts; but he knows that God does
act and that He is just. The difficulties in the notion
of Providence do not disturb his faith, because they are
only great difficulties and not refutations; he submits to
this Providence, although he only perceives some of its
effects and externals; and, judging things he does not see
by the things he does see, he thinks that this Providence
reaches into every place and time.

United in this principle with the rest of the universe, he
does not embrace any of the sects, which all contradict
one another. His religion is the oldest and the most
widespread; for the simple worship of God preceded all the
systems of the world. He speaks a language that all nations
understand, while they do not understand each other. He
has brothers from Peking to Cayenne and counts all sages
among his brothers. He believes that religion consists
neither in the opinions of an unintelligible metaphysics
nor in vain display, but in worship and in justice. To do
good-that is his adoration; to submit to God-that is his
doctrine. The Moslem exclaims to him: "Take care if you
don't make the pilgrimage to Mecca!" "Woe to you," a
Franciscan tells him, "if you don't make a voyage to Our
Lady of Loretto!" He laughs at Loretto and Mecca; but he
helps the needy and he defends the oppressed.

VIRTUE (VERTU)

What is virtue? Doing good to your neighbor. Can I call
virtue anything else but what does me good? I am in need,
you are liberal; I am in danger, you help me; I am deceived,
you tell me the truth; I am neglected, you console me; I am
ignorant, you instruct me: without a doubt I shall call you
virtuous. But then what becomes of the cardinal and theological virtues? Some will be left in the schools.

What does it matter to me that you are temperate? You are
observing a rule of health; it will make you feel better,
and I congratulate you on it. You have faith and hope, I
congratulate you even more on that: they will procure you
eternal life. Your theological virtues are celestial gifts;
your cardinal virtues are fine qualities which help to guide
your course; but they are not virtues in relation to your
neighbor. The prudent man looks out for himself, the virtuous one looks out for mankind. St. Paul was right to tell
you that charity outweighs faith and hope.

What, you admit as virtues only those useful to your neighbor?
Very well, but how can I admit any others? We live in society; therefore nothing is truly good for us that is not
good for society. A hermit is sober and pious; he dresses
in a hair shirt: all right, he is a saint; but I shall call
him virtuous only when he performs some act of virtue from
which other men benefit. As long as he is solitary, he
neither does good nor evil; he is nothing to us. If St.
Bruno brought peace to families, if he aided the needy, he
was virtuous; if he fasted, prayed in solitude, he was a
saint. Virtue among men is an exchange of kindness; the one
who takes no part in this exchange should not be counted. If
this saint were in the world, he would probably do good
there; but as long as he is not, the world will have good
reason not to call him virtuous: he is good for himself, but
not to us.

But, you say, if a hermit is a drunken glutton, given over to
secret debauchery with himself, he is O.K.: therefore if he
has the opposite qualities, he is virtuous. I cannot agree
with that: he is an extremely villainous man if he has the
faults you mention; but he is not vicious, evil, punishable

147

in relation to society, which is not harmed by his infamous actions. We may assume that if he returns to society he will do harm there, that he will be extremely vicious; indeed, it is far more probable that he will be an evil man than it is certain that the other hermit, temperate and chaste, will be a good man; for in society one's faults increase and good qualities dwindle.

There is a much stronger objection: Nero, Pope Alexander VI, and other monsters of this species were lavish with kindness; I boldly answer that on that day they were virtuous.

Some theologians say that the divine emperor Marcus Aurelius was not virtuous; that he was an obstinate Stoic who, not content with commanding men, also wanted them to esteem him; that he claimed for himself the good he did for mankind; that all his life he was just, hardworking, and generous out of vanity, and that his virtues deceived men; to which I exclaim: "My God, give us such rascals often!"

Chapter 8

JEAN-JACQUES ROUSSEAU (1712-1778)

If Voltaire can be considered the mind of the Eighteenth Century, surely Rousseau should be considered its heart; or at least the heart of the second half of the century, since that is when he made the deep impression that was to change the lives of most Europeans from then onward.

Despite the popularity of sentimental works like Prévost's Manon Lescaut or the genre of the "tearful theater" (le théâtre larmoyant), the Eighteenth Century is all too frequently considered a cold, impersonal time during which Reason prevailed in all human relationships. This was the Reason which Descartes outlined in his Discourse on the Method (1635); according to it he applied a scientific, mathematical approach in order to understand all the hitherto inexplicables, including the soul and even God. There was no divine revelation for Descartes; while he did not dare to deny God, he did show man dependent upon his own intellect for finding the values by which to live. Everything in this life could be explained by formula.

But the real importance of this philosophy--its stress on personal responsibility--was pretty much overlooked by this century for which "Cartesianism" provided a means of reasoning in order to free man in society from the restraints and abuses of the past. The "Age of Voltaire" was essentially witty, profane and anti-traditionalist. The general confidence that knowledge of everything was within the grasp of everyone is symbolized by the fascination which the Encyclopedia held for the reading public-each volume being eagerly awaited. Voltaire's writings characterize the period-intellectually brilliant, emotionally superficial.

Rousseau and his works represent the sentimental reaction to the Voltairian atmosphere of the latter half of the Eighteenth Century. His thinking as well as his conduct remind us of Pascal's aphorism: the heart has its reasons which Reason cannot know. Rousseau lived by that principle and his writings carry forward the ideas which he was not able to realize in his own existence.

All of Rousseau's existence illustrates the reason of the heart. He is guided by sentiment in everything that he does, including his writings on morality and politics. He is frequently confusing, contradictory, critical, and even revolutionary. His end is to turn himself and all mankind away from the innate corruption of society and to the natural way of life. Perhaps not a totally natural way of life, but at least a simpler existence than the one available in eighteenth century France (and England, and Switzerland, and Italy). The "noble savages" of America were considered admirable under the influence of this writer, who only knew of them what he had heard and read but who was impressed by the role which natural selection played in their lives.

Rousseau's ideas have influenced all the areas of modern life. He has written on government, society, science, art, self-expression, marriage, love, public morals, music, and education, condemning past practices and suggesting what can be done to improve upon them to make the future better. Republicans, socialists, communists, all owe a debt to Rousseau for having laid the foundations of social reform.

While today Voltaire remains the spirit of the Eighteenth Century, Rousseau is the man of the future. His works are not dated. Rousseau could have appeared at almost any time in history; earlier, more of his books-or perhaps he himself-would have been burned; later, he would simply have seemed a radical theorist treated with great suspicion by many. Rousseau is not a rebel like Voltaire who thrived on iconoclasm and needed enemies to inspire his satire. He is an independent thinker whose enthusiasm comes from within; he bases his thoughts on human nature which knows no historical or social limitations. He wrote, in the preface to his Confessions, that Nature broke the mold in which it had cast him; it would appear that Nature also made the mold in which to create him because he is unique, an original. No one before him reveals a similar combination of virtues, vices, talents, and peculiarities; and no one after him really wants to have that combination in their lives, even though, over the years, everyone seems to have wanted to pick and choose that part of his legacy which they thought most suited their own search for happiness and fulfillment.

Jean-Jacques Rousseau was born in Geneva (1712), the Calvinist capital. His mother died in childbirth and he felt responsible for her loss for the rest of his life. He left Geneva in 1728 by chance; having returned to the city gates after they were closed, he decided to continue on to France. There he met Mme. de Warens, who directed him to the local priest who was to guide him in his conversion to Catholicism. He then travelled to various cities in France and the nearby countries. He later became one of Mme. de Warens' lovers and always referred to her as "Maman" in his writings. He had other loves and one lifelong partner, Thérèse Levasseur, whom, he says, he married in what was a kind of declaration before God rather than a traditional ceremony. From Thérèse he had five children, all of whom he placed in an orphanage, explaining that his erratic lifestyle was not the proper family setting for a child.

For many years Rousseau worked as a music copyist and in 1741 he devised a new form of musical notation which is still included in studies of musical theory. In 1752, he wrote an opéra-comique Le Devin du village (The Village Soothsayer) which is still occasionally performed. His Discourse on the Arts and Sciences (1750) received the prize offered by the Académie de Dijon and Rousseau was launched on his literary career. This lasted until his death (1778) and includes the Letter to d'Alembert on the Theater (1758), Discourse on the Origins of Inequality Among Men (1755), Julie, or the New Heloise (1761), The

Social Contract (1762), Emile (1762), Dictionary of Music (1767).

Rousseau was acquainted with many members of high society, mainly through his association with the Encyclopedia and his different patrons. With the public burning of Emile, 1762, in both Paris and Geneva, he entered into the long period of persecution, partly real, partly imagined, that was to last until he died. His visit to England (1766-1767) at the invitation of David Hume ended in a break-up, as did almost all of his social relationships. Thus began his gradual withdrawal from social activity and the ways of society. In his return to the more "natural" way of life, Rousseau mentions that he threw away his watch, as a symbolic action against the demands of social life. (Antithetically, we may recall that, among his variety of manufactures, Voltaire produced fine watches!)

By 1772 Rousseau was well on his way toward creating his defense before posterity; he had completed the Confessions and was beginning the Reveries of a Solitary Stroller and Rousseau, Judge of Jean-Jacques (The Dialogues), all of which were published after his death (1782, 1789). Posterity has not really been much kinder than his contemporaries. His work is widely accepted--irresistibly--but it is also criticized continuously and frequently condemned. In the final analysis he is as controversial and provocative as he wanted to be: "I should prefer to be forgotten by the whole human race than to be looked upon as an ordinary man."

Rousseau reconverted to his original religion in 1754, but from his later writings, especially Emile, we realize that neither Calvinism nor Catholicism satisfied the kind of faith which he felt. Like so many of his contemporaries, Rousseau is a deist, but unlike them, he has an inner light, "Une lumière intérieure," which affords the possibility to converse with God through the sensitivity of his heart. Most deists have a cold freedom in their reasoning, but Rousseau is dependent upon this communication with God in his reasoning.

The Profession of Faith of a Savoyard Vicar, a brief chapter in the fourth book of Emile, presents the essence of Rous-

seau's religious attitude. The vicar, like Emile and his
tutor, is yet another attitude taken by Rousseau. He presents a religion of submission to natural possibility, to
the recognition that God is good though hardly comprehen-
sible to His creatures. We must accept that He is good and
that we are part of a divine plan, also incomprehensible to
us. Beyond this acceptance, there is a basic moral code:
consideration of others.

All of Rousseau's works are based essentially on this religion of personal faith, and in reading them it is possible
to see his evolution toward the articulation found in Emile
and his total acceptance of this faith in the later works.
It is understandable, then, that the Church would find this
"religion" heretical and that it would condemn Rousseau's
works, especially Emile, for fear of their corrupting the
social order. It is surprising, but eventually understandable as well, that the opposition, the Calvinists, should
condemn his work for essentially the same reason: the direct
revelation of God's will to man's heart with no need for
intermediary control is not acceptable to organized
religion.

The passages presented here are from the Profession of
Faith. In them we find the principal moral precepts that
formed Rousseau's faith. One senses throughout the liberation which is inherent in the vicar's belief; he is free
of the traditionalist subjugation imposed on the individual
by the "old faiths." In listening to him, we may even feel
that he rejects old prejudices along with faiths and wishes
to replace them with a new order based on love, kindness,
simplicity, purity of purpose, natural equality, and personal inspiration.

EMILE: The Profession of Faith of the Savoyard Vicar

How swiftly life passes here below! The first quarter of it is gone before we know how to use it; the last quarter finds us incapable of enjoying life. At first we do not know how to live; and when we know how to live it is too late. In the interval between these two useless extremes we waste three-fourths of our time sleeping, working, sorrowing, enduring restraint and every kind of suffering. Life is short, not so much because of the short time it lasts, but because we are allowed scarcely any time to enjoy it. In vain is there a long interval between the hour of death and that of birth; life is still too short, if this interval is not well spent.

Hence it follows that we are drawn to our fellow-creatures less by our feeling for their joys than for their sorrows; for in them we discern more plainly a nature like our own, and a pledge of their affection for us.

By nature men are neither kings, nobles, courtiers, nor millionaires. All men are born poor and naked, all are liable to the sorrows of life, its disappointments, its ills, its needs, its suffering of every kind; and all are condemned in the end to die. This is what it really means to be a man, this is what no mortal can escape. Begin with the study of the essentials of humanity, that which really constitutes mankind.

First Maxim. - It is not in human nature to put ourselves in the place of those who are happier than we, but only in the place of those who can claim our pity.

Second Maxim. - We never pity another's woes unless we know we may suffer in like manner ourselves.

"Non ignara mali, miseris succurrere disco."
                                        VIRGIL. *

---

* "I myself knowing misfortune, I know how to help the unfortunate." These are the words with which Dido receives Aeneas.

154

Why have kings no pity on their people? Because they never expect to be ordinary men. Why are the rich so hard on the poor? Because they have no fear of becoming poor. Why do the nobles look down upon the people? Because a nobleman will never be of the lower classes. Why are the Turks generally kinder and more hospitable than we are? Because, under their wholly arbitrary system of government, the rank and wealth of individuals are always uncertain and precarious, so that they do not regard proverty and degradation as conditions with which they have no concern; tomorrow, any one may himself be in the same position as those on whom he bestows alms today.

So do not train your pupil to look down from the height of his glory upon the sufferings of the unfortunate, the labors of the wretched, and do not hope to teach him to pity them while he considers them far removed from himself. Make him thoroughly aware of the fact that the fate of these unhappy persons may one day be his own, that his feet are standing on the edge of the abyss, into which he may be thrown at any moment by a thousand unexpected inevitable misfortunes. Teach him to have no trust in birth, health, or riches; show him all the changes of fortune; find him examples-there are only too many-in which men of higher rank than himself have sunk below the condition of these wretched people. Whether this happened by their own fault or another's is for the present no concern of ours; does he indeed know the meaning of the word fault? Never interfere with the order in which he acquires knowledge, and teach him only through the means within his reach; it takes no great learning to perceive that all the prudence of mankind cannot make certain whether he will be alive or dead in an hour's time, whether before nightfall he will not be grinding his teeth in the pangs of nephritis, whether a month hence he will be rich or poor, whether in a year's time he may not be rowing an Algerian galley under the lash of the slave-driver. Above all do not teach him this, like his catechism, in cold blood; let him see and feel the calamities which overtake men; surprise and startle his imagination with the perils which lurk continually about a man's path; let him see the pitfalls all about him, and when he hears you speak of them, let him cling more closely to you for fear lest he should fall. "You will make him timid and cowardly," do you say? We shall see; let us make him kindly to begin with, that is what matters most.

Third Maxim. - The pity we feel for others is proportionate, not to the amount of the evil, but to the feelings we attribute to the sufferers.

We only pity the wretched insofar as we think they feel the need of pity. The physical effect of our suffering is less than one would suppose; it is memory that prolongs the pain, imagination which projects it into the future, and makes us really to be pitied. This is, I think, one of the reasons why we are more indifferent to the sufferings of animals than of men, although sympathy ought to make us identify ourselves equally with either. ... I usually judge the value any one puts on the welfare of his fellow creatures by what he seems to think of them. We naturally think lightly of the happiness of those we despise. Do not be surprised that politicians speak so scornfully of the people, and philosophers profess to think mankind so wicked.

The people are mankind; those who do not belong to the people are so few in number that they are not worth counting. Man is the same in every station of life; if that is so, those ranks to which most men belong deserve most honor. All distinctions of rank fade before the eyes of a thinking person; he sees the same passions, the same feelings in the noble and the ragamuffin; there is merely a slight difference in speech, and more or less artificiality of tone; and if there is indeed any essential difference between them, the disadvantage is all on the side of those who are more sophisticated. The people reveal themselves as they are, and they are not attractive; but the fashionable world is compelled to adopt a disguise; we should be horrified if we saw it as it really is.

Society must be studied in the individual and the individual in society; those who wish to treat politics and morals apart from one another will never understand either. By confining ourselves at first to primitive relations, we see how men should be influenced by them and what passions should arise from them; we see that it is in proportion to the development of these passions that a man's relations

with others expand or contract. It is not so much strength
of arm as moderation of spirit which makes men free and independent. The man whose wants are few is dependent on just
a few people, but those who constantly confound our vain
desires with our bodily needs, those who have made these
needs the basis of human society, are continually mistaking
effects for causes, and they have only confused themselves
by their own reasoning.

Unfortunately, this study has its dangers, its drawbacks of
several kinds. It is difficult to adopt a point of view
which enables one to judge one's fellow creatures fairly.
It is one of the chief defects of history to paint men's
evil deeds rather than their good ones; it is revolutions
and catastrophes that make history interesting; so long as
a nation grows and prospers quietly in the tranquillity of
a peaceful government, history says nothing; it only begins
to speak of nations when, no longer able to be self-suffic-
ing, they interfere with their neighbors' business or allow
their neighbors to interfere with theirs; history only makes
them famous when they are on the downward path; all our his-
tories begin where they ought to end. We have very accurate accounts of declining nations. What we lack is the history of those nations which are multiplying; they are so
happy and so good that history has nothing to tell us of
them. And we see indeed in our own times that the most successful governments are least discussed. We only hear what
is bad; the good is scarcely mentioned. Only the wicked
become famous, the good are forgotten or laughed to scorn,
and thus history, like philosophy, is forever slandering
mankind.

"We must believe in God if we would be saved." This doctrine wrongly understood is the root of bloody intolerance
and the cause of all the futile teaching which strikes a
deadly blow at human reason by training it to cheat itself
with mere words. No doubt there is not a moment to be lost
if we would deserve eternal salvation; but if the repeti-
tion of certain words suffices to obtain it, I do not see
why we should not people heaven with starlings and magpies
as well as with children.

...Peace of mind consists in despising everything that
might disturb that peace; the man who clings most closely

to life is the man who can least enjoy it; and the man who most eagerly desires happiness is always most miserable."

I suppose this prodigious diversity of opinion is caused, in the first place, by the weakness of the human intellect; and, in the second, by pride. We have no means of measuring this vast machine; we are unable to calculate its workings; we know neither its guiding principles nor its final purpose; we do not know ourselves, we know neither our nature nor the spirit that moves us; we scarcely know whether man is one or many; we are surrounded by impenetrable mysteries. These mysteries are beyond the region of sense, we think we can penetrate them by the light of reason, but we fall back on our imagination. Through this imagined world each forges a way for himself which he holds to be right; none can tell whether his path will lead him to the goal. Yet we long to know and understand it all. The one thing we do not know is the limit of the knowable. We prefer to trust to chance and to believe what is not true, rather than to admit that not one of us can see what really is. A fragment of some vast whole whose bounds are beyond our gaze, a fragment abandoned by its Creator to our foolish quarrels, we are vain enough to want to determine the nature of that whole and our own relations with regard to it.

... Where is the philosopher who would not deceive the whole world for his own glory? If he can rise above the crowd, if he can excel his rivals, what more does he want? Among believers he is an atheist; among atheists he would be a believer.

In a word, motion which is not caused by another motion cannot take place, except by a spontaneous, voluntary action; inanimate bodies have no action but motion, and there is no real action without will.This is my first principle. I believe, therefore, that there is a will which sets the universe in motion and gives life to nature. This is my first dogma, or the first article of my creed.

Remember that I am not preaching my own opinion but explaining it. Whether matter is eternal or created, whether its origin is passive or not, it is still certain that the whole is one, and that it proclaims a single intelligence; for I see nothing that is not part of the same ordered system, nothing which does not cooperate to the same end, namely, the conservation of everything within the established order. This being who wills and can perform his will, this being who is active through his own power, this being, whoever he may be, who moves the universe and orders all things, is the one I call God. To this name I add the ideas of intelligence, power, will, which I have brought together, and that of kindness which is their necessary consequence; but for all this I know no more of the being to which I attribute them. He hides Himself both from my senses and my understanding; the more I think of Him, the more perplexed I am; I know full well that He exists, and that He exists of Himself alone; I know that my existence depends on His, and that everything I know depends upon Him also. I see God everywhere in His works; I feel Him within myself; I behold Him all around me; but if I try to ponder Him Himself, if I try to find out where He is, what He is, what is His substance, He escapes me and my troubled spirit finds nothing.

O Mankind! seek no further for the author of evil; you are he. There is no evil but the evil you do or the evil you suffer, and both come from yourself. Evil in general can only spring from disorder, and in the order of the world I find a never failing system. Evil in particular cases exists only in the mind of those who experience it; and this feeling is not the gift of nature, but the work of man himself. Pain has little power over those who, having thought little, look neither forward nor back. Take away our fatal progress, take away our faults and our vices, take away man's handiwork, and all is well.

...Take from our hearts this love of what is noble and you rob us of the joy of life. The mean spirited man in whom these delightful feelings have been stifled among vile passions, who by thinking of no one but himself comes at last to love no one but himself, this man feels no raptures, his cold heart no longer beats with joy, and his eyes no longer fill with the sweet tears of sympathy, he delights in nothing; the wretch has neither life nor feeling, he is already dead.

...We do not hate the wicked merely because of the harm they do to us but because they are wicked. Not only do we wish to be happy ourselves, we wish others to be happy too, and if this happiness does not interfere with our own happiness, it increases it. In conclusion, whether we wish to or not, we pity the unfortunate; when we see their suffering we suffer too. Even the most depraved are not wholly without this instinct, and it often leads them to self-contradiction. The highwayman who robs the traveler, clothes the nakedness of the poor; the fiercest murderer assists a fainting man.

Let us obey the call of nature; we shall see that her yoke is easy and that when we heed her voice we find a joy in the answer of a good conscience. The wicked fears and flees from her; he delights to escape from himself; his anxious eyes look around him for some object of diversion; without bitter satire and rude mockery he would always be sorrowful; the scornful laugh is his one pleasure. Not so the just man, who finds his peace within himself; there is joy not malice in his laughter, a joy which springs from his own heart; he is as cheerful alone as in company, his satisfaction does not depend on those who approach him; it includes them.

There is, therefore, at the bottom of our hearts an innate principle of justice and virtue, by which, in spite of our maxims, we judge our own actions or those of others to be good or evil; and it is this principle that I call conscience.

...Far from throwing light upon the ideas of the Supreme Being, special doctrines seem to me to confuse these ideas; far from ennobling them, they degrade them; to the inconceivable mysteries which surround the Almighty, they add absurd contradictions, they make man proud, intolerant, and cruel; instead of bringing peace upon earth, they bring fire and sword. I wonder what is the use of it all, and I find no answer. I see nothing but the crimes of men and the misery of mankind.

In all three revelations the sacred books are written in languages unknown to the people who believe in them. The Jews no longer understand Hebrew, the Christians understand neither Hebrew nor Greek; the Turks and Persians do not understand Arabic, and the Arabs of our time do not speak the language of Mohammed. Is not this a very foolish way of teaching, to teach people in an unknown tongue? These books are translated, you say. What an answer! How am I to know that the translations are correct, or how am I to make sure that such a thing as a correct translation is possible? If God has gone so far as to speak to men, why should he require an interpreter?

Chapter 9

CHAMFORT (1740-1794)

Although the exact date of his birth remains uncertain,
Sébastien-Roch-Nicolas Chamfort was born around 1740. He
was the illegitimate son of a certain Pierre Nicolas,
Canon of the Cathedral of Clermont; his mother, Thérèse
Croiset, was wed to the grocer Francois Nicolas, a relative
of the canon.

Chamfort lived very briefly with his "foster parents", until
about the age of five, when he received a scholarship to
the Collège des Grassins in Paris thanks to the intervention
of Canon Nicolas. (The Collège had been founded two centuries before specifically to educate poor children, often
from irregular family backgrounds such as that of Chamfort.)
He left the Auvergne for good at this time, but he seems
always to have retained the love for nature and spirit of
self-reliance indigenous to the inhabitants of this rustic
part of France.

Extremely sensitive, intelligent, and independent, he soon
distinguished himself in the classics and in philosophy.
Because he was an excellent student, he was encouraged by
his teachers to enter the clergy and even wore the garb of
an "abbé". Yet he obstinately refused to take the final
step of Holy Orders. "I am, he said, too fond of repose,
philosophy, women, honor, and true glory and not fond

162

enough of bickering, hypocrisy, honors, and money to be a priest."

Upon leaving the college when he was about twenty, he was introduced by rich and titled friends, whom he seemed to attract easily, into the fashionable society of the <u>ancien</u> <u>régime</u>. Through his wit, extremely handsome appearance, and thirst for acceptance by the nobility, he was able to survive in this world through appointments provided by influential patrons: the Prince de Condé, the Comte de Vaudreuil, Mirabeau, Mlle. de Lespinasse, and Helvétius, among the most prominent. A notorious Don Juan in his younger years, he also gained the support and affection of a number of influential women.

Chamfort never forgot, however, that he was not born into this class which granted him limited rights of entry into its circles. To alleviate his nagging poverty and fulfill his aspiration of glory, he avidly pursued a career as a man of letters and eventually assumed the name by which we recognize him, Chamfort, taking it from the small town so named in the Auvergne.

Despite the grinding poverty he constantly had to endure amid conditions which early ravaged his health and altered his handsome features, he soon achieved considerable success in the theater. In fact, several of his plays--<u>La</u> <u>Jeune</u> <u>Indienne</u> (1760), <u>Le</u> <u>Marchand</u> <u>de</u> <u>Smyrne</u> (1770), and <u>Mustapha</u> <u>et</u> <u>Zéangir</u> (1776), for example--were presented many times by the Comédie Française and in his day surpassed in popularity Beaumarchais' <u>Mariage</u> <u>de</u> <u>Figaro</u>. Chamfort also became a well-known journalist-critic winning several prizes from French academies for dissertations written on literary and social topics much in the nature of Rousseau's <u>Discourses</u>. His tireless efforts were rewarded by his election to the French Academy in 1781 at the reatively young age of forty.

But there is a depth to Chamfort that the preceding facts do not fully explain. He was not merely a "joli petit abbé" who, through his clever pen and urbane literary output, rose from obscure origins to gain fame and access to fashionable society; Chamfort became, in fact, progres-

sively more disenchanted and disgusted with the shallow, egotistical, and cruel nature of aristocratic society and, for
all practical purposes, went into seclusion about 1778 when
only thirty-eight. Although he still frequented the smart
gatherings at the home of Helvétius (where he met such intellectual luminaries as Fontenelle, Hume, Diderot, and Ben-
jamin Franklin), he ceased to write plays and articles for
publication.

During this period he began to compose the maxims, thoughts,
and anecdotes which he grouped under the ironic title,
Products of the Perfected Civilization. None of his piquant
and mordant remarks illustrating the gangrenous society to
which he had originally been attracted appeared during his
lifetime. They were, however, collected and published posthumously by his friend and biographer, Ginguené, who like
Pascal's early editors, presented these fragments as the
outline of a major work, which they were never meant to be.

The last decade of Chamfort's life is both tragic and inspiring. An ardent republican and friend of Robespierre,
he was an original member of the Jacobin faction and wrote
stirring journalistic contributions in a series entitled,
"Scenes from the Revolution", which described such events
as the storming of the Bastille.

Offered the post of director of the Bibliothèque Nationale
after the fall of the monarchy in August, 1792, he soon
experienced grave problems with the course of the Revolution.
He never abandoned his adherence to the early principles of
the Jacobin movement and refused to support the apparatus
and extreme measures of the Terror. Refusing to write
against the freedom of the press at the urging of Marat, he
was soon threatened with imprisonment and possible execution.
In May, 1793, he was arrested and forced to stay for a
brief time at the prison of Les Madelonettes, one of the
most unsanitary in Paris. His health broke completely, and
upon his release he vowed that we would rather die than be
imprisoned again.

Under constant police surveillance by an agent actually
billeted with him, he still refused to compromise the frankness of his remarks in daily conversation. And remembering

his oath when the agent decided to arrest him again, he severely wounded himself with a pistol. Still alive, he then attempted to slash his throat and wrists. He miraculously recovered and was permitted to spend the little remaining time in solitude. Three months later he collapsed and died, April 13, 1794.

Though traditionally branded a misanthrope, Chamfort, through his passionate quest for justice and political reform, does not merit this reputation. It is true that he lashed out in fury at the kind of society he had to endure during his lifetime; yet this indicates all the more his ardent hope that a more just society along the lines of the British and American systems would someday emerge in France. An enemy of past tyranny and a victim of the revolution which eventually made light of the very ideals which it had originally fostered, Chamfort witnessed the disintegration of the evil society he had castigated. He was also forced to view the desecration of the revolutionary aims in which he had placed such fervent hope. But in spite of so much adversity, never did he hesitate to contest any ideology that would enslave the human spirit; and to the very end he chose to live freely or not at all.

3. What a curious work it would be which would indicate
    all the corrupting ideas of the human mind, of society,
    of morality, which are presented as facts or theories
    in the most famous writings and the most honored auth-
    ors; the ideas which propagate religious superstitions,
    bad political maxims, despotism, vanity of rank, pop-
    ular prejudices of all kind. We would see that almost
    all books corrupt, and that the best do almost as much
    harm as good.

7. Man, in the present state of society, seems to me to
    be more corrupted by his reason than by his passions.
    His passions (here I mean those that belong to prim-
    itive man) have preserved, in the social order, the
    tiny bit of nature that one still can find there.

9. In general, if society were not an artificial fabri-
    cation, every expression that conveys a true and sim-
    ple feeling would not have the remarkable effect that
    it does. It would please without astonishing, but
    it astonishes and it pleases at present. Our surprise
    is the satire of society, and our pleasure is a hom-
    age to nature.

12. One must admit that it is impossible to live in the
    world without acting a part from time to time. The
    upright man is different from the swindler in this
    respect: he plays a role only when he has to, and to
    avoid danger, whereas the other welcomes the occasions.

14. There are two categories of moralists and statesmen:
    those who have seen human nature only from its spite-
    ful and ridiculous side, and they are more numerous:
    Lucian, Montaigne, La Bruyère, La Rochefoucauld,
    Swift, Manderville, Helvétius, etc.; those who have
    seen it only from its noble side and with its perfec-
    tions: Shaftesbury and certain others. The first are
    not familiar with the court, of which they have only
    seen the latrines. The second are enthusiasts who
    turn their eyes far from what offends them but never-
    theless exists. Est in medio verum. (Truth is in
    the mean.)

17. Philosophy, like medicine, can provide many drugs, very few good remedies, and almost no specifics.

20. He who does not know how to deal in pleasantries and lacks a ready wit very often finds himself faced with the necessity of being either false or pedantic--a troublesome alternative, which any reasonable man escapes, ordinarily, by means of grace and humor.

21. Often an opinion, a custom, becomes absurd to a person in his early youth, and as one advances in life, one learns the reason for it; and it becomes less so. Should we then conclude that certain customs have become less ridiculous? At times one is led to believe that they were established by people who had read the book of life in its entirety, and are judged by others who, despite their intelligence, have read only a few pages.

24. I have read in some traveler, I forget which, that certain savages of Africa believe in the immortality of the soul. Without pretending to explain what becomes of it, they believe that after death it wanders through the underbrush which surrounds their settlements, and for several successive mornings they go to look for it. When they do not find it, they abandon the search and think no more about it. This is more or less what philosophers have done, at their very best.

29. Thought brings consolation to everything and remedies for everything. If it sometimes hurts you, ask it to cure the injury it has done you, and it will do so.

39. In order to pardon reason for the evil it has done to most men, we must consider what man would be without reason. It was a necessary evil.

46. Our reason sometimes renders us as unhappy as our passions, and when this happens to a man, one can say of him that he is like a patient poisoned by his doctor.

49.   You ask how one makes one's fortune. Observe what happens in the pit of a theater, on the day there is a crowd: Some stay in the back, some who are up front move to the rear, and some in the back are pressed forward. So apt is this image that the word that expressed it has passed into the language of the people which refers to making one's fortune as "getting ahead": "My son or my nephew will get ahead." Refined people say "advance oneself," or "succeed"-- gentler terms, which avoid the added idea of force, of violence, or grossness, but keep the main idea.

50.   The physical world seems to be the work of a powerful and good being who has been forced to abandon to a wicked being the execution of a part of his plan. But the world seems to be that product of a devil who has become mad.

55.   Not to be manipulated by others, to be one's own man, to have one's own principles and feelings, this is the rarest thing that I have seen.

67.   Physical disasters and the calamities of human nature have rendered society necessary. Society has added to the evils of nature. The difficulties of society have led to the necessity of government, and government has added to the miseries of society. This is the history of the human race.

71.   Nature, in giving birth at the same time to reason and the passions, seems to have wished, with her second gift, to help man to forget the harm she did him with the first, and in allowing him to live only a few years after the loss of his passions, she seems to have taken pity on him, quickly relieving him of a life reduced to reason as its sole resource.

80.   The most completely wasted of all days is that one in which we did not laugh even once.

83.   The philosopher who wishes to snuff out passions is like the alchemist who would like to work without fire.

168

87. In learning the evils of nature, one acquires a contempt for death. In learning the ills of society, one
acquires a contempt for life.

102. Fame often subjects an honest man to the same trials
as wealth. It would appear that both, before granting
his request, force him to do or to suffer things unworthy of his character. And so the man undaunted in
virtue rejects the one as the other and wraps himself
in obscurity or misfortune, and sometimes in both.

104. The opinion of the public is an authority that an
honest man should never entirely accept and which he
should never discount.

110. There are few vices which will prevent a man from having many friends as will the possession of too many
unusual talents or virtues.

113. Living is an illness which sleep alleviates every
sixteen hours. It is merely a palliative. Death is
the remedy.

115. There are two things which we must get used to or we
shall find life unbearable: the ravages of time and
the wrongs of men.

124. It must be admitted that, in order to be happy in
this world there have to be sides of one's soul
which are totally paralyzed.

126. In regard to things, everything is a mixture, and with
regard to men, everything is patchwork. In the moral
and physical spheres, everything is mixed. Nothing
is whole, nothing is pure.

129. A man without principles is also usually a man without character, for had he been born with character,
he would have felt the need to create principles for
himself.

135. Celebrity: the advantage of being known by those who
do not know you.

140. It is not true (as Rousseau said, referring to Plutarch) that the more one thinks, the less one feels; but it is true that the more one judges, the less one loves. Few men offer exceptions to this rule.

150. Maxims are to life's conduct what practice is to the arts.

153. Pleasure may be based on illusion, but happiness reposes on virtue.

158. Love: pleasant folly; Ambition: serious imbecility.

159. Prejudice, vanity, scheming, these are what govern the world. He who recognizes as his rule for conduct only reason, truth, and sensibility has almost nothing in common with society. It is within himself that he must seek out and find virtually all his happiness.

192. Fashionable people are no sooner herded together than they imagine they are in society.

194. Society is made up of two great classes: those who have more dinners than appetite, and those who have more appetite than dinners.

198. When at times one sees the skilful thieveries of inferiors and the robberies of men in office, one is tempted to regard society as a wood full of thieves, among whom the most dangerous are the constables or men of the law put in charge there to arrest the others.

201. The world is so contemptible that the few honest people who can be found in it esteem those who despise it and become influenced by this very contempt.

202. Court friendship, faithfulness of foxes and society of wolves.

252. Courtiers are poor men who have become wealthy by begging.

271.   One is happier in solitude than in the world. Is that
       not because in solitude one thinks about things, where-
       as in the world one is forced to think of men?

273.   A man who persists in keeping both his reason and his
       integrity, or at least his fastidiousness, intact
       despite the pressure of all the absurd and dishonest
       conventions of society, who never bends when it is in
       his interest to do so, invariably ends up without any-
       one taking his part, and with no friend except an
       abstract being that is called virtue, who will let
       you die of hunger.

277.   A man of intelligence is lost if his intelligence is
       not accompanied by energy of character. When one has
       Diogenes' lantern, one also needs his stick.

285.   He who has no character is not a man but a thing.

302.   Calumny is like an annoying wasp against which one
       must make no move unless one is sure to kill it, or
       else it will return to the attack more furiously than
       ever.

308.   The new friends that we make after a certain age, by
       whom we hope to replace those we have lost, are to
       our old friends as glass eyes, false teeth, and wooden
       legs are to real eyes, natural teeth, and legs of
       flesh and blood.

319.   Enjoy and give pleasure, without harming yourself or
       anyone else, this is, I believe, the sum total of
       morality.

335.   My entire life is a tissue of apparent contrasts with
       my principles. I do not esteem princes, yet I am
       attached to a princess and a prince. I am well known
       for my republican maxims, and several of my friends
       wear decorations presented by the monarchy. I love
       voluntary poverty, yet I live with rich people. I
       flee from honors, yet some have come to me. Letters
       are almost my only consolation, yet I do not frequent
       wits or attend the Academy. Add to this that I believe

171

illusions are necessary for men, yet I live without illusions; or that I believe the passions to be more useful than reason, yet I no longer know what they are, etc.

354. Society which greatly diminishes men, reduces women to almost nothing.

359. Love as it exists in society is merely the sharing of fantasies and the contact of two skins.

370. Perhaps one has had to feel love to know what friendship really is.

373. A woman of wit one day told me what in one sentence could very well be the secret of her sex, which is that every woman, when she takes a lover, is more interested in how other women regard this man than in how she regards him herself.

389. Marriage and celibacy both have disadvantages; one should prefer the one whose disadvantages are not irremediable.

391. Love is more pleasing than marriage for the reason that novels are more amusing than history.

408. In love everything is true, everything is false; it is the only subject about which one cannot say anything absurd.

446. Men of letters who retire from the world are often strenuously taken to task. They are asked to take an interest in the society from which they derive almost no advantages; they are impelled to be eternally present at the drawing of a lottery in which they have no ticket.

474. The natural character of the Frenchman combines the characteristics of the monkey and the bird dog. Comical and frisking about, like the monkey, and as completely malicious at heart as him; like the hunting dog he is of ignoble birth; he fawns, licks his master who beats him, lets himself be put on a chain and

172

then leaps for joy when he is unleashed to go hunting.

493.   France: a country in which it is often useful to show one's vices and always dangerous to display one's virtues.

515.   North America is the part of the universe in which the rights of man are best known. The Americans are the worthy descendants of these famous republicans who exiled themselves to flee tyranny. It is there that men have been formed and reared who were worthy to fight and vanquish conquering the English themselves, at a time when the latter had recovered their liberty and had successfully created the finest government that has ever existed. The American Revolution will be useful to England herself by forcing her to examine again her constitution and get rid of its abuses. What will happen? The English, driven from the continent of North America, will pounce upon the islands and the French and Spanish possessions and will give these their English form of government which is founded on the natural love that men have for liberty, and which increases it. In the Spanish and French islands, and especially in the Hispanic continent, when it has become Anglicized, new constitutions will be formed, based on liberty. Thus to the English will belong the unique glory of having formed almost the only free people in the universe, the only ones, properly speaking, who will be worthy to be called men, they alone will have known and conserved the rights of men. But how many years will it take to bring about this revolution? The French and Spanish will have to be driven out from these vast territories which presently can only be populated by slaves, and Englishmen will have to be transplanted in them to bear the first seeds of liberty. These seeds will grow, and yielding new fruit, will bring about the revolution which will chase out the English themselves from both Americas and all the islands.

612.   It is a certain fact that Madame, the King's little
       daughter, playing with one of her maids, looked at her
       hand and, after counting the fingers said in surprise,
       "What? You have five fingers, too, just like me?"
       And she counted again, just to be sure.

Chapter 10

JOUBERT (1754-1824)

Joseph Joubert lived during one of the most turbulent periods in modern history. During his lifetime, France had
seen four kings and several revolutionary governments, including the Reign of Terror, the Directorate, and the First
Empire. In literature, Joubert witnessed the waning of the
classical period with Diderot, Voltaire, Rousseau, and
Chénier; the growth of the romantic spirit with Madame de
Staël and Chateaubriand; and finally the first successes of
the romantic sensibility: Lamartine's Méditations poétiques
(1820) and Stendhal's Racine et Shakespeare. But little of
these significant literary and political events appears in
the Thoughts (Pensées) of Joubert.

He was repulsed by the realities of the Revolution: "The
Revolution chased my spirit from the real world by making
it too horrible for me." In politics he managed to remain
above it all.

He was friends with Buffon, the naturalist, Diderot, the
encyclopedist, Chateaubriand, Madame de Beaumont, and Fontanes, the classicist. By the efforts of the last, Joubert
became Inspector General of the University, but, in true
classical fashion, none of these facts appears in his non-
epistolary writings: Joubert was, in the final analysis, a
man of his times. He did not look back with deep nostal-

igia, nor did he look very far into the future. In fact, past, present, and future mean little in the content of his aphoristic writings because he looks at man in his eternal incarnation, and finds continuity where others find episodic change.

Like Montaigne and La Fontaine, Joubert can be classified as a provincial, and like them his provincialism is modified by the sophisticating influence of Paris. He is practical without the earthiness of La Fontaine or the extreme reserve of Montaigne. Unlike Pascal, he is able to assume different viewpoints of life and still moralize upon all of them. His variety of subjects brings him closer to Montaigne without being aloof from his subjects.

Outside of his philosophical writings, Joubert's conduct reveals him rather typical of his times with regard to his personal values. He started out life as a Catholic. He was twenty-four years old when he arrived in Paris and came to know Diderot. Around this time his religious attitudes seem indeed to have changed, if not to the atheistic pose of Diderot, at least to the deism which was a common characteristic of contemporaries who considered themselves "philosophes" in the eighteenth century sense. But by 1790 he had again accepted Catholicism as his faith, this time permanently and most profoundly.

In reading about Joubert's life we do not encounter the exciting controversies which entertain us while reading Voltaire or Rousseau, nor the byzantine intrigues which Stendhal thinks he sees everywhere, or the spiritual involvement of Pascal or Francis de Sales. He is much more like Montaigne: a man of pragmatic bourgeois values who attracts us by his calmly reasoned intellectual reactions to life: "Life is a job to do, in which we must eliminate tender affections as little as possible."

Joubert was born in 1754 into a comfortable middle-class family. In a letter to his friend, Madame de Beaumont, he tells her how his mother found him extreme in his sentiments, fearless in his hopes, negligent before dangers, too generous to the point that she wondered how successful he would be in life. He remained a sentimentalist throughout

176

his life and was always attached to his family as well.

His marriage was a marriage of reason to a woman whom he
respected greatly but for whom he never seems to have felt
those tender affections he considered so essential to life.
He had many "loving friendships" with the women who were
frequently attracted to him throughout his life. Whether
any of them were true mistresses still remains a question.
All we know is that Joubert found great satisfaction in the
friendship of women and that his wife accepted the situation
with no outward signs of displeasure.

Like so many of our writers, Joubert was destined to be a
lawyer but from the beginning his preference for letters was
evident. He studied with the Pères de la Doctrine and became a scholar and teacher, a humanist. Eventually, through
the auspices of his close friend Fontanes, he was appointed
Inspector General and Conseiller at the newly formed University (1809). Writing was obviously not a big career for
him. Though he did publish some of his scholarship, it remained for another of his friends, Chateaubriand the author
of The Genius of Christianity, made famous by René and
Atala, to publish his Thoughts shortly after his death, in
1824.

Joubert's life was not truly dull, but it was not one to
stir the soul of the reader; rather it was a life lived
fully, but from within. He was perhaps too friendly, too
compassionate, too considerate of others, this man whose
last written words are: "The true, the beautiful, the just,
the saintly."

It is difficult to classify Joubert. He is, of course, a
moralist. His formative years with the Doctrinaires must
have inspired his natural talent for sermonizing concisely:
"If there ever was someone tormented by the cursed ambition
to put an entire book into one page, an entire page into
one phrase, and that phrase into a word, it is I." But
then, what kind of moralist is he? In this anthology alone
we have already passed through the works of different types
of moralists: Pascal, the Jansenist; de Sales, the Catholic
humanist; Voltaire, the deist; Rousseau, the sentimentalist,
etc. In the end, Joubert may prove to be the liberal

Catholic, a man of his own times with no extreme or revolutionary ideas, a man who sought to define clearly and simply the matters which touch the lives of others like himself.

His Thoughts cover a wide variety of topics. Reading La Rochefoucauld and Voltaire, we soon realize that such authors have a point to make and all of their works make the point again and again. Not so with Joubert who always seems to remain receptive to the possibilities which any situation of life has to offer. He is an optimist in true Christian fashion. When he condemns, unlike La Rochefoucauld, he condemns with compassion; he is never vindictive. In his unswerving conviction that man is salvable, Joubert reminds us of Vauvenargues' faith in mankind's infinite, if occasionally unrealized, capacity for good and ability to live virtuously.

Beyond considering Joubert a moralist whose views reflect a middle-of-the-road moderation, we find it difficult to characterize his philosophy. In this, too, he reminds us of Montaigne who, in his Essays, sought to bring out the just reason of the everyday person, as opposed to La Rochefoucauld who is readily obvious as the bitter, disappointed courtesan. Joubert is best understood when he speaks for himself.

When my friends are one-eyed, I look at their profile.

I still prefer those who make vice likable to those who degrade virtue.

Will God put beautiful thoughts in the rank of beautiful actions? Will they be rewarded, who have looked for them, who are pleased by them and are attached to them? Will the philosopher and the politician be paid for their plans, as the wealthy man will be paid for his good works? And do useful works have merit, in the eyes of God, as good moral habits do? Perhaps yes; but the first prize is not as certain as the second and will not be the same; God has not put the hope and certainty of this in our souls; other motives determine our actions. Nevertheless, I can very well imagine Boussuet, Fénelon, Plato, bringing their works before God, even Pascal and La Bruyère, even Vauvenargues and La Fontaine because their works depict their souls and can be counted for them in heaven. But it seems to me that J.-J. Rousseau and Montesquieu would not dare to present theirs: they have only included their wit, their mood and their efforts. As for Voltaire, his also depict him and I think that they will be weighed in his case, but against him.

Superstition is the only religion of which base souls are capable.

Which is more deformed, a religion without virtue, or virtues without religion?

There are two kinds of atheisms: one which tends to do without the idea of God, and one which tends to do without His intervention in human affairs.

To arrive in the regions of light, it is necessary to pass through the clouds. Some stop there; others know how to pass beyond.

It is only by our faces that we reveal who we are, and
that barely. The body reveals the sex more than the per-
sona, the species more than the individual.

There are light minds who do not have light opinions;
their doctrines and their virtues make them grave, when
necessary. On the contrary, there are serious and somber
spirits who have very futile doctrines, and then all is
lost.

We are never mediocre when we have lots of common sense
and lots of good sentiments.

There are heads which have no windows and which the light
from on high cannot penetrate. Nothing comes to them
from heaven.

There are some minds similar to those convex or concave
mirrors which represent objects such as they receive them,
but which never receive them such as they are.

Those who always love do not have the leisure to complain
and to feel unhappy.

It is a cruel situation not to be able to resolve to hate
or scorn a man that one can neither love nor admire.

Do not admit the greedy either among your friends, or
among your followers, because they are incapable of wisdom and faithfulness.

The hate between the sexes hardly ever subsides.

The punishment of those who have loved women too much is
to love them forever.

Tenderness is the repose of passion.

Hidden perfumes and secret loves reveal themselves.

If apathy is, as some say, egoism in repose, activity,
some people boast of so much, could well be egoism in
movement. It would, therefore, be egoism in action to
complain of egoism in repose.

People are only good out of pity. Therefore, it is necessary that there be some pity in all our sentiments, even when we are indignant and when we hate the wicked. But is it necessary that there also be some in our love for God? Yes, pity for ourselves, as there is always some in gratitude. Thus all our feelings are marked by some pity for ourselves or for others. The love that the angels bring to us is itself only continual pity, in the guise of compassion. Each of us is compassionate towards the evils that he fears.

Do not possess wit more refined than your taste, and judgment more severe than your conscience.

The heart should walk before the mind, and indulgence before truth.

Wishing to do without all men and not being obliged to anyone is the certain sign of a soul bereft of sensitivity.

Every man ought to be the author, if not of good works, at least of good deeds. It is not sufficient to have one's talent in manuscripts, and one's nobility on parchment.

God! How chastity produces some admirable loves! And of what rapture our intemperance deprives us!

The passions of the young are vices in old age.

The evening of life brings its own lamp.

It seems that, for certain accomplishments of the mind, the winter of the body is the autumn of the soul.

Good breeding smoothes the wrinkles.

It is not true that old age is necessarily devoid of grace. It can be so in looks, in language, in a smile. The harmony of action and the kind of tempered candor which produce gracefulness can occur at any age between our mind and our words, between our soul and our manner.

A little vanity and a little voluptuousness, that's what makes the life of most women and men.

Everyone is his own fate, and spins his own future.

Think of the past when you consult, of the present when you enjoy, but in everything you do, think of the future.

To love only beautiful women, and to tolerate bad books: signs of decadence.

We must die pleasant, if we can.

Few men are worthy to be head of the family, and few families are capable of having a head.

One should choose for a wife only the woman that one would choose for a friend, if she were a man.

Nothing is so honorable in a woman as her patience, and nothing does her so little honor as her husband's patience.

Contradiction only irritates us because it troubles the peaceful possession that we have of some opinion or of some pre-eminent quality. That is why it irritates the weak more than the strong, and the sickly more than the healthy.

One must always have a free and open place in his mind to provide a place for the opinions of his friends, and to lodge them there as they pass through. It becomes really unbearable to converse with men who have, in their heads, only compartments where everything is occupied, and where nothing from the outside can enter. Let us have hospitable hearts and minds.

Seriousness is only the outer shell of wisdom, but it is protection.

One can never regret the time necessary to do good.

Virtue without rewards does not complain, become indignant or excited; injustice does not produce in it any resentment, just a sweet melancholy.

Everything is learned, even virtue.

One should never draw attention to and make people remember bad maxims that are well expressed.

Do not exaggerate the evils of life, and do not fail to recognize its good, if you are trying to live happily.

Truth takes the character of the souls it enters. Rigorous and severe in arid souls, it is tempered and mellowed in loving souls.

Presumption causes as many errors as credulity; but it is better to be mistaken about others' errors than about one's own; from which I conclude that credulity is still preferable to presumption.

It is not about truth and deceit that we should be concerned above all else, but about evil and good; because it is less error that we should fear than evil itself.

How many people make themselves abstract in order to appear profound! Most abstract terms are shadows which hide voids.

Every philosophical system is an artifice, a fabrication which interests me little; I examine what natural riches it contains, and only watch for the treasure.

Politics is the art of knowing and leading the multitude or the plurality; its glory is to lead it, not where it wishes, but where it should go.

In governments which obey the superiority of numbers, it is a statistical or arithmetic dignity, a rough or quantitative preponderance, which judges human things.

Men are born unequal. The great benefit of society is to reduce that inequality as much as possible, while obtaining for all security, necessary goods, education, and assistance.

Liberty! Liberty! Justice in all things, and that will be enough liberty.

The French are born fickle, but they are born moderate. Their minds are sharp, pleasant and hardly imposing. Among them, even the wise, in their writings, seem to be young.

Outside of domestic affections, all lengthy sentiments are impossible for the French.

We live in a century where superfluous ideas proliferate, and where necessary ideas are lacking.

Making one's mood the standard for one's judgments, and one's fantasies the motive of one's actions, such is a dreadful habit of the times.

When custom and authority are destroyed, each one takes on habits and manners according to his inclinations; vulgar, if he is naturally vulgar. Deplorable epochs, these, when everyone weighs everything by his own values, and walks, as the Bible says, in the light of his own lamp!

To be capable of respect today is almost as rare as to be worthy of it.

In raising a child, think of his old age.

To teach is to learn twice.

We cannot find poetry anywhere when we do not carry it within.

There are simple words in the French language which almost no one knows how to use.

Men who only have ordinary thoughts and dull brains ought to use only the easiest words. Brilliant expressions are natural to those who have colorful memory, sensitive hearts, enlightened minds and keen eyes.

The art of articulating well what one thinks is different from the faculty of thinking: the latter may be very great in depth, height, extent, and the former may not exist. The talent to express well is not that of conceiving; the first makes great writers, and the second great minds.

Add that even those who have the two qualities in their power do not always have them in practice, and often experience that the one operates without the other. How many people have a pen and no ink! How many others have a pen and ink, but have no paper, that is to say, no subject on which their style can act.

Wisdom is the beginning of beauty.

Genius begins the beautiful works, but work alone completes them.

The bee and the wasp suck the same flowers; but both do not know how to find the same honey.

Let us recall the word quoted from St. Francis de Sales, about the Imitation: "I have sought repose everywhere, and I have only found it in a little corner, with a little book." Happy the writer who can create a beautiful little book.

Voltaire conserved for his entire life, in society and in business, a very strong impression of the cleverness of his first masters. Impetuous as a poet, and refined like a courtesan, he knew how to be insinuating and tricky like a Jesuit. No one has observed more carefully, but with more art and proportion, the maxim which he himself mocked so: to become all things to all people. He had the need to please, even more than to dominate, and found more pleasure in putting his seductive qualities into play than his strengths. Above all he gave great care to controlling men of letters, and only treated as enemies those minds which he could not win over.

An irreligious piety, a corrupting severity, a dogmatism which destroys all authority: that is the character of Rousseau's philosophy.

185

Chapter 11

STENDHAL (1783-1842)

Henri Beyle, who signed most of his works <u>Stendhal</u>, was in
his fifties when he wrote that, sitting on the steps of a
little church in Italy, he asked himself what he had been
and what he was. He would answer, in his autobiography,
that he was a man of great passion; not simply amorous passion but the attitude as it applied to his outlook on life,
to his search for happiness in all phases of life.

He suggested for his epitaph: <u>Wisse</u>, <u>Scrisse</u>, <u>Amo</u>, "He lived,
he wrote, he loved," which remains the best summation of
Stendhal's career even after a century and a half. And he
was also a traveler. As adjunct to the War Commisioner he
spent several years in Germany and Austria, took part in
Napoleon's Russian campaign, visited England, and spent
about twenty years in Italy. But travel was for him a form
of research; it provided the scenario for his life, his
writings, and his loves.

Life, literature, and love, these three elements cannot be
separated when we talk of Stendhal. He is not like so many
other writers who either are born esthetes watching life
from a privileged position or who, early in life, are ambitious participants (La Rochefoucauld, Pascal) and later on
withdraw from it all to write about their experiences.
Stendhal is more like Hemingway and Malraux for whom action
is its own poetry and literature merely expresses it in
186

another mode. Love is one of life's activities that is to be pursued and studied with passionate drive; it is not, for Stendhal, an emotion that one simply awaits and rhapsodizes about; love, too, is part of his ideal of action.

Man's spiritual nature is not of great importance to Stendhal. He is profoundly effected by those philosophers who see man in control of his own destiny: Helvétius, Hobbes, Destutt de Tracy. His preference for Pascal is not for the latter's spiritual, religious, fervor; it results from his ability to express so clearly the dilemma of man in this world: "I believe that he is the one, of all the writers, whom I resemble most in my soul." And when, in The Just Assassins (Les Justes) Camus paraphrases Christ by saying, "My kingdom is of this world," it is possible to see Stendhal as part of a continuing line of activist-writers who conceive of literature as part of the living process not just a written record of the past or a prediction of things to come.

Born in 1783, Stendhal was six when the Revolution began. He was seven when his mother died and nine when the king of the old French monarchy was beheaded. He was raised by his father, a legal advisor to Parliament, who spent some time hiding from the forces of the Revolution, an aunt whom he detested and a grandfather and great-aunt whom he adored. Amidst the turmoil of the times, the boy understood that his family--especially his father--struggled to maintain traditional bourgeois values: work, propriety, and their own morality. The society of the city of Grenoble was built around these values and the Beyle-Gagnon family was a prominent family there. Henri began by loathing his father and his father's values and eventually he came to despise the entire city along with its hypocritical priests who tried to give him the "proper" education. At sixteen he was sent to Paris to continue his studies, but shortly thereafter he joined the army and was soon a second lieutenant in Italy. By 1802 he was out of the army, living in Paris and beginning to dream of what he could do with the rest of his life. His Thoughts (Pensées: filosofia nova, 1801-1804) reveal these wishes and at the same time contain some of the moral observations that he had already made and that would remain part of his philosophy until his death.

187

Two of his wishes came to pass, though not exactly as he had conceived them. He wanted to write comedies like those of Molière; instead he created his own original style. He wanted to have a mistress in Italy, he did and, in fact, had more than one over the long periods of time spent in his adopted country.

And so, he began to write in 1801 while serving time in military positions and later in government positions. His writings include works on painting and music, literary criticism, travel, several novels (<u>The Red and the Black</u>, <u>The Charterhouse of Parma</u>), and autobiography (<u>The Life of Henry Brulard</u> and an unusual work with a classical title: <u>On Love</u>. His busy schedule accounts in part for the fact that some of these works were left incomplete at his death, but his passionate nature--passing from one intense interest to another--surely accounts for the incompletion also because each of his works is related to episodes in his life and the career and loves that formed them.

There were serious differences between Stendhal's vision of what society should be and what it actually was. One result was that his published works sold very poorly. Undaunted, Stendhal proclaimed that he wrote for "the happy few" who could understand him and that his works would be "discovered" in 1880 and that his talent would find recognition in 1935. Both predictions came true.

Though his writing career (1801-1842) coincided very closely with the appearance, establishment, and collapse of the romantic period in France, Stendhal shunned most of the elements which made up that school of thought. And because of his passionate nature, he also avoided the cool self-effacement of the classicists and their strict observations of rules. In the final analysis, he belongs to no philosophic tradition or contemporary school of thought. His very personal philosophy has been called <u>beylisme</u> and it is under that rubric that we observe a fascinating combination of passionate epicurianism (his famous "chasse au bonheur"), individualism (culminating in egotism), energy, a refinement in all dealings with others; he is anti-vulgar and anti-bourgeois. Stendhal himself associated his personal idealism with the customs and practices of the Italian Renaissance and the later French Renaissance.

188

Beylisme is a way of life, but it is also reflected in the author's approach to writing. The result is a simple, natural style reminiscent of the prose of Napoleon's Civil Code the style of which he studied carefully, a direct style which at first encounter may seem devoid of art altogether. But shortly one senses that this simplicity is in reality restrained flamboyance.

While his works are always about himself, he avoids the self-apologetic tones of the romantics and with the naturalness of his style he looks at himself as he would look at another person.

In the case of the maxims found in the Thoughts and On Love, his personal presentation does not lend itself to the epic universality achieved by earlier moralists, but Stendhal's universal appeal lies in his ability to show a person in the struggle to find values by which to live. Without being bitter or cynical, he notes the personal guidelines which one should follow. He analyzes society, life, and love. The stress is always on the last mentioned, love, just as in his epitaph, because for Stendhal all of happiness in life comes down eventually to love; not that banal interpretation of love which one falls "into" or "out of", to use the everyday jargon, but the emotion whose essence is conceived of in the intellectual observation and analysis made by the individual seeking to understand the machinations of the mind in the act of "creating" such an emotion, so that he might be able to evoke it on the level he wills at a chosen moment in order to assure the pleasure sought.

The maxims presented here are taken from the Thoughts (1801-1804) and On Love (1822). The ideas found in these works are essentially those found in all of Stendhal's works, including the last one, The Charterhouse of Parma (1839).

THOUGHTS (Filosofia Nova I)

The importance of the crime increases in proportion to the ties which the guilty party has broken.

If the allied forces had prevailed against France, that would have been the end of beauty in the world.

You return to the vulgar by your love of society and pleasure
It is necessary, however, to see them as often as possible
for the experience and to be disgusted by them.

The free citizen of a republic has greater thoughts than the
courtisan who only thinks of little things in a monarchy. It
is necessary, therefore, to become a citizen and, in the process, to flee those more powerful than oneself.

The hate that the vulgar person has for the man lacking in
social graces, does it not come in part from the fact that
it is proof that the latter is less bored than he?

The more the government is despotic, the less the people are
sensitive to the description of great passions.

In every sort of composition, the perfection of art is to
conceal art.

The passions are forces which can be mixed in an infinity
of ways in man.

No enjoyment without action.

As soon as we fear ridicule in friendship, it is no longer
friendship.

THOUGHTS (Filosofia Nova) II

The art of comedy does not consist, I think, in having a
protagonist perform extraordinary actions, but rather in
rendering very likeable, very hateful or very ridiculous,
the perpetrators of actions whom we see everyday in society.

Men will never have perfectly good or perfectly bad conduct
until they are guided by one single principle.

Indignation is the displeasure caused us by the idea of the
success of one whom we judge to be unworthy of it.

Pity is the fear of a future misfortune for ourselves,
caused by the feeling of the misfortune of another.

Our passions, and consequently our states of passion, are not voluntary. They are the cause and not the effect of the will.

Man lives according to what he thinks himself to be and not according to what he really is.

There is only one law concerning sentiment. That is to create the happiness of the object of one's love.

ON LOVE

The Birth of Love. This is what goes on in the mind:

1. Admiration.
2. One says to one's self: "How delightful to kiss her, to be kissed in return," etc.
3. Hope

One studies her perfections. It is at this moment that a woman should surrender herself, to get the greatest possible sensual pleasure...

4. Love is born...

We take a joy in attributing a thousand perfections to a woman of whose love we are sure; we analyze all our happiness with intense satisfaction. This reduces itself to giving ourselves an exaggerated idea of a magnificent possession which has just fallen to us from Heaven in some way we do not understand, and the continued possession of which is assured to us.

This is what you will find if you allow a lover to turn things over in his mind for twenty-four hours.

In the salt mines of Salzburg a bough stripped of its leaves by winter is thrown into the depths of the disused workings; two or three months later it is pulled out again, covered with brilliant crystals: even the tiniest twigs, no bigger than a tomtit's claw, are spangled with a vast number of shimmering, glittering diamonds, so that the original bough is no longer recognizable.

I call crystallization that process of the mind which discovers fresh perfection in its beloved at every turn of events...

6. Doubt is born...

7. Second crystallization.

Now begins the second crystallization, producing as its diamonds various confirmations of the following idea: "She loves me."...

Every great poet who possesses vivid imagination is shy, that is to say, he is afraid of men for the interruptions and worries they can bring to his delicious reveries. He is afraid that his <u>attention</u> will be distracted. Men with their coarse interests drag him from the gardens of Armida[*] and plunge him into a filthy quagmire, and they can never attract his attention to themselves except by irritating him. It is only by the habit of nurturing his mind with entrancing dreams, and by his horror of all vulgarity, that a great artist keeps in such close touch with love.

The greater artist a man is, the more he ought to want titles and decorations as a bulwark against the world.

As for me, I always come back to the physical laws. In men the nervous fluid is used up by the brain, in women by the heart; which is why they are more sensitive. Hard, necessary work in the profession we have followed all our lives consoles us, but only distractions can console women.

The most common mistake is to treat women as though they were a species of man, only more generous, more variable and above all with whom there is no possibility of rivalry. We are too easily apt to forget that there are two new and peculiar laws which tyrannize over these fickle creatures, conflicting with all the ordinary tendencies of human nature; I mean these:

Feminine pride and modesty, and the habits, often quite inexplicable, engendered by modesty.

---

[*] Armida seduced Rinaldo in her enchanted gardens, thus preventing him from joining the army of the Crusaders. (Tasso, <u>Jerusalem Liberated</u>)

The whole art of love reduces itself, it appears to me, to saying exactly what the degree of intoxication of the moment suggests, that is to say, in other words, to listening to the dictates of one's heart.

Everyone in France knows the anecdote of Mademoiselle de Sommery, who, surprised in the very act by her lover, denied the fact brazenly and, when he protested, exclaimed: Ah! how well I see you don't love me any more; you believe what you see sooner than what I tell you!"

Pique, being an infirmity of honour, is much more frequent under monarchies, and must make a much rarer appearance in countries where they have acquired the habit of judging actions by their degree of utility, as, for instance, in the United States of America.

Nothing is so odious to medocrity as intellectual superiority; in our present-day world this is the chief cause of hatred; and if we do not owe the most desperate feuds to this principle, it is solely because the people it estranges from one another are not compelled to live together.

Pedants have kept on telling us for two thousand years that women have more refinement in their ideas and men stronger powers of concentration. A certain city dweller in Paris who used to stroll occasionally in the gardens of Versailles similarly came to the conclusion from his own observation that trees came up already clipped.

So far as real morality is concerned, the more intelligence we possess, the more clearly do we see that justice is the only road to happiness. Genius is a power, but even more is it a torch with which we discover the great art of being happy.

MAXIMS from ON LOVE

One can acquire anything in solitude, except character.

The majority of men in this world, through vanity or diffidence or from fear of failure, only abandon themselves to their love for a woman after intimacy with her.

The more people one attracts, the less deeply one attracts them.

In Europe desire is sharpened by restraint; in America it is blunted by liberty.

The only unions that are always legitimate are those which are ordained by true passion.

To be happy with a loose moral code requires the simplicity of character found in Germany and in Italy, but never in France.

The dictionary of music has never been written; it has never even been begun; it is only by chance that one finds phrases which mean: I am angry or I love you, in varying degrees. The maestro only hits on these passages when they are dictated to him by the presence of passion or the memory of passion in his heart. Men who spend the ardent days of their youth in study instead of in feeling cannot, therefore, be artists: A very simple instance of cause and effect.

I call pleasure every sensation which the mind would rather experience than not.
I call pain every sensation which the mind would prefer not to experience.

Love is the only passion which pays itself in a coin which it mints itself.

I am inclined to think that the merits of any system of life should be judged by the character of the individual professing it: for instance, Richard Coeur de Lion was the perfection of heroism and of chivalrous valor on the throne, but he was an absurd king.

There is much less envy in America than in France, and much less intelligence.

Chapter 12

PAUL VALÉRY (1871-1945)

Among the great writers of twentieth century France, Paul
Valéry stands out as the greatest poet of the century. This
judgment was made early in the century, but as we near the
end of it, there is no suggestion that it will be revised.
Valéry continues to hold the title, just as Proust is considered the greatest novelist and Gide the most important
theorist and essayist. And as with these writers and so
many others, Valéry did not limit his writing to poetry; he
has produced essays, thoughts, and fiction, to mention those
works which are easily classified. But in his poetry he
reveals the essence of his attempts at clear thinking and
perfected technique.

Writing poetry was not an easy task for Valéry. Nor is
understanding his poetry easy for us. At first glance,
Valéry's poetry may suggest the subtly obscure images of the
symbolists: Valéry was greatly influenced by Mallarmé. But
on closer reading we find that he was not at all a symbol-
ist. He wrote with the intention of being absolutely clear
in his use of words, though he did try to create new images
by new combinations of words. For him the importance of art
lies not so much in producing a significant oeuvre but in
the act of composition itself. Technique is a key word in
understanding Valéry. He is a technician of language and
expression.

It is not surprising, then, that Valéry lacks--or shuns--the emotional involvement that we associate with the majority of poets. Nor are we surprised to learn that he rejects the heartfelt reasoning of Pascal. And needless to say, he is at the far end of the spectrum from the sentimental Musset. The art of writing for Valéry is really the craft of composing: "Nothing has influenced me more than the work of this Wagner, or at least certain characters of his work." And his subject is not the fruit of having lived and experienced life in social relationships; it is more the desire to express the result of his thought processes, to witness the inner life of the mind. Others count for very little in his literature. He remains preoccupied with his intellectual activity.

Valéry does not conceive of his intellect as simply superior to that of most other human beings--though he frequently refers to his awareness of his special situation--but he treats it as another artist would treat moral problems. It is something that he feels requires all his attention lest he fail to live up to its demands. With it he seeks to create literature of the utmost clarity and obvious meaning, a literature based on reason the way Descartes approached reason-- with the mind--not as Pascal did, with a reasoning heart.

The result of Valéry's search for absolute clarity of expression is a body of literature--the best of which is his intricate poetry revealing brilliantly his philosophy of life at the same time that it illustrates his deep concern with composition--that has led scholars and critics to consider him as the most important French poet of this century.

Biographical data on Valéry reveals that his was not the exciting, adventuresome life we frequently seek--and find-- among writers. Compared to his friend Gide or his contemporary Claudel, Valéry appears to have led a relatively sedentary life. Indeed, among writers, his life story is most reminiscent of the life of his most immediate poetic influence, Stéphane Mallarmé who taught English in a lycée to support his little family in their modest apartment. Valéry did not quite exist so humbly, but his life is so entwined in the activity of his mind that at times it may seem that he only really lived within himself. Certainly his collected works stress such an inner life and his Monsieur

Teste, the title of which contains an ambiguous reference to intellectuality as well as to sexuality, can be seen especially as a work with autobiographical dimensions.

Valéry was born in 1871, in the city of Cette (today it is Sète) on the sea in southern France, of an Italian mother and a French father. His achievements as a student were not remarkable. He began writing his first verses in his thirteenth year and though he later undertook painting and had more than a passing interest in mathematics ("For me mathematics is often like opium"), he eventually accepted that he was indeed a poet. Between 1892 and 1917 there is relatively little literature from Valéry, though his notebooks reveal that he was contemplating works which appeared later. At the same time, while existing as others do--marriage, children, a position by which to support the everyday existence--he was searching for an absolute value in his life. It is in this period that his fascination with mathematics became manifest. And when he returned to literature, his work was received as the revelation of his genius. He himself considered his poetry as the realization of his failure to attain the absolute he sought and questioned whether he was capable of attaining that absolute, wondering whether a truly intelligent man would write poetry.

But he continued to write poetry--sparingly--and permitted the publication of his notebooks and essays while lecturing and teaching in France and abroad. In May, 1945, at the beginning of his last illness he commented: "I see nothing at present which demands a tomorrow. What remains to me of living cannot be anything more from now on but time to kill. After all, I have done what I could." He died in July and was accorded the rare distinction of a state funeral, on the insistence of General De Gaulle.

Valéry expressed surprise when, in 1932, the literary critic and author Edmond Jaloux referred to him as a moralist. The publication of his essays and especially of the collection of his notebooks under the general title Such as it is (Tel quel, 1941, begun in 1910) only serves to reinforce what Jaloux perceived years earlier; Valéry is truly a moralist in the tradition of Montaigne and even Pascal.

Free of what seemed to be the inevitable association of passion and woman, or love for woman, Valéry meditates passionately about many subjects. The search for the full potential of his mind predominates all his thinking and expressing
it clearly is his next dilemma. Secondarily, he discusses a
great variety of subjects, usually closely associated with
himself: intellect, intimate friendship, God, religion. The
usual subjects of the moralist--love, women, society, social
friendships, social recognition--do not occupy much space in
his work just as they did not occupy much space in his life.
It is probably for this reason that his writings give the impression of a cold, selfish, indifferent individual on first
reading. But his notes reveal a man endowed with a full
range of passions arranged in an unusual proportion, deeply
involved in his intellectuality but certainly not withdrawn
from life.

When Proust died (1922) Valéry was hard-put to say much
about the author of Remembrance of Things Past. First, like
most others, he had not read much of Proust but respected
him for what he had done with style and language. More important, however, despite their being of the very same generation, both were born in 1871, Proust seemed to him to be
a man of the past or, at least, a man who needed the past
in order to comprehend the future while Valéry himself wanted little to do with the past. He is more absorbed by his
ruminations on his present existence and his future.

By his concern for moral stability in the absence of personal
religious convictions in order to evaluate the meaning of
his life, Valéry's thoughts reveal some of the same concerns
as those of the Absurd writers whose works began to appear
in the thirties: Malraux, Sartre, Camus. But if their tragedy is an inability to solve the Absurd dilemma faced by
modern man, Valéry's tragedy is his feeling of inability to
articulate the problem itself.

Valéry's audience is not made up of casual readers. To
understand Valéry one must read his work several times in
order to appreciate the depth of ideas and phrases which
may, at first, seem insignificant because of an everyday
simplicity or totally obscure because of the author's excessive involvement in intellectual self-scrutiny. Neither

198

judgment is correct and repeated readings will gradually reveal the sense which he sought to convey. Valéry himself was aware of the special difficulties which his work presented, but he insisted that he preferred "to be read several times by one sole person, than to be read one sole time by several."

SUCH AS IT IS

Taste is made of a thousand distastes.

In all useless things, one must be divine. Or not meddle
with it.

Beautiful works are daughters of their form, which is born
before them.

Some works are created by their public. Others create their
public.
The former respond to the needs of the average natural sensitivity. The latter create artificial needs which they satisfy at the same time.

Our disciples and our successors would teach us a thousand
times more than our masters, if we could live long enough
to see their works.

In the end every poet's value will be equal to his value as
a self-critic.

About a modern writer:
His chance creations are admirable, but his substance is of
little consequence.

A poetic idea is one which, put into prose, still demands
verse.

The expression of true sentiment is always banal. The more
truthful one is, the more banal one is. Because one must
seek to avoid it.
All the same, an unsophisticated person is truly unsophisticated, or if the sentiment is strong enough to avoid even
banality, even the memory of what commonly suits the circumstance, then this blind groping for words can produce, by
chance, some truly beautiful expressions.

Perfection is a form of defense. We put perfection between
ourselves and others. Between ourselves and ourselves.

One should be light as a bird, not as a feather.

The greatest men are those who have dared to follow their own judgment--and the same is true for the greatest fools.

A man who has never tried to make himself like the gods is less than a man.

True pride is the cult of what one would like to do, the scorn for what one can do, and a lucid, fierce, implacable preference for one's "ideal". My God is stronger than yours.

If the I is hateful, "to love one's neighbor as oneself" is an atrocious irony.

A person's true secrets are more secret to him than to others.

We never know with whom we are sleeping.

Sincerity.
Intentional sincerity leads to reflection, which leads to doubt, which leads to nothing.

Cool-headed men, almost always mediocre, are good in critical circumstances in order to steady the others and give them calm and sometimes the simple, stupid idea which saves the day.

Intellect cuts through conventions, beliefs, dogmas, traditions, modesties, habits, sentiments and social codes, the way an engineer cuts through forests, mountains, and all the peculiarities and local forms of nature which he tunnels through, slices and clears, imposing by force the shortest route.

A very dangerous state of mind: believing we understand.

Depth.
All the depth that we assign to certain states of mind is due only to their distance from the state of normal life, and not to their proximity to very important and secret things.

Philosophy and Science would not exist, if men who did not bother about them, who were unaware of their need for them,

201

of their existence and even their possibility, had not, by
their own life and action, established the fundamental basis,
the subject matter, the language, the obscurity and the jus-
tification.

Variations on Descartes.
Sometimes I think; and sometimes, I am.

If a human being could not live a life other than his own,
he would not be able to live his own.
Because his own is made only of an infinity of accidents
each of which can belong to another life.

Thought escapes in sobs, in laughter, in action, in swooning,
in the throat which tighteens, in the fist which strikes, in
the heart which stops.
It also escapes in the spoken word, but then it is a transformation which permits a resumption and returns to the
source. It is a relay.

There are doctrines which cannot survive translation into a
language other than their original one, and which do not
carry over with them the magic, discretion and customary
acceptance which they enjoyed from their crystallization
into words which were mysterious and reserved to them.

The most difficult thing in the world: putting all one's
intelligence and all one's inventiveness into service.

The most elegant, superficial, fickle, and useless society
is the best milieu for the proper judgment of things in
general.

To know oneself is not to reform oneself.
To know oneself, a detour for absolving oneself.

Everyone as an assassin.
There is a secret little movement, a reflex which destroys--
totally effaces, abolishes the one who tells you something
you do not wish to hear.

How many children there would be if looks could fecundate!
How many dead, if they could kill!
The streets would be filled with corpses and pregnant women.

The "reasons" which cause us to abstain from crimes are more
shameful, more secret than the crimes.

Moral.
The moralist is a difficult amateur. He does not savor a
moral without struggle, danger, trouble, remorse and pangs
of conscience. Repugnance, torment, labor, ill winds are
essential to the perfection of this art. Merit counts, not
just conformity. It is the energy spent descending the
slope which counts.
His moral, therefore, is really pride in taking a contrary
stance. It would follow logically that a naturally moral
person forcing himself into immorality is similar to an
immoral person who forces himself into morality.
Nothing is simple. There is, however, a certain marked penchant revealed by instincts and needs. Here we begin the
case against the nervous system.

Virtues without cause.
It is not out of charity that we must love our enemies..it is
by full control of our own motives and in order to get a
reign on nature.--Besides, there is scorn in the love of
one's enemies.
It is not out of humility that we should judge ourselves
base, it is by prudence and experience. And one must not
believe in one's personality, in oneself, in one's importance, or to consider oneself a work signed--by the Author--.
First, because one should not multiply entities, because one
must believe as little as possible in and only give credit
to whom and to what is worthy of it.--But also because we
must be fair.

To do one's duty by contrariness, to do "good" despite those
who do it stupidly, pompously, piously,--or by fear.--To do
good as a man who can do evil.

Man cannot sincerely sell himself to the devil or give himself to God.

The rare man is truly good who never blames people for the
evils which befall them.

No true hate is possible toward those that one has not loved,
--that one would not have loved... Nor extreme love for anyone who would not be worth hating.

Love always includes a potential for hatred; and I know
states of mind in which they are so poorly distinguishable
that it would be necessary to invent a special name for the
complex forms of passionate attention.
Perhaps we are inevitably contradictory when we try to express what is closest to us. Close up, hate and love have
their meaning.

What one loves, _inspires_.--To be loved, is to inspire, to
make someone inventive--productive of images, kind atten-
tions, trickery, superstition,--and violence.

What is difficult for me is always new to me.

Everything has recourse to the brain. The world in order to
be and to recognize itself as best it can; the being in order to contact itself, communicate with itself, and to com-
plicate itself.--The human brain is a place where the world
pricks and pinches itself in order to ascertain its existence. _Man_ _thinks_, therefore _I_ _am_, says the Universe.

Thought.
Thought is like a gesture or an action more or less prompt;
more or less deferred or glimpsed; a gesture that has all
possible things for limbs and parts; _time_ for articulation
field of action; _reality_ for its frontier and forbidden
territories.

The inferiority of the mind is measured by the apparent importance of the objects and circumstances which it needs
to be roused to action. And above all by the enormity of
the lies and fictions which it needs in order not to see
the simpleness of its means and its desires.

One says: "my mind," as one says: "my foot, my eye."
One says: "He has a bright mind," as one says: "He has
blue eyes." "What a genius!" as one says: "What hair!"--
What is stranger and more profound than to say: "My memory?"

I have written: "Man is absurd for what he seeks; great for
what he finds."
We should, then, practice concentrating on what was found,
and neglect what is sought.
We should consider that which has been found as what was supposed to be found. And, therefore, we should ascertain
whether the bearing, the nature, the general aspect of what
has been found so far ought not modify the usual sense of our
searches.
Perhaps transform our problems?--Our curiosity?
--Answer.--But the transformation takes place by itself.
Look around you.

Objections are often created by this simple cause: that those
who make them have not themselves found the idea that they
are attacking.

We can only call Science that combination of recipes which
always succeeds. All the rest is literature.--

View from high.
Men in high places only see fools: either natural fools or
fools by calculation,--or fools by timidity.--
And whoever speaks to them becomes a fool.

Boredom is the feeling that one has of being a creature of
habit, and of living...a conscious non-existence, as if one
had the ability to perceive that one is not. To perceive
that one does not exist!
In the last analysis, boredom is the answer of same to same.

Wealth is an oil that lubricates the wheels of life.

The optimist and the pessimist are only at odds on that which
does not exist.

They are modest those in whom the feeling of being men first
is stronger than the feeling of being themselves.
They are more aware of their resemblance with the common people than of their differences and idiosyncrasies. They min-
gle with the group more than they separate themselves from
it. The sensitivity to difference causes pride or envy; to
resemblance causes modesty or insolence because there is an

insolence which is based on equality, asserted and demanded.

All that we notice of living things is their means of defense and organs of attack: their hide, their warning sig-
nals, their motor extensions, their weapons, their tools.

There are two kinds of men--those who feel themselves to be
men and need men--
And those who feel themselves--alone, and not men.--
Because the one who is truly alone is not a man.--

We must always excuse ourselves for doing good.--
Nothing hurts more.

Nothing is more common and easier than to attribute to
strength what arises from weakness. Violence always marks
weakness. The violent-minded always stop at the first
stages of their thoughts. Delicate terms and fine nuances
escape them; and we know that the most precious clues and
deepest relations are concealed in those fine subtitles.

That which has been believed by everyone, always everywhere,
has every chance of being false.

The Church does not authorize suicide. Still it does not
prevent us from saying (it advises us to say): I am a fool,
a brute, a miserable sinner: so many suicides.

God created man, and not finding him lonely enough, He gave
him a companion to make him more aware of his loneliness.

Thanks to the vulgar myth of happiness, one can do almost
anything one wants with men, and anything one wants with
women.

Growing old means experiencing the changes in the permanent.

Books have the same enemies as man: fire, humidity, animals,
time...and their own content.

Thoughts, naked emotions are as weak as naked men.
It is necessary to clothe them.

It is perfectly useless for me to know what I cannot change.

"Genius" is a habit that certain people acquire.

Only extremes give value to this world and only by the ordinary does it endure.
Only the extremists give it value and only the moderates help it endure.

In the end, all morals are based on the human capacity to play several roles.

Youth is finished as soon as what I think imprints itself on what I do--while what I do encrusts itself on what I think.

Power without abuse loses its charm.

Great men die twice; once as men, and once as great.

Every moral prophesies.

Politics is the art of preventing people from getting involved in what concerns them.

I have known a bizarre creature who believed everything that he read in a certain newspaper, and nothing of what he read in another.
A real character; has since been committed.

Without parasites, thieves, singers, mystics, dancers, heroes, poets, philosophers, business people, humanity would be an animal society; or not even a society, a species; the world would be without salt.

One must be profoundly unjust. --If not, don't get involved. Be just.

What one regrets of life is what it has not given--and never would have given. Calm yourself.

Theology plays with "truth" the way a cat plays with a mouse.

One can judge men by the amount of seriousness they reveal in the act of eating.
The more animal they are, the more serious they are. They masticate.

Frankness means behaving and speaking as if others had no nerves.
There is little frankness in those very sensitive people who suffer as though they were in the skins of others.

We must not refer to people as imbeciles--the word incomplete would generally be more appropriate.
We realize this when we feel that we do not have all our faculties.

By means of man, the impossible infringes upon the real.

The "I"
It is in the Scriptures that one finds the cult of the Self expressed in the most naive, the most brutal, most absolute way.
But it is a question of God's Self.

Chapter 13

ALAIN (EMILE CHARTIER) (1868-1951)

Alain was not only a major philosopher and moralist but a
much venerated teacher who exercised an extraordinary influence on many generations of French youth. In fact,
a number of his former students became important writers
and thinkers in their own right: Simone Weil, André
Maurois, Jean Prévost, Henri Massis, Pierre Bost, and
Maurice Schumann emerged from his classes as did a large
number of future teachers who passed on his method of rigid
inquiry and fervent love for truth in virtually all the
academic disciplines. He therefore became well before his
death almost an institution in his own country where his
philosophical and political attitudes permeated to the very
core of French thought. His ardent espousal of republican
principles, his deep-rooted pacificism and hatred of war,
and his personal philosophy stressing the power of the will
to initiate decisive action for the purpose of transforming
the individual and his society, all became powerful modes
of thought highly prized by French intellectuals of the
period between the two World Wars.

A former student, Gilbert Spire, characterized his influence as follows: "Alain inculcated in all the men he
taught a certain number of principles, certain convictions
free of any sort of attachment, any religious or political
label. We learned from him that probity and courage are

the primary virtues of the mind, that each individual has the powers of mind he deserves, that no one of us was excepted from the danger of stupidity through ill-temper, conceit, fear, or lack of faith in oneself, that the simplest questions are difficult if one examines them closely, that the knottiest problems become simple if one attacks them in an orderly and persistent fashion; and finally, that freedom is man's greatest attribute."

Alain was a product of French rural society. He was born of humble origins in the town of Mortagne (Orne) on March 3, 1868. His father was the local veternarian from whom the boy received his power of concrete observation of the natural environment as well as a solid contempt for social striving of any kind. He received his early education from priests of the local College of Martagne. In his early youth he was deeply attracted to the mysticism of Catholic ritual and was a fervent participant. Upon his entry into the Lycée of Alençon in 1881, he seems to have lost once and for all his faith in formal religion yet never his deep appreciation and reverence for a religious spirit which, he felt, characterized man's deepest desire to understand the universe.

A brilliant student, he was soon tapped to prepare for entrance to the Ecole Normale in Paris--the least "normal" of French institutions of higher learning and a fiercely competitive hothouse where the cream of French intelligentsia has traditionally been trained. With little difficulty he completed his studies in philosophy and literature there with distinction and embarked upon a career in teaching that led him to accept teaching posts in philosophy first in the provinces: at Pontivy, Lorient, and Rouen, and eventually Paris (the Lycée Condorcet, the Lycée Michelet, and finally at the prestigious Lycée Henri IV where he filled the chair of philosophy and trained students for entry to his alma mater, the Ecole Normale). He also taught a class of girls at the Collège de Sévigné, and thus shaped minds of some of the most outstanding Frenchmen and Frenchwomen until he retired from teaching in 1933.

Alain soon developed a style of lecturing that was informal, spontaneous, and permeated with illustrations from literature, poetry, current events, and phenomena of everyday

life. The classroom was never divorced from the world outside and the students were inspired to view philosophy not
as an arid or abstract exercise but rather as a means of
coming to grips with the reality of the world about them.
His reputation as a teacher soon spread throughout France
and many of his former students, now enrolled in universities
in Paris, regularly returned to his lecture hall.

It would be a vain exercise to formalize Alain's "philosophy",
and he would be the first to deny that he held any system.
Yet there are broad principles that can serve to summarize
his approach. Alain imbued his students with the fervent
conviction that philosophy in its most authentic dimensions
provides a discipline for life. Echoing Plato and Montaigne,
he insisted that man, in order to become fully human, must
know and fully possess himself. When we are victims of
passion or fantasy, we do not truly exist or understand ourselves. It is therefore incumbent on all to gain mastery
of the self through constant effort and vigilance. And this
implies a momentous struggle since the human mind, enveloped
in the sack of flesh and victim of diverse imaginations, is
not by nature in control of itself.

The key which he proposed to gain access to truth and wisdom
is simply the ability to recognize the world and the role
which we play in it. To attain this clarity of vision,
Alain evolved his celebrated system of perception. To perceive the world means to take an active role in it, to ex-
plore and be aware of the position of objects, their use,
and our potential to act upon and influence them. It also
necessitates a relentless pursuit of truth, without which
there can be no progress; and the truth itself must be ac-
tively reconstructed at every moment by adjusting, weaving,
and justifying the relationship of things one to another
since all that exists is bound to other existents.

In the human realm to perceive means to make a connection
with other human beings in a universe that is shared. Every
perception is rooted in perception for the other, and the
fact that we perceive in common is ultimate proof that we
belong to a common world. By perception we draw together
the universe of things and of other human beings in the most
simple acts and thoughts. The world and ideas thus have

coexistence; ideas are inseparable from the world and only
have reality in their application to a common experience.
When we cease to form our thoughts in the prism of action
or experience, they are no longer thoughts but merely isolated fantasies.

From this concept of perception Alain derived his program of
active commitment to transform the social and political order. Perception implies a sizing up of a given situation
and contains an appeal to action. Just as a wound or lesion
demands the intervention of the surgeon, so in the human
realm the sight of misery demands help and calls to mind
justice and the means to attain it in a better world. "To
be just, you must strive to perceive the world," he declared,
and this implies a full assumption of responsibility for
what is seen. The will to change is nothing unless translated to action, and all domains that one perceives call
forth a responsibility to act in order to attain a fuller
measure of justice. Hence we are never justified in finding
solace in mere contemplation and any philosophy which en-
courages a flight to solipsism is unworthy of man.

Despite the pressure of teaching, Alain became a prolific
writer. His works can be divided into two categories: the
brief Propos, or essays, that he wrote from 1904 to approximately 1940, as almost daily columns in newspapers, and
more formal philosophical or literary treatises and studies:
Mars ou la Guerre jugée (1921), a sharp attack on war in
general; Système de Beaux Arts (1931), a major work on
aesthetics, his important work on religion, Les Dieux (1934),
and some critical works on major authors: Stendhal (1935),
En lisant Dickens (1945), and Avec Balzac (1935), all of
which indicate a profound grasp of literary form and meaning for these authors whom he especially admired and whom
he read and reread constantly during his life.

Alain's work as moralist is best exemplified in the hundreds of propos that have been preserved and gathered in
various collections: Les Propos d'Alain (1920); Les Propos
sur le Bonheur (1928); the Propos de littérature (1934),
Propos d'Economique (1935), and Propos sur la Religion
(1938), to name the most important.

As early as 1904 he devised the genre of the propos which can be characterized as short, aphoristic pieces that generalize from a concrete fact or set of circumstances to specific proposals for action in the moral, political, and social spheres. These brief essays of about two pages written every evening for several daily newspapers gained a tremendous vogue and established his reputation as a major essayist and moralist. Extraordinarily varied in topic and written in simple and concise prose, the propos provided wise and incisive comments on all manner of human foibles and attitudes and held up for study and criticism French institutions and political realities. Often using homely and familiar matters--the grooming of horses, the act of yawning, the phenomenon of laughter, the song of a bird, animal fables, and attitudes in love--, Alain advanced his central philosophical ideals and, in his own words, attempted to "change philosophy into literature, and conversely, literature into philosophy." Rich in historical relevance and most valuable as reflectors of the French political scene in the first half of the century, the propos combine the moralist enterprise of observing man and his world and offering prescriptions to better the state of things. Reflective and filled with good humor, they are never pompous nor strident. And they are filled with observations that display a profound understanding of the human condition without recourse to rigid ideological or doctrinary theories of any kind.

Like Montaigne, whom he closely resembles by his emphasis on a man-centered philosophy, Alain prescribes a non-dogmatic method to find happiness and to enhance our human faculties through proper judgment and understanding. Yet as a man of the modern age, he refuses to find repose in Montaigne'e personal cultivation of the self or to come to terms with the world through the consolation of religion or any other doctrine. Rather he emphasizes a full scale program of social concern and reform based on the necessity to bring will to action. With Alain the French moralist becomes a committed writer whose scope must include the political and social realities of the age.

PROPOS

"The Art of Being Happy"

We should certainly teach children the art of being happy.
Not the art of being happy when misfortune falls on one's
head; I leave that to the Stoicians, but the art of being
happy when circumstances are tolerable and when all the bitterness of life is reduced to small vexations and slight
discomforts.

The first rule would be never to talk to others of one's own
ills, past or present. We should consider it impolite to
describe for others a headache, an upset stomach, heartburn,
or colic even in restrained terms. The same is true for injustices and misunderstandings. We should explain to children, to young people, and also to grownups something that
they forget too often, which is that complaints about ourselves can only sadden others and displease them even if
they seek out such coincidentals or seem to take pleasure in
consoling. For sadness is like a poison; we can be fond of
it but will not find any good in it. And the strongest sentiment wins out in the end. Everyone desires to live and
not to die, and seeks out the living, I mean those who say
they are happy and show themselves to be content. What a
marvelous society this would be if everyone put some wood
on his fire instead of whining in the ashes!

Notice that these rules were part of a polite society, and
it is true that people used to be bored through lack of
frank speech. Our bourgeoisie succeeded in granting to our
conversations all the frankness that was necessary and
that's a fine thing. This is no reason, however, for everyone to bring his miseries to the pile, and it would only
result in a more gloomy situation. And this is one reason
to enlarge our society beyond that of the family, for often
in the family circle, through too little restraint or too
much confidence, we come to complain of little things which
we wouldn't even give a thought to if we had any desire to
please. The pleasure of plotting with the powerful is
doubtless derived from the fact that one forgets by necessity
the thousand petty misfortunes which would be annoying to
tell. The intriguer gives himself, as we say, trouble and

214

this trouble is transformed to pleasure like that of the musican or the painter; but the intriguer is first of all delivered from all his minor afflictions which he had neither the time nor the occasion to recount. This illustrates the following point: If you don't speak about your troubles, I mean your minor ones, you will not think about them for long.

In this art of being happy, which I have in mind, I would also include some useful counsels on using bad weather to good advantage. At the very moment that I am writing, the rain is falling and beating on the tiles of the roof; a thousand small ditches are splashing. The air is washed and filtered and the clouds resemble magnificent tatters of clothing. We must learn to appreciate such forms of beauty. But, says one, rain spoils the harvest, and another: mud dirties everything; and a third: it is so nice to sit down on the grass. Of course we know all that; yet your complaints in no way alter what is happening, and I receive a storm of complaints which pursues me into my own house. Certainly it's especially during rainy weather that we look for cheerful expressions. So, put on a happy face in bad weather.

"Laughter"

I've read dissertations on laughter too remote from the phenomenon itself. In order to understand what laughter is we
must attentively watch a man who laughs, and understand that
the convulsive movement of the shoulders is its principal
feature. The movements of the nose and mouth are only acces-
sory effects resulting from the fact that, when one laughs,
the chest breathes and inhales tumultuously. This is essentially what laughter is.

Now we have to analyze these movements. They occur in two
stages. During the first the shoulders are raised and the
chest dilates and is filled with air. In the second the
shoulders are lowered and the chest emptied. In short,
laughter consists of raising the shoulders many times. But
why do we raise our shoulders? Each time that a man prepares
himself for some difficult act, the chest is filled with air
and the shoulders rise; this gives a solid support to the
muscles of the arms by the rigidity of the torso. Try to
lift something heavy and you will see that your respiration
stops and the chest is inflated with air. Sighs then follow
the action. We might conclude from this that sighs signify
resignation and the fact that we're giving up the effort
after having thought a bit about it. But let's get back to
the matter of laughter.

Everyone has the habit of quickly filling the chest when he
is surprised. This is a defense mechanism much like tighten-
ing our fists. But if the perceived object were only the
shadow of a wolf, if the danger were only the shadow of a
danger, then this first movement of defense is corrected;
the chest is once again in repose, the shoulders are lowered.
This double movement of the shoulders thus signifies its
very nature: "It was only that; I am really stupid to get
upset." Then the sign is soon willed and simplified naturally like all signs; sometimes it changes our disposition
more than we think by ventilation, expansion, or suppleness.
It disposes us as it occurs. Thus whoever imitates its
movement understands it; but no one can understand it who
does not go through the process. Such is the property of
signs. And this particular one signifies that an object or
another human are not worth bothering oneself about, with

the same intensity that we were tempted to believe was the case.

We are still not quite at the point of dealing with laughter but we are approaching it. With laughter there is surprise which completely disappears, returns, and then disappears again. The clown falls; I laugh because I am, in a very brief period of time, frightened and much reassured many times. Someone narrates a play on words; I laugh because I alternately hear two things, one that I was expecting and the answer that I was not. Laughter does not occur unless we hesitate between two situations--one very ordinary and the other absolutely unexpected--and the two are parts of a whole.

What proves that laughter is certainly this is the fact that, in order to make us laugh artificially, one only needs to multiply with the finger turned to the chest of the other, a number of lively threats that surprise without giving fright. That is how we make children laugh. But that which makes a man laugh always conceals in its appearance some threat which reoccurs and which is groundless. We believe we are rid of it because we've understood that it is not real; but not totally so because its appearance comes back immediately to astonish us. We have to conquer it again and again. Everything stems from this: In laughter there are always flashes of terror. The illustrious Mark Twain once said: "We were two twin brothers perfectly similar; as they were taking a bath one of them drowned in the bath-tub; I don't know if it was him or me."

"The Misfortunes of Others"

I believe that it was the moralist La Rochefoucauld who wrote, "We always have sufficient strength to bear the misfortunes of others," and he surely said something true; yet it is only half true. An even more pertinent remark is that we always have enough strength to bear with our own misfortunes. And do this we must. For when necessity lays its hand on our shoulder, we are caught. We must either die or live as we can. And most people never let things go that far, for the will to live is admirable.

Recent victims of floods adapted. They did not moan on the gangplank but stepped firmly on it. Those herded into schools and other public buildings camped out with cheerful spirit and ate and slept with good heart. Veterans from the war tell the same story. Great trials don't arise because one is in battle but because one's feet are cold. All you can think about is making a fire and you become totally content when you can warm yourself.

We could even say that the more existence becomes difficult, the more we bear up under misfortune and the better we enjoy pleasures. We don't have the time to anticipate future evils when we are held in check by necessity. Robinson Crusoe only begins to miss his own country after building his house. It is doubtless for this reason that the rich enjoy the hunt; pains such as sore feet or pleasures of eating and drinking will come later, and, for the present, action absorbs everything and everybody. Whoever gives all his attention to a rather difficult act becomes perfectly happy. He who thinks about the past or the future cannot be totally happy. We either are happy or perish according to the extent that we can bear the weight of circumstances. And as soon as we bear the weight of self with worry or trepidation, every path is rough. The past and the future weigh heavily on our path.

In short we should not think about ourselves. What is fortunate is that others put us back in touch with ourselves by recounting their own experiences. To act together is always good, but to converse with each other, to talk, to whine, or to complain is one of the great scourges of life. Add to this the fact that the human face is devilishly

expressive and succeeds in arousing sadness that our own
circumstances make us forget. All of us become egotists
in society through contact with one another, or by res-
ponding to one another--by the mouth, by the eyes, or by
a fraternal heart. One complaint evokes a thousand complaints and one fear a thousand. The entire troop runs in
each lamb, and that is why a sensitive heart is always a
bit misanthropic. These are the things that friendship must
always be aware of. We tend too quickly to label as egotistical the sensitive man who seeks solitude as a precaution against these human messages. He may not have a
dry enough nature to bear without great difficulty worry,
sadness, and suffering mirrored in the face of a friend.
And one even doubts if people who willingly associate pub-
licly with unhappiness pay less attention to their own
misfortunes, or are more courageous or indifferent. This
moralist was only malicious. The misfortunes of others are
indeed heavy to bear.

"Of What is Natural"

A very good friend of mine often expresses the very strong
opinion that men don't change and that from their twenties
up to ripe old age they always think the same thing, if indeed they think. This idea is a bit shocking at first, but
once everyone tests it by applying it to his friends or to
himself, he will understand in what sense it is true.

There are common ideas and there are individuals. As soon
as an individual is endowed with intelligence, he can understand everything; and in this sense, if he works at it, he
will enrich his entire life. But everyone has his own way
of seizing hold of a common idea, and everyone leaves his
own imprint on it, or he in fact does not have a solid grasp
on it. In the case of the friend that I've mentioned, he
and I understand each other almost instinctively; there is
not one important idea that we don't come to agree upon
after a few words, as if we were both running on the same
track and towards the same goal. Sometimes he gets there
first, and sometimes I do; but it's always the same goal
post and one of us places his hand on the hand of the other.
I can mention a third friend with whom I have enjoyed a shorter period of familiarity but whom I also find along my path
of thought. By this experience I've been able to learn what
is meant by common sense.

But this being so, we are three musketeers who write with
different pens because of tastes, tone, and style. After
twenty years I see them again as they were, but even more
defined; each of them is himself, as a crocodile is a crocodile, or a horse is a horse.

One therefore has to say that certain ideas have more roots
than others in a man and grow better. Each intelligence
yields its own natural products as does each plot of land.
You may sow other ideas and successfully grow them through
cultivation, but the plant that is natural to the terrain
also profits from this gardening and grows even more stur-
dily. Perhaps one could say that cultivation is more useful
to the individual for his own happiness and balance, but
that the wild stock that he grows is more beneficial to
others.

But let's leave aside this question of gardening. Everyone has ideas which suit him and which his nature produces more willingly; he may understand others but he will never express them as well as his own, with happiness and force through the harmony of his disposition, gestures, and being. What furnishes him the precise image? Instinct must be a force, but one may also possess a personal genius and never use it through excessive cultivation. As a result we have these hollow thinkers.

Genius supposes a common idea carried along and nourished by instinct and temperament. If the idea is not a common one, it is only foolishness or fantasy. But when the common idea goes against one's instinct and temperament, it makes an individual reasonable but at the same time tedious. One needs the two. The passions must be in agreement with a true idea; and without this, you will possess neither eloquence, poetry, nor gain hold over others. In this way a commonplace, old as the hills, may be attractive and profound because it is natural.

"Christianity and Socialism"

"A socialist is really a Christian without knowing it." I'm
not so sure. I can think of so many conciliators who applied
a poor and only too well-known method: "Let's hold on to
what unites us and forget what divides us." In my experience I've never seen either any good or progress emerge
from conciliation; common stupidity rather than common wisdom is brought together by this means. I expect something
better from opposing forces, especially when they have been
sharply drawn. That is why I reject this unsavory mixture
in which both Socialism and Christianity lose their own
virtue.

What is common to both, and indeed to all practical doctrines
is goodness, a feeble abstraction which doesn't solve anything. For me socialism is essentially political in that
it relies a great deal on organization. The cooperative is
the experience from which the socialist derives his strength
having observed and still observing every day that only
participation in this reasonable system gives to each a bit
more temperance, order, and political wisdom. Departing fro
this, I would even say that the socialist mentality always
seeks to modify the human order by taking it by the arm.
For example, let's not wait until the worker has a taste for
study before we give him leisure; let's not wait until the
level of instruction and culture of each bring into being a
better political system. Rather let's change the political
order to effect these ends; the education and cultivation
of everyone will thus result. We must first modify the conditions of labor which affect everything else. A powerful
idea which one must be careful not to weaken.

The Christian idea is totally opposite to this. The political organization, in the mind of the Christian, is always
mediocre and often even evil because everyone's soul tends
to function contrary to the way it should. We must first
rehabilitate the individual so that he can judge as vile
what is vile and venerable that which is venerable. When
the notion of values is reestablished, when individual judgment will recognize what is precious in man, then legal systems, always extraneous and contemptible, will become tolerable, and that is all that they can ever be. Everyone

must therefore have for his goal his personal salvation, and avoid vanity, anger, and lust. By thus putting his own house in order, he will work to change the political order to the extent that he can; and the letter of the law is of slight importance in this regard. Every constitution is good when interpreted by the spirit and evil when by the letter of the law. Of such consists that evangelical movement, in whose opinion every form of socialism is merely pharisaical ostentation.

Two views on war: The socialist says: "Organize the means of production justly and there will no longer be wars." The evangelist says: "Let everyone be peace-loving in spirit and truth, and wars will no longer exist." And it is rather clear that socialism carries the seeds of war in itself through its strong passions that one can recognize in its most insignificant statements. Yes, socialism even wages war against war through its well disciplined masses. It is also rather clear that evangelism is helpless against war because of lack of organization. It makes an appeal to the individual, to inner justice and charity. It therefore can have no hope in force; and it has no army. The opposition between the two being so constituted, we can only hope for some authentic ideal that will bring them together. The catholic idea, considered in the light of the christian ideal, resulted from an attempt to organize following the spirit. We are now at the point where the socialist and catholic principles must unite. The true judgment we will make of the two will result from such a union. Whether noble or efficacious, or lacking, history alone will tell.

"Bucephalus"

When a tiny infant cries and does not want to be comforted, the nurse often formulates the most ingenious theories about his youthful character and about what pleases and irritates him. She may even bring heredity to bear by claiming to recognize the father's characteristics in the son. These attempts at psychological analysis are prolonged until the nurse has discovered the pin--the real cause of everything.

When the famous horse Bucephalus was presented to the young Alexander, no groom could ride this fearful animal. For this reason a man of limited understanding might have said: "There is a mean horse." Alexander looked, however, for the pin and soon found it by noticing that Bucephalus was terribly afraid of his own shadow; and since fear caused the shadow to jump, there was no end to the matter. But Alexander turned Bucephalus' nose toward the sun, and, maintaining it in that direction, was finally able to reassure and tire out the horse. Thus this pupil of Aristotle already had learned that we can bring no power to bear on the passions until we understand what causes them.

Many men have contested fear by solid reasoning; the person who is afraid does not listen to reasons but to the beating of his heart and the coursing of his blood. The pedant reasons from danger to fear and the man of passion from fear to danger; both want to be reasonable and both are in error. The pedant, however, is twice mistaken: he ignores the true cause and does not comprehend the other's error. A man who is afraid invents some danger in order to explain a real and amply felt fear. But the slightest surprise arouses fear, without any presence of danger: for example, a pistol shot at close quarters and which we don't anticipate, or simply the presence of someone where he is not expected. Masséna* was terrified by a statue in a badly lit stairwell and fled as fast as his legs could take him.

---

*André Masséna (1756-1817), duke de Rivoli; maréchal de France, he distinguished himself in several important battles of Napoleon, who called him "Victory's darling."

224

A man's impatience and bad humor often are caused by having
to stand too long. Don't try to reason with his irritation
but offer him a seat. Talleyrand, expressing the opinion
that manners are everything, said more than he imagined.
By continually trying not to give discomfort he looked for
the pin and succeeded in finding it. All these diplomats
presently on the scene have a pin uncomfortably placed somewhere in their underwear and this is the cause of Europe's
problems and complications. Everyone knows that a child
who cries causes the others to do the same; even worse, they
cry for the sake of crying. With professional instinct,
nurses place children on their stomachs; and there are other
movements that immediately follow. Such is an art of persuasion which does not aim too high. The ills of the year
1914 stemmed, in my opinion, from the fact that important
men were taken by surprise and thus were made afraid. When
a man is afraid, anger is not far away; and irritation follows excitation. It is not a happy circumstance when a
man's leisure and repose are brusquely taken away; he is
often too radically transformed. Like a man awakened by
surprise, he becomes too awake. But never say that men
are evil or that they have such and such a character. Rather
look for the pin.

Chapter 14

ANDRÉ GIDE (1869-1951)

André Gide is that rarity in French letters, the Protestant
writer. There have been a few others, Rousseau and Mme. de
Staël to name the most outstanding, but it does seem
that Gide's religion is responsible for the special philosophical angle with which he looks at life or, to be more
precise, his life. Whereas Rousseau and de Staël limit
their discussions of religion to certain areas of their
writing because they are more interested in the relationship
between the individual and society, Gide appears to be a lay
theologian always involved with the moral consequences of
his actions and their significance for a God who surely exists but who does not become involved in the individual's
life.

As a writer, Gide ranks among the four or five greatest literary figures of twentieth century France. His literary re-
nown rests on his masterpieces, such as The Immoralist,
Lafcadio's Adventures (Les Caves du Vatican),Pastoral Sym-
phony,and especially The Counterfeiters. His Journal, along
with some smaller works is known but usually to a smaller
circle of readers; not all his writings have been translated.

Gide is perhaps better known by reputation than through his
writings. It is because of his reputation as a disciple of
rebellious freedom that Gide became a prophet for the youth

of several generations. And those who read his works were all the more convinced that his reputation was justly earned and that he did indeed preach and practice his theory of freedom.

Moral questions pervade the work of Gide from the early Notebooks of André Walter with its subtle suggestions of frustration through the Fruits of the Earth with its hedonistic overtones and all the novels which he refused to consider as novels because they are so simple in development. He did present The Counterfeiters as a novel because of its complicated plot and it does offer a variety of moral dilemmas. Then there are the essays and plays and, of course, the Journal which covers half a century, and each of these works is steeped in moral soul searching. Finally, a brief work of Gide's late maturity, Theseus, stated quite succinctly that he had no regrets in living as he had and that he expected to be judged on what he had done in this life as this was the only way that he could be judged.

It is not surprising, then, to find in Gide's writing a moralist, a philosopher who is always ready to make a precise comment on the state of mankind. Who is to say exactly why he takes the position that he does? That would be like attempting to define art or to explain genius. Suffice it to say that what he does he does brilliantly and with wit. Why? There are a few indications in his biography which may serve to suggest that he found himself in a special situation but which can hardly account for his genius. He was a Protestant in a Catholic society. French Protestants (Huguenots) are known for the severity of their reservation in dealing with life's problems. Catholicism tempted Gide by its warmth and understanding of human nature which for this man seemed like indulgence of his weaknesses. But, as we see in his writings, the temptations of the world weigh heavily on this Protestant esthete, and most specifically he is drawn into the world by the temptations of the flesh.

André Gide was born in 1869. His father, a lawyer, died just as André was entering adolesence. The boy was raised by his mother and an aunt in the conservative atmosphere that is characteristic of the minority Protestants of

France. He seems always to have been a sensitive person -
not necessarily sensitive to others but always aware of the
nuances of meaning in any human relationship. The quote,
"I am not like the others," which he uttered while still a
child playing with neighborhood children, is often used by
critics to prove that Gide's homosexuality was already apparent at an early age. But when we look at Gide's life
from the present vantage point, the phrase seems more pro-
phetic than simply revelatory for Gide was indeed different.
He was a creative genius who in his mind explored the limit-
less possibilities of human relationships, who in his actions tried to experience as many of these situations as
time, physical energy, and his own morality would permit.

His first book, entitled the Notebooks of André Walter
(1891), reveals youthful frustrations expressed in lyrical
outbursts. In 1893 and again in 1895 he visited Algeria,
the first two of many trips he would make to Africa. The
principal reason for going to Africa was his fragile health;
he was threatened with tuberculosis. During this time he
acknowledged the latent homosexuality which his mother always tried to suppress as part of his moral education and
accepted that his sexual preferences were definitely for
males. Rather than see this as a fault in his character
as Proust did, Gide saw it as a form of liberation, as did
he new friend, Oscar Wilde. The frustrations of André
Walter and the physical weakness associated with tuberculosis gradually disappeared from Gide's works and his life.
He credited these changes to his acceptance of the truth
of his existence; he was indeed different intellectually,
morally, physically.

In 1897 he published his first significant work, Fruits of
the Earth (Les Nourritures Terrestres), which is an unabashed exaltation of life. The scandal it occasioned was
the first of many that would greet just about all of his
publications. (Gide's works, *opera omnia*, were later put
on the Index of the Roman Catholic Church.) In the following years Gide worked intermittently on a similar work,
New Fruits (Les Nouvelles Nourritures), which was published
only in 1935. This second work differs from the original
in that it is more subtle in its message and more mature in
its attitude. But the lyricism of the first is still visible in the second.

In 1902 he published The Immoralist, a work of fiction which attempts to define just what immorality is for him. The hero, Michel, insists that he, as a person, is entitled to pursue the enjoyment of life as he conceives it. He refuses to assume the responsibility for his wife's death. This is another story which reveals Gide's fascination with North Africa, and Michel settles into life in Algeria and the physical pleasures offered by the natives.

Other trips to Africa inspired Gide to write works on oppression and intolerance (Voyage to the Congo (1927), The Return from Chad (1928)). And the search for personal freedom of expression in all aspects of life also led him to consider Communism as a social ideal. The Return from the USSR (1936) marks his disillusionment with Communism and the resumption of his search for freedom.

Two important fictional works, Lafcadio's Adventures (1914) and The Counterfeiters (1925), illustrate Gide's theory of availability, or disponibilité. The theory is that one should never reject the possibilities that life offers, but should be willing to consider them to see what they might offer by way of sensual and intellectual enrichment. In these two books Gide offers for the reader's consideration a man free of family ties, several people who break family ties, a gratuitous murder, a suicide, a boy who discovers his illegitimacy and other unconventional prospects to make us question whether the status quo of everyday life is really to be preferred.

The last fictional work from Gide is Theseus (1946) in which he expresses satisfaction with the writings and social examples he has left behind.

Finally, having omitted many fascinating and entertaining pieces, we must mention that along with the fiction and the essays Gide worked on his Journal from 1889 to 1949. In this diary he has recorded some minor happenings and some major ones. Some of his most important moral ruminations are found in the Journal. It is one of the four great literary diaries written in French (the others: Montaigne's Essays, Rousseau's Confessions; Stendhal's Life of Henry Brûlard) and positively the one containing the greatest detail of personal psychological revelation.

229

Like the moralists who preceded him, Gide's interest in
writing is not limited to creating a beautiful piece of
literature. "We live to express.... Any work which does
not express [its author's views] is useless and consequently bad. Any man who does not express [his true self] is
useless and bad." He admires Montaigne ("I should never
travel without a copy of Montaigne."), Pascal, Racine, and
the Stendhal of the Journals. Freedom is probably the most
important word in his vocabulary but other concepts are also dear to him: beauty, pleasure, enjoyment of life. He
disagrees with Pascal, however. In reaction to the latter's
"The ego is hateful," Gide writes, "The ego is hateful, you
say. Not mine. I should have liked it in another...."

He contributed to the cult of youth which has marked the
Twentieth Century in the western world. Like the young
people he so admired, he could say at any point in his life:
"I never am, I am becoming." He never abandoned hope in the
face of intolerance, tradition, oppression, and the narrow-
minded Protestant ethic which had caused him so much suffering especially in his youth.

The passages which follow are drawn from five works, only
one of which, Theseus, is fictional. The Fruits of the
Earth and The New Fruits pretend to be the lessons of a
modern day "Greek philosopher;" So Be It...is a posthumously published work (1952) which again states his satisfaction with life as he chose to live it; the Journals are
jottings in his diary which provide a view of Gide's life-
long concerns.

THE FRUITS OF THE EARTH

Do not hope, Nathaniel, to find God here or there - but
everywhere.

Every creature points to God, none reveals Him.

Every creature we let our eyes dwell on distracts us from
God.

Act without judging whether the action is right or wrong.
Love without caring whether what you love is good or bad.

Nathaniel, I will teach you fervor.

Nathaniel, let your waiting be not ever a longing, but simply a welcoming. Welcome everything that comes to you, but
do not long for anything else. Long only for what you have.
Understand that at every moment of the day God in His entirety may be yours. Let your longing be for love, and your
possession a lover's. For what is longing that is not
effectual?

As women in the pale East wear their entire fortune on their
persons, so I have always carried with me all my possessions.
At every smallest moment of my life I have felt within me
the whole of my wealth. It consisted, not in the addition
of a great many particular items, but in my single adoration of them. I have constantly carried my whole wealth
in my whole power.

Look upon the evening as the death of the day; and upon the
morning as the birth of all things.

Let every moment renew your vision.

The wise man is he who constantly wonders afresh.

A LAY

Worshipping What I Have Burned

Some books one reads sitting on a narrow bench
In front of a school desk.

231

Some books one reads out walking
(A little too because of their size);
Some are for the woods,
Some for other country places -
Nobiscum rusticantur, says Cicero.
There are some I have read in stagecoaches;
Some others lying in a hayloft.
There are some that make us believe in the
        existence of the soul;
Others that make us despair of it.
Some that prove there is a God;
Others that fail to.

Some that can only be admitted into private libraries
Some that have been praised by many eminent critics.
There are some that treat of nothing but apiculture
And might be thought a little technical;
Others in which there is so much talk of nature
That after reading them there is no need to go out
        for a walk.

There are some that are despised by wise men,
But that thrill little children.

Some are called anthologies
And contain all the best sayings
On everything under the sun.
There are some that try to make one love life;
Others after writing which
The author has committed suicide.
There are some that sow hatred
And reap what they have sown.
Some, as one reads them, seem to shine,
Charged with ecstasy, delicious with humility.
There are some one loves like brothers
Who have lived more purely and better than we.
There are some written in such strange languages
That even after a deep study of them
They are impossible to understand.

Nathaniel, when shall we make a bonfire of all our books?

Some there are not worth a penny;
Others extremely valuable.
Some speak of kings and queens,
And others of the very poor.

There are some whose words are sweeter
Than the rustle of leaves at noon.
It was a book that John ate on Patmos,
Like a rat (as for me, I prefer raspberries).
It made his belly bitter
And afterwards he had visions.

A bonfire, Nathaniel, for all our books!!

It is not enough for me to read that the sand on the sea-shore is soft; my bare feet must feel it. I have no use for knowledge that has not been preceded by a sensation.

When you cannot say: so much the better, say: so much the worse. That way lie great promises of happiness.

Some people look upon their moments of happiness as given them by God--and others as given by--Whom?

Nathaniel, do not distinguish between your happiness and God.

I can be no more grateful to "God" for having created me than I could be to Him for not existing--if I did not exist.

Nathaniel, you should only speak of God naturally.

Everything comes of its own hour, Nathaniel; everything is born of its need and is merely, so to speak, the outward expression of a need.

But you must understand that it takes a great deal of joy to purchase a little right to think. He who counts himself happy and who yet thinks, he shall be called truly worthy.

...I believe the path I follow is my path and that I follow it as I should. A vast confidence has become habitual to me which I should call faith if it has subscribed to any vows.

Throw away my book; say to yourself that it is only one of the thousand possible postures in life. Look for your own. Do not do what someone else could do as well as you. Do not say, do not write, what someone else could say, could write, as well as you. Care for nothing in yourself but what you feel exists nowhere else, and out of yourself create, impatiently or patiently, ah, Nathaniel, the most irreplaceable of beings.

NEW FRUITS

Very few monsters deserve to be feared as we fear them.

Monsters engendered of fear--fear of the dark and fear of
the light; fear of death and fear of life; fear of others
and fear of ourselves; fear of the devil and fear of God--
you will cease to impose upon us. But we still live in the
reign of bugaboos. Who was it said that the fear of God
was the beginning of Wisdom? Imprudent wisdom, true wisdom, you begin where fear ends, and you teach us life.

Corrupters, debilitators, wet blankets, retrogrades, tardi-
grades, and scoffers become my personal enemies.
I detest everything that belittles man, everything that
tends to make him less wise, less confident, or less prompt.
For I cannot grant that wisdom should always be accompanied
by slowness and mistrust. And this indeed is why I believe
that there is often more wisdom in the child than in the
old man.

It is not only the world that must change, but man. Where
will he come from, this new man? Not from the outside.
Comrade, you must discover him in yourself, and, as the native ore casts its dross and emerges pure metal, you must
call up out of yourself this coming man. Obtain him from
yourself. Have courage to become yourself. Do not let
yourself off too easily. There are great possibilities in
every being. Believe in your strength and youth. Keep
saying to yourself: "It lies with me."

A man's life is his image. At the hour of death we shall be
reflected in the past, and, leaning over the mirror of our
acts, our souls will recognize what we are. Our whole life
is spent in sketching an ineradicable portrait of ourselves.
The terrible thing is that we don't know this; we do not
think of beautifying ourselves. We think of it in speaking
our ourselves; we flatter ourselves; but later our terrible
portrait will not flatter us. We recount our lives and lie
to ourselves, but our life will not lie; it will recount
our soul, which will stand before God in its usual posture.

This can therefore be said, which strikes me as a kind of
reverse sincerity (on the part of the artist):

Rather than recounting his life as he has lived it, he must
live his life as he will recount it. In other words, the
portrait of him formed by his life must identify itself
with the ideal portrait he desires. And, in still simpler
terms, he must be as he wishes to be.

Every action must find its purpose and its end in itself,
and must not be self-seeking. One must not do good or evil
for reward; the work of art for action; love for money;
struggle for life. But art for art, good for good, and bad
for bad; love for love; struggle for struggle and life for
life. Nature takes care of the rest and this rest does not
concern us. All things are bound together and interdepen-
dent in this world; we know that; but doing everything for
itself is the only way to justify its value.

Our actions are part of us like the flame of phosphorus.
They provide our splendor, it is true; but only after we
have used them.

Doctrine of sin: being capable of all evil and committing
none; that is the definition of good. I do not like this
merely negative exercise of the will. I prefer that blindness to evil should result from being dazzled by the good;

otherwise virtue   is ignorance--poverty.

I can no more be grateful to God for having created me than
I could hold it against Him for my not existing--if I did
not exist.

It is frustrating to believe that man needs tradition, history to understand an eternal God.   The history of God can
only be the history of what men have believed it to be.

As soon as a man has an idea he writes a whole volume not
so much to explain it as to excuse himself for having it.

"The ego is hateful," you say.   Not mine.   I should have
liked it in another; should I be hard to please simply because it is mine?   On what worse ego might I not have fallen?   (To begin with, I am alive, and that is magnificent.)

I pity you if you find something to hate in yourself.   I
hate only such sorry ethics.   If I like my ego, do not think
for a moment that I like yours any the less, or that this
is because of my more or less happiness.

But you are alive too, I believe, and that is magnificent.

Social question?   Yes, indeed.   But the ethical question is
antecedent.

Man is more interesting than men.   God made *him* and not
them in His image.   Each one is more precious than all.

To love the true is to refuse to let oneself be saddened by it.

Honor, integrity, good faith--merely to pride oneself on them amounts to relinquishing them somewhat.

In reading Valéry one acquires that wisdom which consists in feeling a bit more stupid than before.

From the moment when I realized and convinced myself that *man is responsible for God...*

And the wonderful thing is that by believing he was saving humanity Christ did actually save it.

Likewise it may be said that prayer creates God.

It is good to let the child think God sees him, for he must act as if within the sight of God and make of that his *conscience*.

When, upon leaving my next to the last year of school, I began to go out and to frequent a few salons, I readily realized that the thing most needed in them is an ear, each person being more attentive to what he says himself than to what others say. Nothing flatters people more than the interest one takes, or seems to take, in their conversation.

The young people who come to me in the hope of hearing me utter a few memorable maxims are quite disappointed. Aphorisms are not my forte. I say nothing but banalities, nothing but platitudes to them; but, above all, I question them; and that is just what they prefer; talking about themselves. I listen to them and they go away delighted.

"I am only comfortable with myself when I do what I ought to do." (Diderot Lettres à S.V., 8 oct. 1760)

This is very well put, but the annoying thing is that one does not always know what he should do.

Activity or passiveness in the practices of love more clearly marks the men themselves than the object of their desires.

Law and censure compromise freedom of thought much less than fear. All divergence of opinion becomes suspect and only a few rare spirits do not force themselves to think and judge "properly".

"Will you sing when you are vaporous?" writes Valéry in an admirable sob, which is tantamount to saying: "Alas, great soul that I loved, I know that, without the vibrant body, the soul is absent." Now, that soul that I know to be unable to exist without the body, how could it then be immortal? I have already written, I don't recall where, that there is probably no word of the Gospel which I earlier or more completely adopted, subordinating my being to it and letting it dominate my thoughts: "My kingdom is not of this world." So that "this world," which, for the mass of human beings, alone exists--to tell the truth, I do not believe in it. I believe in the spiritual world, and all the rest is nothing to me. But that spiritual world, I believe that it has existence only through us, in us; that it depends on us, on that support which our body provides it. And when I write: "I believe that..." there is no question whatever of an act of faith. I say: "I believe" because there is no other way of expressing the establishment, by my reason, of that obvious fact. What have I to do with *revelations?* I want to appeal solely to my reason which is the same and was the same at all times and for men.

Beneath which sprawls at ease my constant sensuality.

I believe that there are not two separate worlds, the spiritual and the material, and that it is useless to oppose them.

Diary of Goebbels:

"In reality, we carry the flame which lights the way for humanity." What is more dangerous than an ideologist in action?

SO BE IT...

Richepin is credited with a clever comment: "We all resemble our bust." How well said that is! How rare is the artist who, in life, does not give any attention to the greater or lesser effect that he might create.

THESEUS

"Weapons," he said, "count for less than the arm that wields them, and the arm in its turn for less than the thinking will that directs it. Here are the weapons. Before giving them to you, I was waiting to see you deserve them. I can sense in you now the ambition to use them, and that longing for same which will allow you to take up arms only in defense of noble causes and for the weal of all mankind. Your childhood is over. Be a man. Show your fellow men what one of their kind can be and what he means to become. There are great things to be done. Claim yourself."

If I compare my lot with that of Oedipus, I am content: I have fulfilled my destiny. Behind me I leave the city of Athens. It has been dearer to me even than my wife and my son. My city stands. After I am gone, my thoughts will live on there forever. Lonely and consenting, I draw near to death. I have enjoyed the good things of the earth, and I am happy to think that after me, and thanks to me, men will recognize themselves as being happier, better and more free. I have worked always for the good of those who are to come. I have lived.

Chapter 15

JEAN ROSTAND (1894-1977)

Scientific research and methodology have had an immense impact on French thought and culture since the Nineteenth
Century. August Comte's positivist philosophy which exclud-
ed everything but the natural phenomena of properties of
things knowable from the domain of what is real became a dominant means to study man and his institutions in the second
half of this last century. Medical science aided and abet-
ted these positivist theories by stressing a behavioral explanation of human nature to the detriment of traditional
religious belief in the soul as a distinct spiritual faculty
setting man apart from the rest of the animal world. So
strong was this current of thought that major novelists such
as Zola, Maupassant, and Roger Martin du Gard applied its
basic theories to their literary craft in developing the
school of naturalism with its stress on the overwhelming
influence of heredity and environment on human development.

In fact, a veritable crisis of religious belief pervaded all
levels of French society in the early part of the Twentieth
Century, and many of the young intellectuals of the pre-
World War I period anguished over a perceived conflict between traditional faith and scientific positivism which
greatly eroded their faith in and adherence to traditional
Christian beliefs. Some, like Alain and Martin du Gard,
lost their faith and replaced it with various forms of humanistic ideals; others like Claudel and Maritain, after

years of alienation and doubt, returned to their religious
convictions through personal, and mystical conversions.

Especially devastating in aggravating the conflict between
traditional belief and positivism have been the scientific
breakthroughs in the area of biology. Not only France but
all of Western Civilization has been embroiled in the de-
bate between Darwinians, who advanced the theory of evolution as the definitive explanation of man's long physical
history of development, and their opponents, who viewed the
theory as anathema to Christian revelation. And though
the facts seem to be decisively on the side of the biologists in this instance, dissension is still bitterly
voiced in many quarters. The recent attempts by biologists
to construct the DNA molecule--the essential building block
of life--in the laboratory and subsequent dramatic advances
in artifical insemination have given rise to deep-set fears
that biologists are revamping (some would say tampering
with) the very process of human procreation.

A brilliant biologist and eminently cultured man of letters,
Jean Rostand, has given minute and critical attention to the
impact of biological discoveries on the reality of what man
is and has written specifically on how he, as a biologist,
applies this fruit of investigation to philosophical and
ethical concerns. In the process he has vastly extended the
moralist observations of man by offering valuable and extremely challenging insights based on the vision and wisdom
of natural science--an element hitherto absent in a strictly
professional sense.

The second son of the famous poet and playwright Edmond
Rostand, Jean was born in 1894 and grew up in a cultured
Parisian family dedicated to the arts. His elder brother,
Maurice, in fact, would become a well-known poet and novelist
in his own right; but Jean was drawn to the study of science,
though not without himself developing a deep love for literature and a most extensive background that has ever since
been reflected in his philosophical and moral works.

Jean Rostand became a pioneer in his research dedicated to
parthenogenesis--that area of biology that investigates re-
production by means of an unfertilized egg. His work in

244

this area led to the splitting of chromosomes by the process of congealing the egg. He also investigated hereditary variations in the cellular composition of toads and
frogs and thence to research on cellular conservation. His
research has had vital application to subsequent investigation of human heredity and genetics.

An "immortal" of the French Academy, he has published over
fifty volumes of works dealing with pure science, studies
of the lives of animals, philosophical and moral treatises,
biographies, and essays of psychology. He therefore approx-
imates to a very impressive degree the Renaissance man,
l'uomo universale, by his tremendous erudition and extremely
broad areas of interest in science and the humanities. His
works that are especially relevant in the moralist tradition
consist of collections of thoughts, reflections, and aphorisms composed in the two volumes, Thoughts of a Biologist
and Notebooks of a Biologist. In them he brilliantly offers
the fruit of his scientific and philosophical reflections.
A non-believer but a fervent humanist, he engages in a
broad continuing dialogue with many of the French moralist
voices and views, past and present, and he provides a unique
vision of man as a biological and genetic reality.

THE SUBSTANCE OF MAN

Where politics, morals, or philosophy are concerned, I view
with suspicion the judgment of those who know nothing about
their own composition.

Knowledge should come before dreaming.

The two infinites that Blaise Pascal trembled to think of
are today the familiar ground of science. The infinite of
bigness is the province of astronomers; that of smallness
falls to the physicists. The biologist stands midway between; yet it is he who, without ever quitting the realm of
living matter, comes in touch with the prodigious. Man
has no need to plunge into the two Pascalian abysses in order
to be appalled by what he is: let him merely scrutinize his
own substance.

The number of hereditary combinations capable of arising
from the union of two human beings is not less than several
hundred trillions. A single couple could give rise to
enough offspring-no two alike-to people several planets as
vast as ours with their heterogeneous crowds. Every man
has trillions of possible brothers.

All human diversity results from the virtually infinite combinations of genes. All of us are formed of the same chromosomal dust; none of us has a single grain of it that he
can claim as exclusively his own. It is our ensemble that
belongs to us and makes our separate identities; we are an
original mosaic of banal elements.

Everyone shares the essentials of his being with others; all
men are essentially consubstantial.

Through his hereditary make-up each individual may lay claim
to a basic originality. He is the only one of himself.
"Nobody is my like," said Max Stirner; "my flesh is not
their flesh, nor my thought their thought." And biologi-
cally, the fierce theoretician of *The Unique* could not have
spoken more truly.

Even if the earth were to last all those millions of centuries predicted by the astronomers, there is no apparent
likelihood that the blind caprices of heredity would repeat
any individual's precise combination of chromosomes and thus
give him a second chance at life. Chance may have produced
man-but it cannot make two identical samples.

The biologic singularity of the individual is so strong that
a morsel of flesh from one man's body perishes when grafted
on another's. Our humors are poisonous to our fellows.

At the onset each of us was pregnant with a multitude of
possible beings. If our potential personality was first determined from among many possibilities by the accident of
the germinal meeting, the accident of circumstances will
later pick out our true personality from another similar
multitude.

As Le Dantec said, an individual is a history: indeed, the
incomparable history of an incomparable egg. We are ourselves, in the first place, because of the particular germinal inheritance that happened to be ours, and, in the
second, because of all the particular circumstances of our
individual lives. We are doubly unique: in our chromosomal
make-up and in our personal life experience.

The differentiating influence of environment is at least
to a small extent qualified by the fact that the milieu in
which we spend the first months of existence is exactly the
same for all of us. However different are to be the conditions of our lives afterward, we are all denied privilege
during the nine formative months-all treated alike, warmed
alike, nourished alike. One womb is just as good as another.
And in this we may note an equality in principle which is
neither fictitious nor political,but biological and real.
There is no equality of lot for humans except before birth
and after death: in the womb and in the tomb.

Whatever the importance of germinal "grace," we must be on
guard against the kind of biological Jansenism that would
tell us the creature was predetermined in the egg. Environment is powerfully operative in human development. That
is why, in a society such as ours, governed by such a great
diversity of conditions, we cannot hope to make even a

rough calculation of the intrinsic value of individuals. How many well-conceived creatures have had the misfortune to be ill-born! One man is different from another at birth, certainly; but as long as each is not treated like every other, we shall be wrong to attribute patent inequalities to origin. Let us beware of drawing conclusions about the egg from what we perceive in the adult.

Men will never sufficiently realize the contingency of their persons, nor to how slight a matter they owe it that they are not precisely what they despise.

What an individual is-good or bad-has no causes other than the molecular make-up he received from his parents, and the external influences that have worked on him. Our thanks or blame must fall to chemistry and luck.

Society has the right to protect itself against antisocial protoplasma; but it had better realize that when it thinks it is punishing a man, it is only chastising an egg or a set of circumstances.

That man who offends you-either he was born of a race different from yours or else he is your strayed brother: doesn't he, in either case, deserve your compassion?

To condemn the guilty is a necessity. But it is odious, since the culprit himself was predetermined. There is no human solution in a region where the *given* is inhuman.

We are the more pitiless with moral "monsters" the less remote they seem from us ourselves. Our harshness declines as we move along the scale from the human to the inhuman.

Perhaps our desire to punish a man stems not so much from his crime as from the discomfort he causes us by not differing from us except in his misdeed.

There is no creature so odious that he doesn't deserve to be pitied for his enforced membership in existence: miserable packet of sensitive jelly, tossed upon a hostile earth and obliged to cope with all the inward and outward business of it-with love, hate, fear, desire, other men, society, morality, ideas, the universe, death. Mitigating circumstance in all that a man may be: he is.

Our duty is this: to expedite the future. The first anthropoid that stood upright served morality better than the most affectionate of the four-handed creatures.

Science had better not free the minds of men too much, before it has tamed their instincts.

Can the individual who has reached a high degree of fulfillment because of a propitious environment expect to have superior offspring by comparison with the one who, given unfavorable circumstances, has always fallen short of his capacities? The biologist's answer is a categorical negative. The germ cells are not in the least interested in the individual's life experience; they keep no record of it--and thus, the race has no stake in it. We transmit nothing but what we have received from our parents, adding nothing of our own to the heritage. All we have acquired in our persons vanishes at our death. What is most our own of our "self" is the most perishable part. Our sons are less our sons than the inheritors of our line. Let us cease hoping they will owe something to our own experience. All we can do for them is to choose their mothers well.

The newborn, springing up on the tree of the human species, strikes into our tired old world like a fresh, untrammeled bud. Exempt from all parental influence, free of all pasts, empty of all civilization, he has no solidarity with any part of what has been. Neither perfected nor impaired, he is as ignorant of our achievements as of our blunders. Man, and no more. Uncontemporaneous, intact, innocent...Let us respect this rebeginning, this renewal. Let us guard, as we inform, against deforming, against burdening this baggageless traveler as we provide for him.

The day we are able to fashion human beings, what will be left of our old prejudices concerning merit and blame? What will be the reactions of men who have every right to say: "I was not born as I was supposed to be; I am not I?"

Our way of judging the works of nature must be rather like that of the layman judging a work of art. Full of absurd astonishments. If there is anything to be amazed at in

249

nature, it is surely not where we think.

If God were manifest in the structure of creatures, biolo-gists would have too great an advantage over the common run of men.

I cannot manage to believe that when we are dead we are any less dead than when asleep.

The inert, not the living, has the upper hand in the universe To die is to join the stronger side.

To affirm immortality is to blaspheme against the frailty of the person.

Man has no recourse but to forget the brute immensity that ignores and crushes him-to work at becoming as "uncosmic" as the universe is inhuman.

Human consciousness has given the universe a bad conscience. It won't recover its pristine peace and innocence until the day it will have wiped out the pitiable success of certain cell-agglomerations that took it upon themselves to begin thinking.

Claude Bernard when he was dying said: "It is not suffering I protest, but suffering for nothing." So might humanity say.

The deeper man's thought, the more he is sucked down into the human.

We shall never know everything about anything, said Pascal. But the worst of it is to know that even everything about everything would leave us unsatisfied.

Nothing is more touching than the desperate effort of so many minds to find, cost what it may, a meaning for human existence. Participation in the infinite, collaboration with the absolute...These are the pitiful formulas of think-ers who, without themselves having any strong belief, try to rescue a little of man's noble paraphernalia.

We purify God, we simplify Him, we pick Him bare, we accept the fact that everything goes on down here as though He did not exist. We ask Him merely to keep His name.

It is man's fate to create more and more believable gods in whom he will believe less and less.

I should hesitate to deprive any being of the illusion he lives by; but humanity as a whole interests me only insofar as it can stand up to truth.

Nothing is too little; God would be too much.

Those who would need a God most are neither the worst nor the best.

When I consider the majority of believers, I am astonished that they, who differ from me so much in thought, should differ so little in deed.

Those who believe in a God-do they think about Him as passionately as we, who do not believe in Him, think about His absence?

Complement to Pascal's wager: what if it could cost us our immortality to have subscribed to rubbish?

Human solitude: our pride has the same source as our anguish.

If one knew why one writes, one would by the same token know why one lives. Writing is a biological function in which all the instinctual factors of a being participate.

The work of an author who knows too well what literature should be makes me think of the handwriting of a man who knows graphology.

That the best of our fellows never, or almost never, prefer what is best in us is the hardest thing of all to accept.

The stupidities of the masses cancel out, those of the elite add up.

Even the great dead are not safe from the stupidity of the living.

Unquestionably, suffering goes further than anything else-but toward what?

The one thing from which the sufferer may derive some comfort: having put a great deal of suffering behind him.

Increased courage often means not having even enough energy left to complain.

Those who have not really suffered do not know the comfort of the tolerable.

A single remedy-if one can use it: to love with more strength than one suffers.

If we could make use of human suffering, there would be no need of any other source of energy.

In order to suffer less, *become* suffering....

One can love perfectly only what one has lost forever.

Those one has failed to love enough during their lives--after their deaths one will have to love them a little too much.

Once the nerve centers of happiness have been damaged, a man can know only segmentary joys.

After a certain point in existence, the only gaieties left are sacrileges.

A single misery floors us; several may keep us upright.

I should not know myself without my griefs.

Living has not taught me much about men, but what I knew of them before I now know better.

How easily one would pass for a good man if one could agree to express what one *almost* feels.

Nothing rouses one so to virtue as the lapses of those who make a profession of it.

Society produces reactions in me that make me dislike myself. I prefer myself alone.

The most interesting thing about a human being is the connection between his worst and best sides.

There is no philosophic position that doesn't, in the end, produce a cramp.

Science explains nothing, I agree, yet those who have tried to provide something better might as well have kept quiet. Science or silence.

A philosopher has said: God will be....
The biologist, considering present-day nature and finding little evidence there of forces which could have constructed God, would be more inclined to say: God has been....

I am surer every day that there is almost no love in man's heart, but am also each day surer that there is *some*.

Since the invention of artificial insemination, we can no longer join Novalis in saying that every infant is " a love become visible."

I am all the more afraid of science because I believe in nothing else.

The longer humanity lasts, the further it advances in age and knowledge, the older will grow that *"même homme"* to which Pascal compared it - "that enduring man who lives forever and learns continually" - and the less will humanity be reflected in its young people, who will be unable to escape becoming more and more ignorant and ill-equipped by comparison with the accumulated skills and knowledge of the species.
The older humanity grows, the more it will need its old men.

253

One doesn't know for whom one writes.
Does one ever know for whom one is?

Madness, the psychiatrists teach us, is often bound up with
an incapacity for love. Try to be as little mad as possible.

Chapter 16

ALBERT CAMUS (1913-1960)

As this century approaches its end we can look at the writers whose imprint does not seem to be fading and whose work consequently will probably last to represent certain elements of art and thought which distinguish this period from another. Albert Camus appears sure to hold a place in western literature of the Twentieth Century. Few writers have succeeded as he has in combining in prose the results of a search for the values of life with a lyrical expression while remaining totally committed to the ideal of improving the human condition. At the same time he enjoyed immense popularity as a thinker and writer. And politically he found adherents among most persuasions; only the true totalitarian extremes found in him a dangerous enemy.

His success while he was alive was probably due to his humanism which extended to all phases of life. He was not a humanist by profession; he had just one simple vision of man's existence which he enunciated in the early play, Caligula (1945), "Men die, and they are not happy." To the end of his life, this idea permeated all his writings. His dilemma was how to eliminate death and to show his fellow man how to be happy.

He may have failed to reach his goal but his unflagging conviction that things can improve despite their apparent hopelessness continues to inspire those who have lived after him.

Like his hero, Sisyphus, in the face of failure we are also urged to believe that success is possible on the next attempt; and thus Camus concludes that "we must believe Sisyphus happy."

Albert Camus was born in Algeria in 1913. His father died at the battle of the Marne the following year. He and his family knew poverty during his early years. His uneducated mother labored hard to support them; she was never to read the books her son would later write. Young Albert studied the classics at the University of Algiers, but his plans to teach were frustrated by his first attack of tuberculosis. He then moved into several odd jobs just to support himself, was married briefly, and then turned to the theater as actor-director-playwright of the Théâtre du Travail which he founded.

In 1942 he published The Stranger and moved to France where he edited the underground newspaper, Combat. The following year he became an editor at Gallimard. He remained with that publishing house until his death.

Most of the important dates in Camus's life are related to his publications and recurrent attacks of tuberculosis which temporarily incapacitated him. But 1944 stands out in his career as the year when he met Jean-Paul Sartre. Their relationship lasted eight years. As with the passage of time, Camus came to insist that man's lot could be improved while Sartre continued to cling to his vision of an unchanging destiny which we must endure until death, their intellectual relationship suffered a gradual but definite breakdown. It was left to Sartre to regret the passing of the man whose philosophy he could not accept but whose ideas he could only admire and respect.

In 1957 Camus received the Nobel Prize for "his important literary production, which with clearsighted earnestness illuminates the problem of the human conscience of our time." With characteristic modesty, he felt that this prize should have gone to a writer whose work was complete whereas his own always seemed to be in progress. But within three years Camus was killed in an auto accident and what had seemed incomplete now became, by absurd fate, complete.

Camus's career can roughly be divided into three periods: despair, rebellion, and hope. In each he has written major works in three genres, harmoniously complementing each other: novel (though he did not use the term often), essay, and drama. For example, the first period concerns man's despair: Sisyphus is condemned to eternal punishment for a kindly gesture toward mankind, Meursault (The Stranger) is sentenced for not crying at his mother's funeral (his murder of the Arab is treated as just an unfortunate coincidence), and Caligula is condemned to limits (he cannot have the moon) to which, as a Roman emperor, he thinks he should not have to submit. The result is death for Meursault and Caligula and living death for Sisyphus. Even though Camus describes each hero as being happy at the moment of his condemnation, the absurd situation of mankind is illustrated as each is shown to suffer despite the author's insistence that man is made for happiness, not suffering.

The second period is that of the rebel who refuses to accept punishments such as those mentioned, who struggles against the innate injustices of life and is ready to die if necessary, though life is definitely preferred. Dr. Rieux, in The Plague (1947), refuses to permit the malady to go unchallenged and throughout the story risks his life to save the lives of everyone attacked by the plague. He survives but, as Camus observes, it is by chance, not method.

The third period--hope--is that of heroes who insist that justice is the first step toward the good life which Camus believes is possible. Clamence, the judge-penitent of The Fall (1956), who, having already allowed too many others to die, and who refuses to condemn another human being to death, symbolizes this moment in the author's life.

There was still a fourth and final phase to be characterized by love (Don Juan is mentioned), but the project remained in notes at Camus's death.

Camus's writings are not autobiographical in the usual sense. Only occasionally can we relate a character or incident in his fiction with his own life. But it is undeniable that each of his works reveals the mood he was in at the time he conceived the work. His personal experiences, actions, and reactions are transposed into fictitious and allegorical

situations which permit him to express his ideas while maintaining his personal detachment and establishing a certain
universal quality in his message. His classical training is
obvious in his use of myths, allegory, symbols, and history:
Sisyphus; the Plague and the Judge (two characters in The
State of Siege, 1948); the sun which destroys; the sea which
brings health; Caligula, the megalomaniac who feels entitled
to everything, and who can kill a man just to prove to him
that he is miserable.

Camus's rebellion against what he considered the metaphysical
absurdity of the human condition continues to cause him to
be associated with the existentialist movement, but his humanism, commitment to mankind, and readiness to participate
in its struggles separate him from the stark withdrawal and
despair of the true existentialist. He has much in common
with existentialism, but his obstinate humanism reminds us
also of the reasonableness of Montaigne and the compassion
of St. Francis de Sales. He could not accept the binding
confines of any movement which requires adherents to follow
a "party line" whether it was Christianity, communism, or
existentialism. And he investigated wherever possible to
see if he could find the happiness and freedom from death
that he believed were the true destiny of man: "Camus's
work is a search, a search for a truth felt, which he was
attempting to clarify and communicate through literature."*
If he did not succeed as intended, he did give us the example
of an individual who finds fulfillment as he struggles in
his quest for happiness.

The selections presented here are from Camus's Notebooks
(I, II, III) dated 1935-1942. It is the period from his
break with the Communist Party and his organization of the
Théâtre du Travail until shortly before the publication of
The Stranger. With that latter publication his life
changed greatly; he became a major literary figure. But the
years of these notebooks are the ones during which he form-
ulated the essential ideas of the rest of his life.

---

*Germaine Brée, edit., CAMUS, a collection of critical
  essays, Prentice Hall, Englewood Cliffs, 1962.

NOTEBOOK I

Grenier:* We always have too low an opinion of ourselves.
But in poverty, illness, or loneliness we become aware of
our eternity. "We need to be forced into our very last
bastions."
That's exactly it, neither more nor less.

Vanity of the word *experience*. You cannot acquire experience
by making experiments. You cannot create experience. You
must undergo it. Patience rather than experience. We wait
patiently--or, rather, we are patients.
Every experience: when we emerge from experience we are
not wise but skillful. But at what?

Storm sky in August. Gusts of hot wind. Black clouds.
Yet in the East a delicate, transparent band of blue sky.
Impossible to look at it. Its presence is a torture for the
eyes and for the soul, because beauty is unbearable, drives
us to despair, offering us for a minute the glimpse of an
eternity that we should like to stretch out over the whole
of time.

The theme of comedy is also important. What saves us from
our worst suffering is the feeling that we are abandoned
and alone, and yet not sufficiently alone for "other people" to stop "sympathizing with us" in our unhappiness.
It is in this sense that our moments of happiness are often
those when we are lifted up into an endless sadness by the
feeling that everyone has forsaken us. Also in this sense
that happiness is often only the self-pitying awareness of
our unhappiness.
This is very noticeable among the poor--God put self-pity
by the side of despair like the cure by the side of the
disease.

---

*Jean Grenier, a philosopher in his own right, was Camus's
philosophy teacher in Algiers and exercised a considerable
influence over his thought.

When I was young, I expected people to give me more than
they could--continuous friendship, permanent emotion.
Now I have learned to expect less of them than they can
give--a silent companionship. And their emotions, their
friendship, and noble gestures keep their full miraculous
value in my eyes; wholly the fruit of grace.

A prisoner in the cave, I lie alone and look at the shadow
of the world. A January afternoon. But the heart of the
air is full of cold. Everywhere a thin film of sunlight
that you could split with a touch of your fingernail, but
which clothes everything in an eternal smile. Who am I and
what can I do--except enter into the movement of the branches
and the light, be this ray of sunlight in which my cigarette
smolders away, this soft and gentle passion breathing in the
air? If I try to reach myself, it is at the heart of this
light that I am to be found. And if I try to taste and understand this delicate flavor that contains the secret of
the world, it is again myself that I find at the heart of
the universe. Myself, that is to say this intense emotion
which frees me from my surroundings. Soon, my attention
will be filled again with other things and with the world
of men. But let me cut out this moment from the cloth of
time as other men leave a flower in the pages of a book.
In it, they enclose the memory of a walk in which they were
touched by love. I also walk through the world, but am
caressed by a god. Life is short, and it is a sin to waste
one's time. I waste my time all day long, while other people say that I do a great deal. Today is a resting place,
and my heart goes out to meet itself.

What counts is to be true, and then everything fits in, both
humanity and simplicity. And when am I truer and more transparent than when I *am* the world?

I become aware of the possibilities for which I am responsible. Every minute of life carries with it its miraculous
value, and its face of eternal youth.

There is no pleasure in traveling, and I look upon it more
as an occasion for spiritual testing. If we understand by
culture the exercise of our most intimate sense--that of
eternity--then we travel for culture. Pleasure takes us

away from ourselves in the same way as distraction, in Pascal's use of the word, takes us away from God. Travel, which is like a greater and a graver science, brings us back to ourselves.

Seek contacts. All contacts. If I want to write about men, how can I cut myself off from the countryside?

Grenier on Communism: "The whole question comes down to this: should one, for an ideal of justice, accept stupid ideas?" One can reply "yes," this is a fine thing to do. Or "no," it is honest to refuse.
With a due sense of proportion, one can see the same problem here as in Christianity. Should the believer load himself down with the contradictions in the Gospels and the excesses of the Church? Does believing in Christianity involve accepting Noah's ark and defending the Inquisition? or the tribunal which condemned Galileo?
But, on the other hand, how can we reconcile Communism and disgust? If I try extreme forms, in so far as they reach absurdity and uselessness--then I reject Communism. And this concern for religious matters....

It is death which gives gambling and heroism their true meaning.

One must not cut oneself off from the world. No one who lives in the sunlight makes a failure of his life. My whole effort, whatever the situation, misfortune or disillusion, must be to make contact again. But even within this sadness I feel a great leap of joy and a great desire to love simply at the sight of a hill against the evening sky.
Contacts with truth, with nature first of all, and then with the art of those who have understood and with my own art if I am capable of it. Otherwise, the sea, sunshine and delight, with the moist lips of desire, will simply lie there in front of me.
Smiling despair. No solution, but constantly exercising an authority over myself that I know is useless. The essential thing is not to lose oneself, and not to lose that part of oneself that lies sleeping in the world.

If you are convinced of your despair, you must either act as if you did hope after all--or kill yourself. Suffering gives no rights.

An intellectual? Yes. And never deny it. An intellectual
is someone whose mind watches itself. I like this, because
I am happy to be both halves, the watcher and the watched.
"Can they be brought together?" This is a practical question. We must get down to it. "I despise intelligence"
really means: "I cannot bear my doubts."
I prefer to keep my eyes open.

Civilization does not lie in a greater or lesser degree of
refinement, but in an awareness shared by a whole people.
And this awareness is never refined. It is even quite simple and straightforward. To see civilization as the work
of an elite is to identify it with culture, which is something quite different. There is a Mediterranean culture.
But there is also a Mediterranean civilization. At the
other extreme, one must not confuse the idea of civilization
with that of the people.

Mistake of a psychology which concentrates on details. Men
who are seeking and analyzing themselves. To know oneself,
one should assert oneself. Psychology is action, not thinking about oneself. We continue to shape our personality
all our life. If we knew ourselves perfectly, we should
die.

Logical rule: singularity has universal value.
Illogical rule: what is tragic is contradictory.
Practical rule: an intelligent man on one place can be a
fool on others.

Christianity, like Gide, asks man to hold back his desires.
But Gide finds an extra pleasure in doing this, while
Christianity looks upon it as a mortification of the flesh.
From this point of view, Christianity is more "natural"
than Gide, who is an intellectual. But it is not so natural as ordinary people, who quench their thirst at foun-
tains and know that the aim and end of desire is to have
enough and more than enough (write "An Apology for
Satiety").

How unbearable, for women, is the tenderness which a man can give them without love.
For men, how bittersweet this is.

To keep going to the end means not only resisting but also relaxing. I need to be aware of myself, in so far as this is also an awareness of something that goes beyond me as an individual. I sometimes need to write things which I cannot completely control but which therefore prove that what is in me is stronger than I am.

Every time I hear a political speech or I read those of our leaders, I am horrified at having, for years, heard nothing which sounded human. It is always the same words telling the same lies. And the fact that men accept this, that the people's anger has not destroyed these hollow clowns, strikes me as proof that men attribute no importance to the way they are governed; that they gamble--yes, gamble-- with a whole part of their life and their so-called "vital interests."

If I had to write a book on morality, it would have a hundred pages and ninety-nine would be blank. On the last page I should write: "I recognize only one duty, and that is to love."

If they cast everything off, it is for a greater and not for another life. This is the only meaning which I can accept of a term like "stripping oneself bare." "Being naked" always has associations of physical liberty, of harmony between the hand and the flowers it touches, of a loving understanding between the earth and men who have been freed from human things. Ah, I should become a convert to this if it were not already my religion.

Every time a man (myself) gives way to vanity, every time he thinks and lives in order to show off, this is a betrayal. Every time, it has always been the great misfortune of wanting to show off which has lessened me in the presence of the truth. We do not need to reveal ourselves to others, but only to those we love. For then we are no longer revealing ourselves in order to seem but in order to give. There is much more strength in a man who reveals himself only when

it is necessary. I have suffered from being alone, but because I have been able to keep my secret I have overcome the
suffering of loneliness. To go right to the end implies
knowing how to keep one's secret And, today, there is no
greater joy than to live alone and unknown. My deepest joy
is to write. To accept the world and to accept pleasure--
but only when I am stripped bare of everything. I should
not be worthy to love the bare and empty branches if I could
not remain naked in the presence of myself. For the first
time I can understand the meaning of the word happiness
without any ambiguity. It is a little different from what
men normally mean when they say: "I am happy."

The perfect actor (in life) is the man who is "acted upon" --and who knows it--passive passion.

The demand for happiness and the patient quest for it. We need not banish our melancholy, but we must destroy our taste for difficult and fatal things. Be happy with our friends, in harmony with the world, and earn our happiness by following a path which nevertheless leads to death. "You will tremble before death." "Yes, but I shall leave nothing unfulfilled in my mission, which is to live." Don't give way to conformity and to office hours. Don't give up. Never give up--always demand more. But stay lucid, even during office hours. As soon as we are alone in its presence, strive after the nakedness into which the world rejects us. But above all, in order to be, never try to seem.

The spirit of revolution lies wholly in man's protest against the human condition. Under the different forms which it assumes, it is, in this respect, the only eternal theme of art and religion. A revolution is always carried out against the Gods--from that of Prometheus onwards. It is a protest which man makes against his destiny, and both tyrants and *bourgeois* puppets are nothing but pretexts.

What sordid misery there is in the condition of a man who works and in a civilization based on men who work. But we must hang on and not let go. The natural reaction is always to scatter your talents outside work, to make people admire you the easy way, to create an audience and an excuse for cowardice and play acting (most marriages are organized on this basis). Another inevitable reaction is to try to be clever about it. Besides, the two things fit in very well together, if you let yourself go physically, neglect your body, and let your will power slacken. The first thing to do is to keep silent--to abolish audiences and learn to be your own judge. To keep a balance between an active concern for the body and an attentive awareness of being alive. To abandon all claims and devote yourself to achieving two kinds of freedom: freedom from money, and freedom from your own vanity and cowardice. To have

rules and stick to them. Two years is not too long a time
to spend thinking about one single point. You must wipe out
all earlier stages, and concentrate all your strength on
forgetting nothing and then on learning patiently.
If this price is paid, then there is one chance in ten of
escaping from the most sordid and miserable of conditions:
that of the man who works.

The temptation shared by all forms of intelligence:
cynicism.

The only liberty possible is a liberty as regards death.
The really free man is the one who, accepting death as it
is, at the same time accepts its consequences--that is to
say, the abolition of all life's traditional values. Ivan
Karamazov's "Everything is permitted" is the only expression
there is of a coherent liberty. And we must follow out all
the consequences of his remark.

To increase the happiness of a man's life is to extend the
tragic nature of the witness that he bears. A truly tragic
work of art (if it does bear witness) will be that of a
happy man. Because this work of art will be entirely
wiped out by death.

Thought is always out in front. It sees too far, farther
than the body, which lives in the present.

Kirilov is right. To commit suicide is to prove that one is
free. And there is a simple solution to the problem of
liberty. Men have the illusion that they are free. But
when they are sentenced to death they lose the illusion.
The whole problem lies in the reality of illusion.

A love which cannot bear to be faced with reality is not a
real love. But then, it is the privilege of noble hearts
not to be able to love.

We're living right in the middle of a contradiction, the
whole of our century is stifling and living up to its neck
in this contradiction, without a single tear to relieve its
anguish.

266

Not only is there no solution, but there aren't even any problems.

They have all betrayed us, those who preached resistance
and those who talked of peace. There they are, all as docile
and guilty as one another. And never before has the individual stood so alone before the lie-making machine. He can
still feel contempt and use it as a weapon. And if he has
no right to stand on one side and feel scorn, he still has
the right to judge. Humanity in general, the crowd, can offer nothing. It was treason to believe the opposite. We die
alone. They are all going to die alone. Let the man who is
alone keep his scorn, and the ability to pick out from this
terrible ordeal what serves his own greatness.
Accept the ordeal and everything which it entails. But
swear, in the least noble of tasks, to perform only the
noblest of actions. And real nobility (that of the heart)
is based on scorn, courage, and profound indifference.

It is both impossible and immoral to judge an event from
outside. One keeps the right to hold this absurd misfortune in contempt only by remaining inside it.

Accept. And, for example, see the good side of things. If
they don't want me to fight, it is because my fate is always
to stay on one side. And it is from this struggle to remain an ordinary man in exceptional circumstances that I
have always drawn my greatest strength and my greatest
usefulness.

We can despair of the meaning of life in general, but not
of the particular forms that it takes; we can despair of
existence, for we have no power over it, but not of history,
where the individual can do everything. It is individuals
who are killing us today. Why should not individuals manage to give the world peace? We must simply begin without
thinking of such grandiose aims. You must realize that
men make war as much with the enthusiasm of those who want
it as with the despair of those who reject it with all
their soul.

"We should not bring about the Revolution to give power to
a class, but to give a chance to life."

Christianity has understood. And if it has made so deep an impact on us, it is by its God who was made man. But its truth and greatness come to an end on the cross, at the moment when this man cries out that he has been forsaken. If we tear out the last pages of the New Testament, then what we see set forth is a religion of loneliness and grandeur. Certainly, its bitterness makes it unbearable. But that is its truth, and the lie about everything else.

A time comes when one can no longer feel the emotion of love. The only thing left is tragedy. Living for someone or for something no longer has any meaning. Nothing seems to keep its meaning except the idea of dying for something.

REFERENCES

General Works

Adler, Charles. Les précurseurs de Nietzsche, "Livre deux-ieme-L'influence des moralistes francais." Paris: Editions Bossard, 1920.

Bauer, Gerard. Les moralistes français. Paris: A. Michel, 1962.

Levi, Anthony, S.J. French Moralists. Oxford Clarendon Press, 1964.

Prévost-Paradol, Lucien A. Etudes sur les moralistes français. Paris: Hachette, 1895.

Strowski, Fortunat J. La sagesse française: Montaigne, Saint François de Sales, Descartes, La Rochefoucauld, Pascal. Paris: Plon, 1925.

Williams, W.D. Nietzsche and the French. New York: Oxford University Press, 1952.

Authors

Alain

Bridoux, André. Alain, sa vie, son oeuvre, avec un exposé de sa philosophie. Paris: Presses Universitaires de France, 1964.

Maurois, André. From Proust to Camus, Profiles of Modern French Writers. New York: Doubleday & Co., 1968.

Camus

_____. Notebooks (1935-1943), Trans. Philip Thody. New York: Harcourt, Brace, Jovanovich, 1978.

Brée, Germaine. Camus. New Brunswick: Rutgers University Press, 1961.

Cruickshank, John. Albert Camus. London: Oxford University Press, 1959.

Quilliot, Roger. La mer et les prisons. Paris: Librairie Gallimard, 1956.

Chamfort

_____. Products of the Perfected Civilization-- Selected Writings of Chamfort. Trans. W. S. Merwin. New York: Macmillan, 1969.

Pellisson, Maurice. Chamfort, études sur sa vie, son caractere, et ses ecrits. Paris: Lecène, Oudine et Cie., 1895.

Poulet, George. The Interior Distance. Trans. Elliott Coleman. Baltimore: Johns Hopkins Press, 1959.

Francis de Sales

Brémond, Henri. Autour de l'humanisme d'Erasme à Pascal. Paris: Editions Gernhard Grasset, 1937.

Calvet, Jean. La littérature religieuse de François de Sales à Fénelon. Paris: J. de Gigard, 1938.

Gide

Littlejohn, David, Editor. Gide: A Collection of Critical Essays. Englewood Cliffs, N.J.: Prentice Hall,

Rossi, Vinio. André Gide. New York: Columbia University Press, 1968.

Stoltzfus, Ben. Gide's Eagles. Carbondale: Southern Illinois University Press, 1969.

Joubert

_____. Textes choisis et commentes. Paris: Plan, 1914.

Giraud, Victor. Moralistes français, 1923.

Tessanneau, Reny. J. Joubert, éducateur. 1944.

La Bruyère

Delft, Louis van. La Bruyère moraliste. Geneva: Droz, 1971.

Horowitz, Louise K. Love and Language: A Study of the Classical French Moralist Writers. Columbus (Ohio): Ohio State University Press, 1977.

Knox, Edward C. Jean de la Bruyère. Boston: Twayne Publishers, 1973.

La Rochefoucauld

Gosse, Sir Edmund. "La Rochefoucauld" in Three French Moralists. London: Heinemann, 1918.

Grandsaignes d'Hauterive, R. Le pessimisme de La Rochefaucauld. Colin, 1914.

Zeller, Mary Francine, Sr. New Aspects of Style in the MAXIMS of La Rochefoucauld. Washington D.C.: Catholic University of America Press, 1954.

Montaigne

Frame, Donald J. Montaigne: a Biography. New York: Brace, & World, 1965.

_____. Montaigne's Discovery of Man: The Humanization of a Humanist. New York: Columbia University Press, 1955.

Gide, André. Montaigne, An Essay in Two Parts. London: Blackmore Press, 1929.

Pascal

_____. Pensées. English trans., notes and introduction, Hugh F. Stewart. London: Routledge & Paul. New York: Pantheon, 1950.

Bishop, Morris. *Pascal: The Life of Genius*. New York: Reynal & Hitchcock, 1936.

Brunschvicq, Léon. *Le génie de Pascal*. Paris: Hachette, 1924.

Rostand, Jean

_____. *The Substance of Man*. Trans. Irma Brandeis. New York: Doubleday, 1962.

Rousseau

_____. *Oeuvres Complètes*. Edition publiée sous la direction de B. Gagnebin et M. Raymond Gallimard. Paris: Bibliography de la Pléiade.

Havens, George R. *Jean-Jacques Rousseau*. Boston: Twayne, 1978.

Masson, P.M. *La religion de Jean-Jacques Rousseau*. Paris: Hachette, 1916. 3 vols.

Ravier, André. *L'éducation de l'homme nouveau; essai historique et critique sur le livre de l'Emile de Jean-Jacques Rousseau*. Lyon: Cosc et Riou, 1941. 2 vols.

Wright, Ernest H. *The Meaning of Rousseau*. Milford: Oxford University Press, 1929.

Stendhal

Beyle, Marie Henri. *On Love*. Trans. H.B. Vander, under direction of C.K. Scott-Moncrief. New York: Liveright Publishing Corp., 1947.

Alter, Robert and Carol Casman. *A Lion for Love: A Critical Biography of Stendhal*. New York: Basic, 1979.

Caraccio, Armand. *Stendhal*. Trans. Dolores Bagley. New York: New York University Press, 1965.

Hazard, Paul. Stendhal. Trans. Eleanor Hand. New York: Frederick Ungar Publishing Co., 1965.

May, Gita. Standhal and the Age of Napoleon. New York: College University Press, 1977.

Valéry

_____. Analects. Trans. Stuart Gilbert. Princeton: Princeton University Press, 1970.

Mackay, A.E. The Universal Self. A Study of Paul Valéry. London: Routledge Plaid Kegan Paul, 1961.

Thomson, Alastair W. Valéry. Edinburgh-London: Oliver & Boyd, 1965.

Wilson, Edmund. "Paul Valéry" in his Axel's Castle. New York: Scribner, 1931.

Vauvanargues

_____. Oeuvres posthumes et Oeuvres inédites de _____ avec notes et commentaires par D.L. Gilbert. Furne, 1857.

Gosse, Edmund. "Vauvenargues and the Sentiment of 'La Gloire'" in his Three French Moralists. London: Heinemann, 1918.

Morley, John. Vauvenargues in his Critical Miscellanies. London: Macmillan, 1921. Vol. 12.

Poulet, Georges. The Interior Distance. Trans. Elliot Coleman. Baltimore: Johns Hopkins Press, 1959.

Wallas, May. Luc de Clapiers, Marquis de Vauvenargues. Cambridge: University Press, 1928.

Voltaire

_____. François Marie Arouet de. Dictionnaire philiosphique. Ed. Julien Benda and Raymond Naves. Garnier, 1935-36. 2 vols.

Morley, John. Voltaire (1872). London: Macmillan, 1913.

Torrey, Norman L. The Spirit of Voltaire. New York:
    Columbia University Press, 1938.